Theology and Church

THEOLOGY AND CHURCH

Walter Kasper

Crossroad • New York

1989

The Crossroad Publishing Company
370 Lexington Avenue, New York, N.Y. 10017

© Walter Kasper 1989

Translated by Margaret Kohl from the German
Theologie und Kirche (Introduction and Parts II and III)
Matthias-Grünewald-Verlag, Mainz, 1987

Printed in the United States of America

Library of Congress Cataloging-in-Publication Data

Kasper, Walter.
    [Theologie und kirche.   English.   Selections]
    Theology and church / Walter Kasper.
        p.   cm.
    "Translated by Margaret Kohl from the German: Theologie und Kirche
(introduction and parts II and III)"—T.p. verso.
    Bibliography: p.
    Includes index.
    ISBN 0-8245-0962-5
    1. Theology.   2. Church.   3. Catholic Church—Doctrines.
I. Title.
BT75.2.K3413   1989
230'.2—dc20   89-35014
                                                               CIP

Contents

Part Two: The Church as a Sacrament of Salvation

Contents

Abbreviations

CC	*Corpus Christianorum, Turnhout 1953–*
CD	K. Barth, *Church Dogmatics*, ET Edinburgh and Grand Rapids 1936–69
CSEL	Corpus Scriptorum Ecclesiasticorum Latinorum, Vienna 1866–
DS	*Enchiridion Symbolorum*, ed. H. Denzinger and A. Schönmetzer, 33rd d., Freiburg 1965; ET of 30th ed., *The Sources of Catholic Dogma*, trans. R. T. Deferrari, St Louis and London 1957 (cited by paragraph no.)
EKK	Evangelisch-katholischer Kommentar zum Neuen Testament, Zürich, Cologne and Neukirchen
ET	English translation
EvKomm	*Evangelische Kommentare*
EvTh	*Evangelische Theologie*
FZPhTh	*Freiburger Zeitschrift für Philosophie und Theologie*
HDG	*Handbuch der Dogmengeschichte*, ed. M. Schmaus and A. Grillmeier, Freiburg 1962–; ET, *The Herder History of Dogma*, Freiburg and London 1964–
HerKorr	*Herder-Korrespondenz. Orbis Catholicus*, Freiburg
HNT	Handbuch zum Neuen Testament, Tübingen 1907–
HThG	*Handbuch theologischer Grundbegriffe*, Munich 1962–63
HThK	Herders theologischer Kommentar zum Neuen Testament, Freiburg 1953–
IZK Communio	*Internationale Katholische Zeitschrift 'Communio'*
KatBl	*Katechetische Blätter*
LThK	*Lexikon für Theologie und Kirche*, ed. M. Buchberger et al., Freiburg 1930–
MThZ	*Münchener theologische Zeitschrift*
NHThG	*Neues Handbuch theologischer Grundbegriffe*, ed. P. Eicher, Munich 1984–85
NZSTh	*Neue Zeitschrift für systematische Theologie und Religionsphilosophie*
PhJ	*Philosophisches Jahrbuch der Görres-Gesellschaft*
PL	J. P. Migne, Patrologia Latina, Paris 1845–49
QD	Quaestiones disputatae, Freiburg, Basle and Vienna
RSR	*Recherches de science religieuse*
RTL	*Revue théologique de Louvain*

StZ	*Stimme der Zeit*
STh	Thomas Aquinas, *Summa theologiae*
TDNT	*Theological Dictionary of the New Testament*, ed. G. Kittel and G. Friedrich, trans. G. W. Bromiley, Grand Rapids 1964–76
TheolPhil	*Theology and Philosophy*
ThLZ	*Theologische Literaturzeitung*
ThPh	*Theologie und Philosophie* (until 1965 *Scholastik*)
ThQ	*Theologische Quartalschrift*
TRE	*Theologische Realenzyklopädie*, Berlin 1974–
TThSt	Trierer theologische Studien
TU	Texte und Untersuchungen zur Geschichte der altchristlichen Literatur
WA	Martin Luther, *Werke*, Weimarer Ausgabe, Weimar 1883–
WCC	World Council of Churches
WMANT	Wissenschaftliche Monographien zum Alten und Neuen Testament
ZKTh	*Zeitschrift für Katholische Theologie*
ZNW	*Zeitschrift für die neutestamentliche Wissenschaft*

Translator's Note

Quotations from the Bible have been taken from the Revised Standard Version, except where a modification was required to bring out the author's point.

Quotations from the documents of the Second Vatican Council have been taken from *Vatican Council II: The Conciliar and Post Conciliar Documents*, ed. A. Flannery, revised ed., Dublin, Leominster, New Town NSW, 1988.

Where English translations of books referred to exist, references have been given to these as far as possible, but in many cases quotations have been translated direct from the German.

Margaret Kohl

Theology and Church

Introduction

Systematic Theology Today and the Tasks Before It

I

There is no doubt that the outstanding event in the Catholic theology of our century is the surmounting of neo-scholasticism. Neo-scholasticism was the attempt to solve the modern crisis of theology by picking up the thread of the high scholastic tradition of mediaeval times. The aim was to establish a timeless, unified theology that would provide a norm for the universal church. It is impossible to deny this attempt a certain grandeur. But in the long run a restoration of this kind was bound to fail. By finding a constructive way of coming to terms with modern thinking, the Tübingen school of Catholic theology already prepared the way by which the narrow neo-scholastic perspective could be overcome. In German-speaking theology, it was Karl Rahner and Hans Urs von Balthasar above all who set the standard for the break-through in our century; and this was so even though their ways were later to part to some degree – or perhaps for that very reason.

Many different factors contributed to this upheaval.[1] Some of them were factors belonging to theology itself. Some of them were external. The main theological reason was the rediscovery of Holy Scripture as the soul of all theology and, in that context, the reception into dogmatics of historical-critical exegesis. Systematic theology was once again seen to be a systematic interpretation of Scripture, as it had been earlier, in high scholasticism, when it was termed *sacra scriptura*. Other discoveries were the riches to be found in the early Fathers, the wealth of high scholasticism itself and, not least, the treasures of liturgy and hagiography. All this burst apart the rigid confines of neo-scholastic 'thesis' theology. New ecumenical openness, dialogue with the non-Christian religions, and the task of grafting Christianity into non-European cultures all opened up new horizons and faced theologians with new challenges. Finally we have to mention a growing awareness of the estrangement between church and culture, first of all in Europe (especially in France), and now above all in Latin America. These developments provided the impulse for a new pastoral movement.

All these new approaches have to be judged positively. They were taken up, endorsed and developed further by the Second Vatican Council. From this there cannot and must not be any retreat. On the contrary, it is the function of theology to help these new impulses to prevail and reach their full development.

These processes in the church and in theology have to be seen in the context of developments in the world today, especially in the modern sciences. For theology does not live in a closed atmospheric sphere surrounded by a vacuum. On the one hand today's world has drawn closer together. Modern means of information and communication are bringing men and women closer together than ever before. The questions of peace, justice and freedom in the world, the question about life, and whether men and women can survive in true humanity – all these things have taken on a new urgency. In response, systematic theology has once more taken up the old problem of nature and grace, developing an integral interpretation of salvation; though it is of course true that in recent years specific and often new ethical problems have frequently pushed the more fundamental questions of systematic theology out of sight and out of mind.

On the other hand, however, the world today is characterized by a pluralism of civilizations, religions, ideologies and sciences. It is no longer possible to reduce these to a single common denominator. The more we know the stupider we become – until we reach the point of knowing everything about nothing. So today no single theologian can any longer know even approximately all the facts that are relevant for his theology. And supposing that he actually acquires them in a more or less dilettante way, he is even less able to order them and weigh them up methodically and appropriately. Universal theological geniuses like Origen, Albertus Magnus, Nicholas of Cusa are not merely lacking; nowadays they are hardly conceivable.

Pluralism is really another word for secularization, the phenomenon which was so much discussed in theology during the sixties and at the beginning of the seventies.[2] For if we ask about the real constant of this concept, with its many functions and the political ideas it promotes, we discover that – because of modern processes of differentiation and growing autonomy – religion no longer has the function it once had, when it integrated and determined all the different spheres of reality. It has now become one segment, one sub-section, among other sectors of life which – since the whole has disintegrated – are no longer connected with one another. Generally speaking, religion is now conceded merely a solemnly elevating usefulness. It no longer has a constitutive function. In this now worldly world, God seems to be dead – to have no vital force. So some theologians have made a virtue of necessity and have tried to counter this crisis of relevance with the help of a non-religious, purely worldly interpretation (anthropological and existential, sociological and political, or whatever it may be). In so doing they have of course paid the price of an even more severe identity crisis. For a theology after the death of God is a contradiction in terms, even semantically. So it is no surprise to anyone that the death of God theology should now be dead itself.

Developments both in theology and outside led to the phenomenon which has had the most momentous consequences for the present theological situation. This phenomenon was the breakdown of metaphysics in their classic form. Metaphysics was the study of the final, all-determining and cohering foundations, wisdom about the oneness and wholeness of reality. In the total theological tradition hitherto, metaphysics with its universal categories had provided the instrument with which to render in the medium of thought a theologically appropriate and reflective account of God, the one reality that – itself all-comprehending and all-determining – yet transcends all else. The true and deepest crisis of present theology is that there is now no metaphysics of this kind. One reason for this is to be found in philosophy, which in some quarters proclaims the end of metaphysics. Another reason is that the process of overcoming narrow and encrusted neo-scholastic metaphysics has often led theology to divest itself radically of its Hellenized and metaphysical elements.[3] The result was either a purely biblical theology based on salvation history, or a practical, political theology. Often too hermeneutics and linguistic philosophy, or the modern human sciences (especially sociology and psychology), have become the sciences of reference, usurping the place which had been occupied by metaphysics in the previous history of theology.

The result of this development is the end of theology's previous monolithic unity, and the emergence of a pluralism in theology itself which is in this form new and which it is increasingly difficult to survey and to fathom. It is a pluralism of increasingly specialized and differentiated disciplines and methods. And it is in addition a culturally conditioned pluralism of newly emerging African, Asian and Latin American theologies. Many people feel that this new pluralism is a liberation – a setting sail for new shores, the way to a new diversity and a new wealth. Others lament it, viewing it with critical eyes as a confusion and a collapse, a *carte blanche* for a go-as-you-please, and a susceptibility to fashionable trends. So it goes without saying that 'new' Catholic theology is a source of fierce controversy within the church itself.

The new pluralism is not a purely internal, academic problem. About that there can be no doubt. It is a problem for the church, and for the faith it shares. For it is a plain matter of fact that central truths of faith simply are, *de facto*, expressed in the language of metaphysics, from the *homoousios* (the one substance) of the creed of the Council of Nicaea (325) down to the doctrine of transubstantiation promulgated at the Fourth Lateran Council (1215) and the Council of Trent (1545–63). Even more fundamental is the question whether the one belief in the one God, the one Lord and mediator Jesus Christ, the one Spirit, the one baptism in the one church, does not ultimately become dumb and incapable of communication – whether it does not even become a fiction and a chimaera – without the one, single theology which speaks one single language, at least in the central and fundamental things of faith? Must not a completely unbridled pluralism also lead to a new polytheism of 'anything goes'? Finally, is a pure pluralism which cuts itself off and immunizes itself, no longer stringently and inexorably posing the question about the one truth, not much more static and sterile then everything it purports to overcome? Are there not trans-cultural human values as well? And in the present human situation especially, are we not positively dependent, for good or ill, on making people aware of the trans-cultural dignity of every man and woman? And do we not have to embody this in a universal human solidarity?

This, then, is the question that faces us: how can theology be universal and yet take into consideration the pluralism of languages and cultures which cannot be set aside, and the legitimate autonomy of individual sectors and areas of interest? How can it be pluralist without being relativist? How can theology combine legitimate variety with the necessary unity? And then there is a second question: how can theology escape from the identity-relevance dilemma in which it finds itself? How can it escape the deadly logic of either preserving its relevance at the cost of its identity, or of keeping its identity at the cost of its relevance – and at the price of a retreat into the ghetto? Without a clear, unequivocal, individual identity there is no relevance; but of course without relevance there is no identity either.

II

A return to the ghetto of the old theology of the schools is out of the question. In the long term, the developments of recent years have brought too many positive and promising new approaches. And in any case, we cannot run away from the present situation and its challenges. If Catholic theology is to survive at all, it has to free itself completely from the fetters of the neo-scholastic system. Theology – especially theology in the tradition of the Tübingen Catholic school – is possible only in the open river of time.[4] The unity of theology today can no longer be the unity of a monolithic system. But it can be found, and must be found, in the mutual communication of the different theologies, by way of their relation to a common 'object' and through their application of common, fundamental principles in the pursuit of that object. Consequently, if we are to move forward it can only be through a recollection of the common principles of Catholic theology. Three such principles determine the Tübingen tradition: 1. theology must belong within the context of the church; 2. theology must be scholarly, or scientific; and 3. theology must be praxis orientated, and open to the questions of the time.

1. The principle that it must belong within the context of the church is particularly characteristic of Catholic theology. It is based on the conviction that it is only in and through the testimony of the church that we possess the gospel about God's liberating act of salvation in Jesus Christ, or that we possess its *Ur-kunde* in Holy Scripture – that is (to play on the German word) its original proclamation *and* its documentation. The church is the specific, concrete place of truth. J. A. Möhler long ago formulated the objection to this thesis, and at

the same time justified the thesis itself: 'I hear the contemptuous words: the church, the church, nothing but the church! And I reply: there is and can be nothing other than the church; for without the church we have no Christ and no Holy Scripture . . . There is no other proof except the apagogic one, which tells us that every attempt in any other way to acquire assurance that we possess the true doctrine of Christ is in itself incomprehensible, untenable, indeed impossible . . . But the reason why no other proof is possible I have already given; for the premise of all premises cannot itself also have a premise.'[5]

Theology is therefore possible only within the communion of the church, on the foundation of the church, and in subjection to the norm of the church's living tradition. Theology is, so to speak, the reflected *memory* of the church. This insight distinguishes the genuine Tübingen tradition from liberal theology (with which it is occasionally unjustly confused[6]) as well as from a rigid and petrified dogmatism.[7] For properly understood, being bound to the church does not mean being bound to an abstract system of doctrine. It means being woven into a living process of tradition and communication, in which the one gospel of Jesus Christ is interpreted and actualized. This does away with the false alternative between a subjectivist and an objectivist understanding of truth. The comprehensive 'we' of the church is the conscious subject of faith and the place of truth.[8] This means that tradition is always a living transmission to what is always the present, where interpretation is the condition of tradition.

Within this transmission process, dogma certainly has a particular place. But dogma is by no means the only form which the transmission process takes – not even the most important one. For dogma aims to be understood as the church's binding interpretation of Scripture. It must therefore itself, in its turn, be interpreted in the light of Scripture. The transmission takes many other forms, which come before dogma and run parallel to it, above all the liturgy, the day-to-day proclamation, and the daily lived witness of faith. The fundamental form of the church's interpretation of Scripture is the creed, which to this day is shared by all the churches. The individual dogmas are an attempt to develop the articles of faith which the creed contains. Consequently these individual dogmas have also to be interpreted within the structure of the creed as a whole. All this makes it plain that the doctrine of the church is a whole composed of many strata and many dimensions. This is what is meant by Vatican II's phrase about the hierarchy of truths. Individual truths must not merely be included in this hierarchy; they must be weighed up and given their proper 'status', according to their closeness to the common foundation in Jesus Christ.

In this living interpretation of tradition, theology has an important, relatively independent function within the church. The task of interpretation requires of the Catholic theologian far more than a merely outward, more or less formal obedience to the church's magisterium, or teaching office. That must always be felt as repugnant and off-putting whenever it is seen in isolation from the whole and is left as its ultimate distillation, so to speak. Then obedience certainly becomes incomprehensible and burdensome. But in reality what is required is a *sensus fidei* and a comprehensive *sentire ecclesiam*. This is possible only through life in and with the church in the specific forms it takes – its congregations and fellowships.

A theology is a church theology and a Catholic theology as long as it participates in the processes of communication and consensus within the church – that is to say, as long as it allows itself to be complemented by other theologies in the church and by other charismata and ministries, and – if necessary – permits itself to be corrected. It therefore has to fit into the whole of what is Catholic in a way that may well be full of tension. The borderline is drawn where a polarity and a tension turns into a contradiction that can no longer be integrated. This happens when an individual clings obstinately to his own private judgment, assigning it absolute validity. When this occurs, he is letting his own egoism usurp the place of the ecclesial *communio*;[9] and this means an infringement, indeed a surrender, of the Catholic principle.

In this painful situation, if the church is to preserve the clarity of its witness and its inner unity, all that is left to it is to negate the negation by affirming its own position more sharply. This procedure is especially painful because in the process the *particula veri* of the excluded position is not infrequently disavowed and pushed aside. So in these cases the church's *communio* also has its price. However, liberty is never thereby infringed, especially in our pluralistic society. The church merely makes use of its own liberty and authority to proclaim the gospel, and in doing so also safeguards the right of everyone else to hear from the church, and in the church, the whole gospel in its full, unabbreviated form.

2. Yet Catholic theology is certainly not characterized solely by its relation to the church. It is also marked by a second principle: its scholarly or scientific character. For after all, the Christian faith is not faith in the church. It is a faith which, in the church and with the church, is focused on God himself or, to be more precise, on the God who communicates himself to us through Jesus Christ in the Holy Spirit. So theology certainly starts from the testimony of the church's tradition and is permanently bound to that. But because this tradition is true, it finds its definition in the fact that it points beyond itself to the truth of God which is always greater still. The real object of theology is hence not the faith of the church, but the truth of God's revelation of himself, to which the church's testimonies of faith witness. It is this relation alone which makes theology theo-logy, the study of God. It is this which – entirely in the Aquinas tradition – makes a theological theology necessary, so to speak.[10] This single and unified reference also lends theology's individual statements their inward unity, their harmony, coherence, intelligibility and plausibility. Finally, it confers on theology a relatively independent, even critical stance towards individual traditions which do not correspond to this truth, or only do so in part. Even a theological theology is a critical theology. In fact it is the most critical theology of all.

Belief in God is by its very nature a free act on the part of human beings. It is an act to which no one must be, or can be, forced. Moreover, as free act, belief is an act in keeping with human dignity only if it is not a *sacrificium intellectus*, but is obedience towards the truth in accord with reason. So even though faith is an act wholly and entirely sustained by the light of grace, it is at the same time wholly and entirely a human act, which comes about through the medium of human hearing, understanding, thinking, willing, feeling and speaking. Theology reflects this inward logic of faith. Consequently theology's programme is, in Anselm's phrase, *fides quaerens intellectum*, faith seeking understanding. Theology can realize this programme only by facing up to the dialogue with other disciplines, and by rendering an account of the Christian hope before the forum of reason (I Peter 3.15). And in this it is even today indebted to the spirit of its great master Aquinas.

During the Middle Ages and well into modern times, theology had of course no difficulty in maintaining its claim as science, since it offered a coherent body of knowledge resting on secure principles. This became increasingly difficult to the degree in which the other sciences emancipated themselves from the philosophical premises which all had hitherto shared, and as the scientific ideal put forward by the natural sciences increasingly contrived to present itself as the ideal that was almost exclusively valid. As a result of this process, the humanities also found themselves in troubled waters. In the 1970s, theology faced up to the new challenges of scientific theory;[11] and out of the disputes of that period a number of new paradigms of Catholic theology emerged.

What has been surrendered practically everywhere is the neo-scholastic paradigm, which clung staunchly to the mediaeval understanding of science (though to this it gave a one-sided interpretation, falsifying it from an Enlightenment angle). To give theology a new, modern keynote was the great achievement of Karl Rahner. He took up modern subject philosophy in his own way, building up a theology orientated towards anthropology.[12] In a kindred way, and about the same time, Rudolf Bultmann developed an existential interpretation of the New Testament.

Yet Rahner's own pupils, especially Johann Baptist Metz, already criticized the idealistic-transcendental paradigm because, according to their conviction, it tacitly took its bearings from the 'bourgeois' subject, and did not sufficiently take into account the historical, economic, social and political conditions that go to make up subjectivity. At that time, practical philosophy was undergoing a rehabilitation; and these theologians tried to take that up, and to pose the question of God in a new way in the context of the problem of theory and praxis. It may remain an open question here which other non-bourgeois or post-bourgeois 'ideologisms' played a part in this context, expecially in the reception of this political theology, which was developed in the light of the paradigm of the communicative praxis of freedom. There is no doubt that it extended the theological horizon which the transcendental and existential paradigm had in some respects narrowed down. But on the other hand it also excluded essential dimensions of reality. Among these are above all the natural, 'given' circumstances and conditions of human liberty. These are important not merely in connection with our newly awakened ecological awareness, the discussion about life, the protection of life, and survival in human dignity; nor are they significant solely in the context of the urgently required but badly neglected dialogue with the modern sciences – still the hard core of modern times (C. F. von Weizsäcker). These already existing circumstances are important too for the ever more urgently necessary encounter with the non-Christian religions, and with the new religiosity which is now springing up – often in highly nebulous form.

In the language of Western philosophy, thinking that ponders over the whole of reality in its ultimate foundations is called metaphysics. It is the prime philosophy; it can be disputed only if one does metaphysics oneself – but a different metaphysics. So it is no help to give metaphysics a wide berth, as if it were someone stricken by plague. Nor is there any point in simply vilifying it as a expression of the bourgeois mind. Anyone who has not learnt to distinguish the particular conditions and secondary causes of a mode of thought (which of course always exist) from its objective and valid claims to recognition has not even arrived at the level of metaphysics at all; he is simply disguising the personal, unspoken metaphysics which are his premise. Theology, at least, when it wants to talk about God as the all-determining, all-comprehending and all-originating reality cannot avoid presupposing a metaphysics: not a particular metaphysics certainly; not even necessarily a unified metaphysics; but none the less a metaphysics which, on the basis of its relation to the ultimate ground of all reality, is also open for the discussion with other metaphysical approaches. Metaphysics is certainly not the foundation and ground from which theology draws its nourishment and strength; but it is nevertheless the only air it can breathe. Without it theology gets withdrawal symptoms and suffocates. So this air is not replaceable, not even by a new artificial compound of social and scientific theory.[13]

We do not have to decide here which metaphysics is of consequence today in Asia or Africa or Latin America. Our duty is to our own European tradition, in the transition from the second to the third millennium, and it is from this point that we have to enter into dialogue with the theologies of other continents. Ever since Schelling's later philosophy, the fundamental characteristic of our post-idealist situation has been a growing awareness of the undeducible and unpreconceivable facticity and contingency of reality. This is so in Kierkegaard, Marx, Nietzsche, Heidegger, down to the thinkers of the 'post modern' era.[14] There has therefore come to be a new awareness of the primacy of being before doing. A new reverence for what *is*, is beginning to come to the fore, over against the gigantic will to do, and will to power, of modern times. And this raises the metaphysical question in a new way.

What is in question under the heading of 'faith and history' is therefore a theological paradigm which starts from the reciprocal relationship between the subject and his already given reality – the reality with which he is already presented and for which he is responsible. Freedom is therefore once again the starting point. It is the core of the modern philosophy of history. But it is now no longer a matter of freedom in the abstract. Here what is at stake is the specific, historically existing freedom of the human being. Historically conditioned and contingent freedom of this kind, which nevertheless comes forward with the claim to an unconditional dignity of its own, cannot perfect and fulfil itself. It can find its fulfilment only in 'something' which is itself unconditional and infinite, not merely according to its claim but in reality. So the freedom of the human being points to unconditional and perfect freedom as its ultimate foundation, and its ultimate and final fulfilment.[15] Since being takes precedence over doing, this paradigm cannot be termed a liberation theology;[16] but it can certainly be described as a theology of historically existing, responsible liberty. The liberation of human beings always presupposes their liberty. And conversely, a theology which thinks in the paradigm of specific, historically existing liberty will at the same time commit itself to humane and free conditions in which human beings can live. This leads to the third fundamental paradigm of Catholic theology.

3. These somewhat lengthy reflections about the scientific character of Catholic theology were necessary, since they also lay the foundations for its third principle, which is praxis-orientated openness for the problems of the time.[17] The Pastoral Constitution *Gaudium et spes* has thrown the door wide open for this third aspect. Yet it cannot be denied that there has been a great deal of uncertainty and confusion in the last twenty years about the openness of theology. To say that in all honesty does not mean bringing discredit on a permanently justifiable concern. For we do not do theology in a vacuum, and it is not an esoteric game of arranging thought patterns and spinning words, a game played in an ivory tower. Theology is certainly never a

handmaid, but neither is it a privileged and exclusive club. It has a public responsibility; for it belongs, not merely to the public life of the academic world, but to the public life of church and society too.

Theology's relation to praxis is first of all indispensably rooted in the practice of faith, life, proclamation and worship in the church and its congregations and fellowships. Moreover its relation to these things is one of critical accompaniment and positive inspiration. In this respect it is a practical science, above all in the sense in which practice is conceived in the scholasticism that takes its bearings from Augustine. For theology is not supposed merely to communicate theoretical, speculative insights. It aims at the actual, specific practice of faith, hope and love. Seen under this aspect, what a poor figure is cut by many a fat and learned tome! And how rightly many students, and many 'ordinary' Christians, cry out at the present time for this spiritual and mystical dimension, which is so inexcusably neglected in the conduct of our average academic theology![18]

Theology is practical also because it is related to both the personal and the social practice of living, with the experiences and problems involved. And here it is not merely a matter of understanding the world more profoundly in the light of the gospel. We have also to understand the gospel more profoundly in the light of the 'alien prophecy' of the world. In this task theology is always also part of the culture of its time and the area to which it belongs. Consciously or unconsciously, it will be guided by the prejudices of that culture and region, and by specific interests and concerns that play a part there. For the sake of the universality and catholicity of theology itself, these things have to be thought about self-critically, and the ideology behind them has to be critically judged as well, especially in dialogue with the theologians of other churches in the same region. This is necessary if we are to be in a position to react responsibly to our own situation.

This openness for the problems of the time cannot of course be a wilful, go-as-you-please openness. It is an openness that must be called both dialogistic and missionary. The two are not antitheses, and it is really only superficial minds that think so. For true dialogue means communicating to the other person something about oneself – indeed *communicating oneself*. In this sense the church's theology has to strike out specific ways in which the church can become the universal sacrament of salvation for the world of today. In concrete terms this belongs initially within the competence of moral and practical theology. But the corresponding foundational problems make their full impact in fundamental theology and dogmatics also. Unfortunately in recent years the interdisciplinary discussion in theology has been broken off, rather than revived. At present the unity of theology in all the variety of its disciplines is an urgent but as yet unsolved problem. And at the moment only very few practicable approaches to a solution can be detected.

The old integralistic model is certainly not qualified to solve the problems I have touched on. Its aim was to derive from theological premises direct, practical directions about how to act in the world. It thereby failed to recognize the legitimate autonomy of particular 'worldly' sectors, which Vatican II stressed. But the functional model is certainly equally inappropriate. It banishes the church to a special sector of its own, and has recourse to it only in particular circumstances. These circumstances may belong to the civic sphere, where the church is required to lend a solemnly elevating form to particular situations in people's lives, or to provide comfort in the face of the inescapable contingency of existence. Or – perhaps more radically – the church may be expected to exercise a galvanizing function in the reshaping of social conditions.

But the interpenetration of the world with the light and power of the gospel, about which Vatican II spoke, requires a third model, which may be termed Christian responsibility for the world. Ultimately speaking, what is required here is a link between two theological outlines which at present confront one another in highly abrupt form. One of these outlines is the thinking based on creation theology, which starts from the relatively independent orders given with creation. The other is liberation theology, which is historically determined. Of course if we take the Thomist approach seriously, and assume that grace presupposes and perfects nature, then we must apply this to the relation between liberation, biblically understood, and human freedom, and we must consider the orders in which these things exist in that light.[19] A holistic understanding of salvation and liberation would emerge only from an overall view of this kind. The theological starting point for this is to be found in a wisdom christology and theology. But here again we have not gone beyond the first approaches and preliminary reflections.[20] The crisis in the communication of the church's moral standards is sufficiently striking evidence from the practical side for this largely unsolved problem.

In the practical relationship between church and society, therefore, we find a wide and rugged field for future theological work, a field that will be hard to plough. To make this deficit good is the more urgent, because today evangelization and the implanting of Christian values in society have long ceased to be a task merely for the mission fields of the southern hemisphere. In the last two hundred years, a new culture has grown up in Europe which has hitherto been really very little influenced by the spirit of the gospel. The cleft between faith and modern culture is in fact *the* real drama of our time. If Europe is not to lose its soul, it must be newly evangelized, and Christianity must be newly grafted into its civilization.

III

Does a programme of this kind have the slightest chance? Of course this question is not intended to set bounds to God's unlimited potentialities and the inscrutable ways of his providence. It is no more than a modest attempt to discern the historical signs and tokens of God's ways, and thus to discover how human beings can implement his saving will. So the question brings us back to the situation described at the beginning: the pluralism of a secularized world without God. We can certainly not simply reverse the development which has brought us to this point. In many respects we do not even wish to do so. So, in this situation, how can we be theologians who testify to God in a way that will come home to men and women, and transform the world?

Our purpose here is not to find a comprehensive answer. That would in any case not be possible. But let me point out just one thing. The theory about the irreversible march of secularization has apparently proved not to be true. Sociologists of religion are meanwhile talking about religion's continued existence. A new, often highly nebulous, often also fundamentalist religious form of post-modern life now seems to be turning back to myth, sometimes even to obscurantism.[21] Admittedly, we encounter a no less dangerous obscurantism in certain groups in the church, and in some theological circles: the obscurantism of a blasé, sceptical, late Enlightenment, which is simply not prepared to understand what everyone else is talking about. For it really would seem to be the case that *the* question for the century ahead of us is going to be the question about God (J. Illies).

As always in such processes, this shift in the spirit of the age is prompted by many different motives at many different levels. Some of these are certainly not a cause for rejoicing. One very important motive is undoubtedly the bitter discovery and tardy recognition that a pluralistic, secular world can itself provide no ultimate justification for its values and institutions. It lacks legitimation, and is not capable of satisfying the deeply rooted seekings and strivings of men and women for unity and reconciliation, which is at the same time a longing for redemption. On the contrary, the modern world, at times so banal and one-dimensional, creates the best possible pre-conditions for a new, often 'enthusiastic' search for a new religiosity.

Needless to say, the theologian's task is independent of fashions of this kind, which are often short-lived. He has to speak 'in season and out of season' – whether it is opportune or not. At present he has chances enough. For even the Fathers of the church by no means linked on to the mythical theology of their time – not even on to the political theology that was so closely connected with it. What they took up was the philosophic theology of Stoicism, Platonism and, later, Aristotelianism – the philosophical theology which was 'enlightened' in the sense of its time, and which preserved the heritage of the myth in a critical and reasoned way.[22] It is just such a critical discrimination and differentiation which contemporary theology also requires. Without falling victim to the rationalism which has meanwhile become almost obsolete, theology today must once again take as its concern the reasonable nature of religion and reality. For in the history of both mankind and the church, irrationalism has always done more harm than rationalism. Of course we need a rationality that does not sceptically call everything in question, and which is ultimately without any real substance. It has to be a rationality that lives from the substance of faith and tries to bring this substance into the light and to make its light shine. *Fides quaerens intellectum*, faith that seeks understanding: that is theology's great programme, today as well. And it is also the programme for a new humanism.

Of course the essays in this volume do not fulfil this programme. Prompted by particular occasions, they are steps on the way to its fulfilment. Nor are they the only possible answer. But each of them tries to make a contribution to the great communication process of Catholic theology. They remain true to the fundamental concerns which have impelled me from the beginning. It goes without saying that these contributions see certain things more distinctly, and stress certain things more clearly, than earlier essays. It is no less a matter of course that someone who participates in the *colloquium theologicum* should also correct himself in the case of particular questions and assertions. It is not a matter of whether a statement is conservative or progressive. The sole question is whether it is true or false. But this can be decided, not through polemic, but only through argument.

PART ONE

Theology and Anthropology

I

Revelation and Mystery
The Christian Understanding of God

1. The natural revelation of the mystery of God

The subject we shall be considering here[1] requires a few introductory thoughts. Before we discuss the subject 'revelation and mystery' in the Christian context, we must try to arrive at a preliminary understanding of what is meant more generally by revelation and mystery. We do not do this in order to trace back the Christian interpretation of revelation, mystery and God to a pre-Christian and non-Christian view. We do it so as to find our way into the dimension, and to get on to the wavelength, so to speak, which makes it possible for the Christian interpretation 'to be transmitted' and understood at all.

For the theology of the early Fathers and for scholasticism, this preliminary understanding really presented no problem. Until well into modern times, Christian theology profited from a generally religious, numinous view of the world, in which reality was seen as transparent for the divine, as an epiphany – even a hierophany. In so far reality was viewed as a revelation of the divine in what was at first a very general sense. The pre-Socratic Thales of Miletus (seventh/sixth century BC) found a formula for this numinous and hierophanous interpretation when he said that everything was full of gods.[2]

As early as 500 BC, Heraclitus of Ephesus called this all-pervading and all-sustaining divinity the logos.[3] And in so doing he coined what was to become a constituent, primal word and guiding concept for Western thought. Logos is what might be called the symbolic term for the Greek understanding of reality, which then became the understanding of the whole of the West. It is one of those primal, fundamental words which one understands but can hardly translate into any other terms, let alone define. In its original, literal meaning logos comes from *legein*, which means 'to read', in the sense of collecting, counting, listing, but also telling or saying. So logos is a saying and speaking which collects into one what *is*, and 'tells' it – that is both 'counts' and 'recounts' it. Logos is the one reality in its wholeness, which becomes manifest in saying and speaking; it is the meaning of reality which becomes apparent in language. The nature of the logos can be defined more precisely over against myth. For myth originally means more or less the same thing as a saga, a saying. But whereas the myth is the saying which authoritatively proclaims something, the logos is reasonable, substantiated and substantiating speech, which renders an account of something. The logos places its trust in insight and appeals to the logos shared by all human beings – the reason they have in common. Consequently logos also means cause, reason, significance, coherence, order.

Where does this take us? In the primal word and verbal symbol logos, which determines Western thinking and feeling, reality is manifested as open to the interpretation of reason, because it is itself reasonably ordered. So the very beginnings of Western thinking are marked by *a demythologizing and rationalizing process* which understands reality as a manifestation of meaning and reason, and which assumes that this meaning is manifested in human reason and language. Human reason reflects the reasonable nature of reality. In the human being, reality comes to itself. The scholastic philosophy and theology of the Middle Ages defined what logos meant to the Greeks through the formula *Omne ens est verum* – 'everything that is, is true'. However, Aquinas adds that this truth which is immanent in things finds its realization in thinking and speaking. Truth is therefore the correspondence between reality and reason (*adaequatio rei et intellectus*).[4] *Reason is the place where reality is revealed.* This scholastic thinking, derived from the thought of the ancient world, continued well into modern times. Natural scientists as important and seminal as Kepler, Einstein and Heisenberg saw their scientific work, and scientific laws themselves, in this very same perspective – that is to say as a human formulation of the truth of reality itself, indeed as its revelation, using the word in its widest sense.

This rational view of the world should not be repudiated from the outset as rationalist. On the contrary, Greek thinking was already aware that, when we consider the final ground of all reality and truth, reason comes up against a closed frontier, because here it touches on something that is illimitable and no longer definable. The Greeks realized that infinite reason can only be defined negatively, no longer positively. As early as the sixth century BC, Anaximander of Miletus calls this the *apeiron*, the boundlessly indefinable. About the same time, Xenophanes of Colophon established *the tradition of negative theology*, which makes only negative statements about God, defining him as the wholly Other compared with everything worldly and human: 'A single God, the greatest among gods and men, like neither to the form of mortals nor to thought.'[5] As Socrates put it, the utmost form of knowledge is therefore to know that we do not know,[6] a formula which recurs later in Augustine, Bonaventure and especially Nicholas of Cusa. Negative theology found its classic expression in Neoplatonism. In the fifth century AD, Dionysius the Areopagite (pseudo-Dionysius), who exerted such an influence on scholasticism, defined negative theology as follows: 'With respect to what is divine, negations are true, affirmations insufficient.'[7] As we know, the Fourth Lateran Council (1215) made negative theology the official doctrine of the church, saying: 'For between Creator and creature no similarity can be uttered without this having to embrace a still greater dissimilarity between the two.'[8]

For the early Fathers, this negative theology was already *the connecting link between Greek logos philosophy and biblical revealed theology*, and provided the presupposition for a synthesis between the two. The basic postulate of this synthesis was that the logos which reveals itself fragmentarily everywhere and in everything has appeared in all its fullness in Jesus Christ. The foundation for this synthesis had already been prepared in Hellenistic Judaism, especially by Philo of Alexandria, the Jewish philosopher of religion. The prologue to the Gospel of John takes up this approach: everything that has come into being has come into being through the logos, which was from the beginning. In the logos everything has life and light (John 1.1–14). But in Jesus Christ this eternal logos has become flesh. He has dwelt among us. 'From his fullness have we all received, grace upon grace' (John 1.14, 16). So in the Gospel of John Jesus can say of himself: 'I am the truth' (John 14.6); that is to say, in him the truth about which all ask and for which all seek has been finally revealed. 'In him are hid all the treasures of wisdom and knowledge' (Col. 2.3).

This doctrine about *Jesus Christ* as *the all-surpassing summing-up of the mystery of God* manifested in the world and history was made the official doctrine of the church by the Second Vatican Council. It calls Jesus Christ the key, the centre and the purpose of the whole of human history.[9] 'The Lord is the goal of human history,' it says, 'the focal point of the desires of history and civilization, the center of mankind, the joy of all hearts, and the fulfilment of all aspirations.' As the council goes on to say, quoting Revelation 22.12f., he is 'the Alpha and the Omega, the first and the last, the beginning and the end'.[10]

2. The revelation of the mystery of God in salvation history

The synthesis between Greek logos philosophy and biblical revealed theology which we have just briefly outlined has been determinative for the whole of Christian theology down to the present day. If we look at the synthesis more closely, however, it of course soon becomes evident that in the process of its Christian reception the logos concept has undergone considerable revision. It has in fact been re-minted. For the biblical understanding of word (*dabar*) differs quite considerably from the Greek *logos*. It is true that *dabar* is the Hebrew equivalent, formally, speaking, of *logos* in Greek. Formally, both have to do with the becoming-manifest of the deepest and ultimate ground of reality; and for both this manifestation takes place through the medium of language. Yet materially – that is to say, substantially – the way in which this manifestation comes about differs profoundly. According to the Bible, reality does not interpret itself in the logos that is common to all human beings. The logos the Bible talks about is the *logos tou theou*, the word of God, which is of its very nature *not* shared by all human beings, but is totally undeducible and non-contingent, and is authoritatively proclaimed by quite particular messengers – the prophets whom God calls. This logos cannot be received by way of rational insight, but solely in faith. That is to say, God's word does not articulate the manifest character of the divine which appears everywhere and at all times, as do both the myth and the logos in their different ways. On the contrary, in God's word this revelation takes place – becomes event – in a way never otherwise given.

It has become customary to term this specific biblical understanding of revelation 'historical'. But in this context the word 'historical' is really used to mean five different things.

1. The word of God is a historical event in the sense that it is not given always and everywhere but *here and now*. It goes forth non-contingently, and hence *graciously and freely*.

2. The word of God does not merely interpret already existent reality. It is a *creative* word, which brings, gives, effects and confers what it utters. It is not merely a word *about* grace, life and salvation. It is an efficacious and creative word *of* grace, life and salvation. So the word of God is not a supernatural doctrine. It is itself life, spirit and power.

3. As efficacious word, God's word always issues *in word and in act*. As we know, the Hebrew *dabar* means both. Here word and act belong intrinsically together. In the act the word shows itself as saving word, just as, conversely, it is only through the word that the acts are interpreted as saving acts. Consequently the word of God is not in any way irrational. On the contrary, it proves itself in historical experience, showing itself in history to be true, in the sense of being faithful and reliable; and this faithfulness and reliability is not an irrational feeling but is in its turn itself framed in the word and publicly proclaimed.

4. This historical demonstration of God's word is given in the historical *struggle with error and lies*. The Gospel of John brings out this historical interpretation quite clearly by saying that the light which shines in reality from the beginning 'shines in the darkness, and the darkness did not comprehend it' because human beings loved the darkness more than the light (John 3.19). They suppressed the truth of reality and exchanged the truth and glory of God for that of created beings (Rom. 1.18, 25). So God's original manifestation was eclipsed, and a new historical revelation was needed, to bring the truth of God and the truth about the world and human beings into the light again. God's word is therefore a *prophetically critical* interpretation of reality. The interpretation of Holy Scripture as the determining testimony of the word of God, given once and for all, must be an interpretation of reality as well. Through his word, God does not only reveal himself. At the same time he reveals 'man to himself'.[11]

5. Finally, the revelation of God's word is historical in the sense that it comes about in *the historical sequence of Old and New Testaments*. The beginning of the Epistle to the Hebrews brings out this historical dimension, at the same time linking it with the universal, cosmic viewpoint which we encountered in the Gospel of John: 'At many times and in various ways God spoke of old to our fathers by the prophets; but in these last days he has spoken to us by the Son, whom he appointed to be the heir of all things, through whom he also created the world; he is the reflection of his glory and bears the very stamp of his nature' (Heb. 1.1–3). In other words, *Jesus Christ* is the final and all-comprehending word of God in history, because in him the Word, in which everything was created and which, in fragmentary form, finds expression in everything that exists, has been summed up once and for all, and finds its final utterance.

If we look as a whole at this fivefold interpretation of God's word, we see that there is a very much stronger mutual tension between revelation and mystery than in the Greek view. For according to Christian understanding, the mystery of the divine is simply *not* something that is manifested everywhere and at all times, and which is therefore by its very nature accessible to human reason. It is true that (at least according to the Catholic view) the Bible recognizes that there is a natural revelation of God in creation, so that in creation we can perceive God by the natural light of reason (Rom. 1.18ff.). But this perception brings us only to the 'outer door', as it were, of the mystery of God. It can grasp the fact of this mystery. But the nature of the mystery is closed to it. The innermost nature of the divine mystery cannot be known 'from below'. It must reveal itself and communicate itself 'from above'. The historicity of revelation, which the Christian view maintains, is therefore not merely an external form and configuration. It belongs intrinsically to the inner content of revelation itself. It is a sign of the uncontingent freedom, graciousness, mercy and inexplicable love of God, the God who out of pure goodness turns towards human beings and reveals to them his mystery, which is the mystery of his love. The revelation of God's mystery in history is therefore something different from illumination *about* the mystery of God. It is the actual revelation of the mystery itself. It does not do away with the mystery. On the contrary, it brings out that mystery in all its fullness.

This gives rise to a new Christian definition of the mystery of God as it is disclosed in revelation. In the Bible, the mystery of God is not what it is in Greek philosophy, where it is the furthest horizon of knowledge that can be attained, a horizon that continually eludes us. In the Bible God's mystery is the fundamental content of his revelation. It is not a theoretical, epistemological proposition. It is a theological statement. It is not the final word of human self-perception. It is the first word of the perception of faith, given us by God. This is not a negative statement but an eminently positive one, which says that in his revelation God actually reveals his hiddenness to men and women. The proposition about the mystery and the hiddenness of God therefore does not refer to the nature of God which is withdrawn from human beings, but rather to the nature which is turned towards them. In specific terms: it reveals God as the mystery of freedom in love. 'God is love' (I John 4.8, 16) is therefore the biblical phrase which sums up the nature and content of Christian revelation, and the nature and content of the mystery uttered in that revelation.

Understood in this way, the revelation of the mystery and the hiddenness of God is anything but a theoretical speculation. It is both a word of judgment and a word of grace. It is a word of judgment because it says quite definitively that human beings cannot exercise control over the mystery of God, either through what they know or through what they do. In this sense the revelation of the mystery of God is the judgment on human hybris, which wants to be like God (Gen. 3.5). It is a judgment on all self-made idols, on all our images of God, and on all absolutizations of finite powers, which do not set us free but enslave us. In this act of judgment, by reminding human beings of their limits, the revelation of God's mystery is at the same time salutary and speaks a word of grace. It revokes the law of achievement, and tells us that we can never ultimately achieve 'life', and ultimately have no need to do so because we are definitively and absolutely accepted and affirmed by God, accepted with all our limitations. Thus the revelation of God's mystery is the revelation of the mystery of our salvation. It is *the* fundamental and central saving truth of the Christian faith, whose central utterance is that God the Father, through Jesus Christ his Son, has in the Holy Spirit finally pledged and communicated himself to us.

3. The personal character of the divine mystery

In this final section we shall try to define a little further what we have just said about the revelation of God's hiddenness. Really, everything that has been said can be summed up in a single sentence: in the historical revelation of his hiddenness, God, the deepest ground of all reality, shows himself to be *a personal being*, an 'I', whom men and women may address as a 'Thou'. For in the self-revelation of his mystery, God does not reveal *something*, not even something of himself and about himself. Here, rather, he becomes manifest in that which he *is*: as the mystery of love. So God does not reveal something, in the sense of some supra-rational and supra-natural truths and realities: he reveals himself. According to the Christian understanding, revelation is the self-revelation of God, in the sense of God's personal communication of himself to human beings.

We shall go on to explain a little what this central thesis means, and shall try to bar the way to some possible misunderstandings. But first we have to justify the thesis rather more precisely on the basis of the biblical writings. This is necessary for a number of different reasons. For one thing, the Bible is not familiar with the *concept* 'person', either in its application to God, or in its application to men and women. For another, there are trends today, even in Christian theology, which cast doubt on the personal character of God. Yet in the biblical revelation, God indisputably speaks as an 'I'; and it is equally indisputable that he permits himself to be addressed as 'Thou'. An operation designed to cut the personal character of God out of the Bible could only end up with a corpse. This is the case even though we do not find the *term* 'person' in the Bible. For the Bible has an equivalent: the concept '*name*'. God has a name, he calls us by name, and we can call him by his name: for the Old Testament and for the New, this is so fundamental that any attempt to term the biblical God an 'it' is doomed to failure.

But this brings us all the more inexorably up against the question: what does the term 'person' mean when we apply it to God? And how can we objectively justify its application to him? This question brings us face to face with the fundamental difficulty of every dialogue between biblical and Asian religiosity. But the discussion is also to be found within modern Western thinking itself. In modern times there have been influential pantheistic philosophies whose influence on the thinking of modern times can hardly be overestimated – the philosophy of Giordano Bruno, for example, or Spinoza. Much was already anticipated in the discussions about the mystical thought of Meister Eckhart, who in his turn exerted a lasting influence on German Idealism. Pantheistic thinking influenced Goethe's writings, for instance, as well as the atheism dispute triggered off by Fichte in 1798. And the classic objections to the use of the term 'person' in talking about God are to be found once again, finally, in the philosophy of Karl Jaspers. The standard objection is that this term projects finitude into God, because a person only exists within given limits and in distinction from the world and other persons. 'Personhood', it is said, includes individuality, and therefore inevitably means limitation; and consequently it has to be excluded as a predicate for God.

We shall try first of all to go into this basic objection, deliberately starting from the classic concept of person that is usually applied in Christian theology. Boethius gives a definition of person which is determinative for the whole theological tradition when he writes: *persona est naturae rationalis individua substantia*,[12] 'The person is the individual being, the unique form in which the spiritual nature is realized.' What this definition intends to say, therefore, is that what is meant by spirit is present in the person in a completely unique and non-communicable way.

So two things belong to the person. The first is *individuality*, in the sense of uniqueness; every person is 'an original', something that exists only once. Consequently, according to the general mediaeval understanding, a person cannot be defined – that is to say, captured in a general concept. But on the other hand the person is also characterized by *spirituality*, and that means infinity. For it belongs to the nature of the spirit to reach out beyond everything finite to the infinite, to break down its limitations, and to be free. Consequently modern anthropology defines the human being as the being open to the world, the being who – unlike all other living things – does not belong within any particular environment but who can 'call in question' every specific environment and change it. Human beings are open for reality as a whole. So even in the finite sphere, the person is characterized by the tension between the specific individual, for whom there is no substitute, and that individual's openness towards the whole of reality. In other words, in the person the whole of reality is present in a way that is unique in every given case. The person is *Da-sein*: the German word means existence, but its literal meaning is 'being there'. The person is the 'there' of being. Because in the person the whole of reality is 'there' in a special way, the person can never be the means to what is considered to be a greater end. The person is an end in himself, and that is the reason for his always unique, unconditional and uninfringeable dignity.

If we now apply this concept of person to God, then – as with all human concepts – we can do so only in an analogous sense. That is to say, all similarity embraces an even greater dissimilarity. So God is not a person as we human beings are persons. God is a person in an incomparably higher, more comprehensive and more profound way, a way which for our 'person-ness' can be no more than an image and a simile. In this analogous, figurative way, the personal nature of God means that in him the whole of reality is present in an utterly unique way. So to apply the concept of person to God is not intended to limit him – quite the reverse. The intention is to preserve God's infinity, but at the same time to say that the infinity of God is not identical with the infinity (real or supposed) of the world and the human spirit. God is infinitely different from the infinity of the human spirit in the world. He is absolutely and utterly unique. The concept of person therefore preserves both things at once: God's *transcendence* – the infinite qualitative difference between God and the world – and his *immanence*. That is to say, he is the one who is infinite, all-encompassing and all-embracing, the one who is present in all things, and of whom traces may be discerned everywhere, and who yet eludes us in everything, being accessible to men and women in his innermost mystery only through himself, through his free self-revelation.

If we take all this into account, the category of person, when it is applied analogously to God (that is, in a figurative way), is capable of three things:

1. The category of person makes it clear that *God is not an object*, not a 'thing' that can be established and thereby pinned down. He is a subject, who speaks and acts in absolute and non-contingent freedom. The category of person therefore preserves the undisposability and hiddenness of God in the revelation of his name. It is the concept of person above all which resists the notion that God could ever be imprisoned in any general concept or in any system. To define God as a person therefore paradoxically makes it plain that God cannot

ultimately be defined. As person, God is absolutely and incomparably unique.

2. The category of person also establishes that *God is not a predicate*, neither a predicate of the world, nor a predicate of human beings. God is not the transfiguration and ideologization of the world, or of human beings, or of any ideas, movements and concerns. This means that he must not be ideologically claimed for any 'worldly' interests. His name must not be taken in vain and misused. It must be hallowed – kept holy. So God must be distinguished from idols which are the absolutizations of worldly forces (power, money, sexuality, fame, success, and so forth). We may put it in modern terms and say that to be critical towards every ideology is one of the functions of faith in God as the Bible defines it.

Through this prophetic criticism of all the idolatries and absolutizations which enslave men and women, the proclamation of God helps to make human beings free. For to recognize the rule of God liberates men and women from the world and in the world. To recognize the personal nature of God preserves the dignity of the personal nature of the human being. But since God is a person in incomparably higher measure than any human person, he is also, in incomparably higher measure, an end in himself. God is never the means to an end. Consequently evidence that faith in God is important for the world has a merely provisional function. The concept of person before all else resists any functionalizing of God, whether its intention be conservatively affirmative or progressively critical. The first thing and the last is not God's significance for us. It is the recognition that God is God, the adoration of God and the praise of God. 'We give thanks to thee for thy great glory.' It is in this way that the concept of person brings out God's glory and his holiness.

3. The category of person does not merely preserve the unique subject-ness of God. It also says that God is *the all-determining reality*. It takes seriously the insight that he is not merely a being in the world beyond, and is therefore not solely a personal counterpart, but that he is in all things, that we find him in everything, and that we can encounter him especially in all human beings. But not only that. By defining God, the all-determining reality, in personal terms, *being as a whole* is personally defined.

This means a revolution in the understanding of being. It is not substance that is ultimate and supreme, but relation. To put it in more concrete terms: *love is the all-determining reality* and the meaning of being. This gives the biblical idea of God a positive importance as well as a critical one. For it tells us that the human person is as person absolutely accepted and loved. So wherever there is love, we already find, here and now, the ultimate meaning of all reality. There the kingdom of God has already come, if only in a fragmentarily provisional way. To believe in God, the almighty Father, therefore also means believing in the almighty power of love and its eschatological victory over hate, violence and egoism; and it means the duty and commitment to live with that as our goal. Whatever is done out of love becomes enduringly part of the whole body of reality. So faith in God does not mean alienation from reality. On the contrary, it means the charge to turn to reality in love, and to contribute to a civilization of love.

In closing, it must of course be said that to show the importance of the concept of person in talk *about* God and in talking *to* God is no more than the beginning of an account of the Christian understanding of what God is. For in the nature of things, to talk about God as person inevitably leads immediately to a series of other questions. The most important of these questions is this: if God is a person, and if a person is only conceivable together with other persons, and in relation to other persons, who is God's counterpart? In other words, if God is love, who is the eternal Thou of that love? If it were the human being, then the revelation of God's love would be for God no longer free but necessary. Then God could no longer be thought without human beings and without the world. God and the world would then stand in a necessary connection to one another. If we are to avoid this conclusion (and it is one that is quite impossible for biblical thinking) we can do so only through *the acknowledgment of the triune God* – an acknowledgment whose foundation is already laid in Scripture. This acknowledgment says that from eternity God is in himself the event of love. It is impossible here to go into the specific form given to Christian talk about God as person by the doctrine of the three-person God. This acknowledgment also affects the Christian discussion itself, more than the dialogue with other religions.

In our present context, it must suffice to have shown that the mystery which God is for the religious man or woman generally, is interpreted by the Christian faith as the mystery of an unfathomable and incomprehensible love, and hence as a personal mystery. *This mystery of God's love is the answer to the mystery of the world and human beings*, the answer to the deepest human longing for acceptance and love. But if God is love and accepts men and women in infinite love, then for human beings the ultimate meaning, fulfilment and bliss is not to be absorbed and diffused in God. It is community and friendship with him. According to the Christian view, this is the nature of grace and salvation, and represents the beginning and foretaste of eternal bliss and eternal life.

So according to Christian understanding, revelation and the mystery of God are the revelation and mystery of God's love; and everything else which Christian theology and the Christian creed have to say about God, his personal nature, and the threeness of his person, are no more than the unfolding – founded on revelation itself – of that single statement in the First Epistle of John: God is love. Anyone who has understood this sentence has understood everything; though to understand it will require a whole eternity, and will indeed be our eternal bliss.

II

Autonomy and Theonomy
The Place of Christianity in the Modern World

1. The urgency of the modern problem of autonomy

Theology has the task of rendering an account of the Christian hope to every human being (cf. I Peter 3.15). So if it is to make the Christian message universally communicable, it has to do so through the medium of the reason which all human beings share. It is through the reason that it must interpret the uncontingent uniqueness of the hope given by God through Jesus Christ in the Spirit. But since human reason interprets itself in a historical context, theology is also partly determined by its historical situation.

Even the New Testament writings already try to be all things to all men, and to proclaim the message of the gospel to the Jews in Jewish ways of thinking and speaking, and to the Gentiles in the language of Hellenistic culture (cf. I Cor. 9.19–22). In the period succeeding New Testament times we do not merely find a history of theology which continually takes new forms with every epoch; there is a history of dogma as well – that is to say, a history of the church's own understanding of its faith.

The catchword and slogan which sums up the modern history of emancipation (as well as the modern reason that goes with it) is 'autonomy'.[1] Consequently the relationship between Christian theonomy (or government by God) and autonomy (or self-government) stand imperatively first on today's theological agenda. We are indebted to Alfons Auer for having emphasized this situation, which presents a problem, not merely for moral theology but for theology as a whole.[2]

Auer has of course also made it plain from the outset that this problem cannot be solved by reducing the Christian claim.[3] Yet the fact that the programmatic stress on the catchword autonomy is open to misunderstanding cannot in itself be regarded as an objection. The words *logos* and *cosmos*, even the supremely orthodox *homoousios* of the Council of Nicaea, were in their time extremely loaded terms, highly open to misunderstanding. As we know, *homoousios* was a term deriving from Valentinian Gnosticism, and had been solemnly condemned at a synod in Antioch only fifty-seven years before Nicaea. In Aquinas' time, Aristotelianism was extremely suspect; it was considered 'leftist' because of the use made of it by Arab philosophers, and it was even officially condemned by the church's magisterium. The courageous theologian has to face up to questions as they are, not as he would like them to be, and must stand their test as best he may.

Urgency was lent to the modern problem of autonomy by the Second Vatican Council.[4] Breaking away from the restoration mentality of official doctrinal statements which were polemically and apologetically closed to the modern history of freedom, the council recognized two things: first, that the demand of modern men and women for autonomy can find its justification in the Christian message itself; second, that in modern times there has been a progression in the awareness of freedom which for a very long time the church undervalued.[5] But the council does not talk merely about the autonomy of the different cultural spheres (science, art, economics, politics, and so forth). It also talks about the inalienable dignity of the human person and his or her liberty, which the church knows it is explicitly sent to protect.[6] So the council does not see theonomy and autonomy as antitheses. And for that very reason it dissociates itself explicitly from atheistic humanism and autonomism.[7] This paves the way for an extremely differentiated, open and yet critical definition of the relationship between the church and modern culture; and it is the task of theology to clarify this definition more precisely.

The new openness on the part of the council has triggered off a keen, and also confusing, discussion about a new relationship between the church and theology on the one hand, and the modern world, with its culture, science and politics, on the other. The point at issue is how Christianity can be grafted into the cultural world of today. Of course this subject takes a different form in different cultural areas. But one

question is always at the centre of the discussion: since the Christian
message is theonomous through and through, how can it meet the
autonomous claim of any culture, or any particular political interest?
More: how can it meet the autonomous claim of the human
conscience? The confusion which has grown up round this question is
due not least to the circumstance that the word autonomy is used to
mean a number of very different things. We shall therefore first of all
try to clarify the problem presented by autonomy in its modern form.
We shall then go on to discuss the different solutions put forward in
present-day systematic theology. And we shall finally suggest an
approach of our own to the solution. In this attempt to define the place
of Christianity in the modern world, the definition we are seeking is
ultimately a practical one: how can the Christian cry for liberty be
channelled in a liberating way today? How can we today give an
account of the hope that is in us?[8]

2. The origin and character of the modern autonomy problem

(a) Its Christian roots

The problem of autonomy in its modern form has quite evidently
Christian roots. Among the Greeks, autonomy was pre-eminently a
political category. It was the ideal, never completely achieved, of the
Greek city states: to reach inward and outward independence and to be
able to live according to their own laws. At first it was only here and
there that the concept of autonomy had an ethical significance too – for
example when Sophocles calls Antigone's attitude of mind autonomy –
life according to one's own law.[9] It was only in the late period of the
ancient world, in Stoicism, that this interpretation came to be generally
accepted. When the earlier civilization of the *polis* collapsed, the
human being was on the one hand individualized; on the other hand he
became the 'cosmopolitan' who in his inner life participates in the law
of the cosmos and so has to live according to his own law.[10]

In the 'cosmos' thinking of the ancient world, the question about the
relationship between autonomy and theonomy could not yet be posed,
for in the ancient world the divine and the worldly ultimately formed a
unity. According to the testimony of Thales of Miletus (the first Greek

philosopher known to us) 'everything is full of the gods'.[11] For Plato the cosmos is a god perceivable through the senses.[12] For the Stoics he is the totality of heaven and earth, the divine and the human.[13] In this world picture, God is not so much the subject of the cosmos as its predicate.[14] God, or the divine, is a dimension of reality – its numinous depth. The gods are forms of being in which the divine depth of reality manifests itself in concrete form.[15] In this ancient interpretation the human being is still completely integrated and embedded in reality in its wholeness.[16] We cannot as yet talk about a direct relationship between God and every individual person.

But for the Bible the world is not *cosmos* but *ktisis*, or creation; not *natura* but *creatura*. The biblical account of creation is certainly woven into the mythological cosmogonies of its environment in many different ways. But the essential difference is that, unlike the mythologies, the Bible draws a dividing line between theogony and cosmogony. Or, to be more precise, it shows no awareness of any theogony at all. 'Before Israel and outside Israel people spoke of the creation of the gods in the same way as they spoke of the creation of the world or of humanity. But this is not possible in Israel. Creation, therefore . . . has different overtones. The object of creation is without exception something outside the divine. The action of God as creator is directed exclusively to the world. God is outside creation; to be created means to be not-god.'[17] So for the Bible there is an infinite qualitative difference between God the creator and the world as creation. Because in the Bible God is thought of as wholly divine, the world can for the first time be thought of as wholly worldly.

So it was precisely when God's divinity was taken seriously that the world could be demythologized and denuminized.[18] And the logical result was that the worldliness of the world could be taken seriously too. It is precisely the world's radical dependence on God which makes its genuine independence before God possible: this is the special character of the Bible's definition of the relationship between God and the world. As what is radically dependent, the world is what is not divine. It therefore stands over against God in relative independence. 'God establishes the creature and its difference from himself. But by the very fact that God establishes the creature and its difference from himself, the creature is a genuine reality different from God, and not a mere appearance behind which God and his own reality hide.'[19] The basic law of the relationship between Creator and creature is therefore: 'The radical dependence and the genuine reality of the existent coming from God vary in direct and not in inverse proportion.' Indeed it is even true that '. . . here genuine reality and radical dependence are simply two sides of one and the same reality, and therefore they vary in direct and not in inverse proportion.'[20]

When Christian belief in creation overcame ancient thinking in terms of the cosmos, the result was above all to free human beings from the clutches of a cosmos that was sacrally interpreted, and which was directly related to God. This becomes especially clear in the biblical version of the teaching that human beings are made in the image of God (cf. Gen. 1.26). For the ancient world, the king was God's image and hence his representative on earth. He represented the cosmic and metaphysical order. If the idea of the image of God is now transferred to every human being, the result of this 'democratization' is that everyone, irrespective of his ethnic, racial or religious affiliation, is God's direct partner, and as such enjoys an unconditional dignity over which no one can dispose (cf. Gen. 9.6).[21] According to Paul (who is here picking up the language of the Stoics), this dignity is expressed not least in the fact that the Gentiles, who do not know the Jewish law, are 'a law to themselves' (Rom. 2.14f.). And being a law to oneself is precisely what is meant by moral autonomy.[22]

Like all great ideas, the notion of the autonomy established with creation needed time before it could become a part of the general awareness. The Christian doctrine of natural law initially adopted a synthesis between biblical and Stoic ideas. Augustine especially – *the* Father of the Western church – maintained a view of the human being totally aligned towards God. This view was unable to bring out the relatively independent values of human beings and the world. All the same, in the theology of the twelfth century the independence and autonomy of created reality was already clearly formulated.[23] This insight acquired its classic form in the thirteenth century with the great mediaeval theologian Thomas Aquinas, who heads the theology of the church's teaching office as *the* teacher.

Aquinas' theology is no longer cosmocentric, like Greek philosophy. It is biblically theocentric. Thomas ponders over the notion that everything proceeds from God and returns to him.[24] But, starting from the idea of creation, he corrects and modifies this circular mythological pattern (which was given philosophical form in Neoplatonism especially) and now includes human freedom as a constitutive element in the whole process.[25] For Thomas, the human being is actually the pivot and hinge of this total movement, which proceeds from God and returns to him.[26] But it is only as free beings that men and women can know God as origin and goal, and can trace back reality to God.[27] So in Aquinas theonomy presupposes the autonomy of human beings. The material theocentricism is matched by a formal anthropocentricism. This means that the human being is not merely a link in the cosmos, not even the supremely important link (the Greek notion). He is – biblically – designated lord of the world.[28]

In Aquinas this conception has far-reaching consequences for the way human beings arrive at moral norms.[29] For he does not deduce these norms directly from the *lex aeterna*, nor does he make human reason a purely receptive instrument for reading the natural order. Since in their reason human beings participate in the divine reason, their insight into the moral order is certainly mediated through the natural order, but at the same time it is an active and creative procedure, the possibility for which is based metaphysically on the *lex aeterna*. Specific moral precepts therefore do not emerge from the eternal law directly and deductively, but merely by way of reflection and reduction.[30] As the image of God, and participating in the divine archetype, human beings are, however, pointed beyond everything that is purely 'natural', and are pointed beyond themselves as well. They are given over to a dynamic which cannot find fulfilment in any finite value, however elevated. This is the beginning of the Thomist doctrine about positive law, especially the *lex divina* of the new covenant. This *lex evangelica* is not a written law. It is unwritten. It is a law of liberty, which can be understood as law merely in an analogous sense.[31] It is the inner dynamic of love, given in the Holy Spirit, which directs the law perceived by reason towards the beatific vision of God, which surpasses natural reason and is itself the no-longer-surpassable consummating goal. So where it is a question of arriving at moral norms, Aquinas is able to unite in a brilliant synthesis the theonomy which accords with both creation and the gospel on the one hand, and, on the other, the autonomy which has its origin in that theonomy. It is a synthesis which resists all the objectivism of natural law, and all clerical positivism.

Unfortunately this brilliant conception did not come to be accepted in later scholastic theology, not even among the Thomists.[32] On the contrary, in late mediaeval Nominalism, this supremely rational model was forced to give way to a voluntarism which strained the Christian idea of theonomy to an unbearable degree, and in so doing profoundly misunderstood the true nature of the concept. According to Nominalist doctrine, God could if he wished command the human being to do what was untrue, unjust and immoral, and the human being was none the less bound to perform what he was commanded, out of pure obedience.[33] In practice too the liberating impulse of the gospel remained ineffective in wide areas of life. Slavery and serfhood, as well as the depreciation of women, continued to be legitimated for many centuries. Religious freedom and liberty of conscience were denied to Jews and heretics. The papal commission *Justitia et pax* has issued a working paper on *The Church and Human Rights* (1974), which states self-critically that the church's attitude towards human rights in the last two centuries 'has all too often been characterized by hesitation, objections and reservations'. Indeed the paper does not talk merely about caution and rejection. It even speaks about open hostility and condemnation by certain popes.[34]

Much of this is understandable, historically speaking. Yet we have to say that Christianity has often failed miserably to put across its own deepest concern: the message of the God who in his divinity liberates us for a humane humanity. And the tragedy of the modern development is that essential humane Christian impulses have had to be asserted in the face of Christianity in its mainstream form. The protest against a Nominalist, arbitrary God and the criticism of an authoritarian ecclesiastical system therefore led to a type of autonomy which was no longer theonomally based but was constituted autonomistically. And this lent the problem of autonomy an entirely new form.

(b) Modern emancipation

The motives, impulses, strands of tradition and immediate causes which led to the development of the specifically modern interpretation of autonomy vary enormously, and are indeed sometimes contradictory. On the one hand the after-effects of Christian impulses are unmistakably evident, particularly in the traditions of the English-speaking countries. We see this especially in America in the Virginia Bill of Rights of 1776.[35] Something similar may be said of the struggle waged by the Dominican Bartholomé de las Casas for the recognition of the human rights of the Indians, against the unbelievably cruel practices of Spanish colonial policy.[36] On the other hand the Protestant Reformation, and the religious wars of the sixteenth century that followed, meant that on the continent of Europe the Christian religion increasingly failed to offer a legitimation for socially relevant norms.[37] As a result Christianity was privatized, while society was constituted on the foundation of a purely rational, autonomous order of reason which was applied *etsi Deus non daretur* (as if there were no God).[38] The Renaissance of classical humanism, and especially the reversion to the Stoic doctrine of natural law, contributed to this situation.[39] In addition, in France particularly, the church's alliance with the *ancien régime* and – in the dispute with the newly developing natural sciences – its authoritarian and reactionary insistence on a world picture that had meanwhile been superseded, led to an aggressively anti-church form of autonomy.

The development of a modern autonomous interpretation of autonomy is therefore also an act of humane self-assertion against an understanding of theonomy which had meanwhile become repressive.[40] And yet the ideology and utopia of autonomism were themselves again mediated through Christianity, even in the antithesis and radicalism of their absolute claim. Indeed it is the tragedy of modern times that the liberating impulse of the Christian faith was so often forced to prevail in the face of Christianity in its mainstream form.

The modern era cannot therefore be traced back to any single principle, as if to a single cause. It has grown up out of a multiplicity of the most widely varying traditions, some of which are connected with one another and some of which are mutually conflicting.[41] Taken as a whole, these traditions have led to an immanentistically orientated culture, emancipated from the tutelage of religion and the churches, and to an emancipatory view of autonomy.[42] So even if it is impossible to arrive at a unified theory of modern times, we can still elicit a number of important fundamental motifs in the modern understanding of what autonomy is. Here we shall confine ourselves to three stages in the development of the modern autonomy problem: Descartes, Kant and Nietzsche.

Descartes is of fundamental importance for the modern interpretation of autonomy. He experienced the breakdown of all the order and
certainty that had hitherto existed. He was tormented by the Nominalist notion of a supremely powerful and cunning trickster who was
deliberately deceiving him. Yet in the end, in the face of this arbitrary
God, Descartes triumphantly proclaims: 'Let him deceive me as much
as he will, he can never cause me to be nothing as long as I think that I
am something.'[43] In the *cogito ergo sum* (I think, therefore I am),
Descartes finds a new unshakeable stance.[44] However great the power
of God may be, a minimum of our own remains to us. The need for
self-assertion leads to the autonomy of self-assurance. This is at first
completely independent of God's existence or his non-existence, or of
his being one thing or perhaps another. It is only at a second stage that
Descartes feels compelled to reintroduce the idea of God. For he
discovers that without the idea and reality of God, the 'I' cannot be sure
either of itself or of the world. In the act of apprehending himself, the
human being also apprehends the idea of God.[45]

In Descartes too, therefore, certainty of the self is based on certainty
of God. But if we compare him with Aquinas, we can see that the
direction of his thinking is reversed. Aquinas maintains an autonomy
that is founded on theonomy, Descartes a theonomy founded on
autonomy. In Aquinas the movement starts from God and returns to
God by way of the human being. In Descartes the movement begins
with the human being and returns to the human being by way of the
idea of God. In Aquinas God is the premise for human beings. In
Descartes the human being presupposes God, as the condition that
makes him possible. So in Descartes we see a Copernican revolution
resulting in a new anthropocentricism. The human being becomes the
starting point of reality and its point of reference. He is the subject that
confronts all other reality, making it his object.

Kant was already compelled to master the ethical consequences of
this turn to anthropology. For to the degree in which all external
authority collapsed, and all external order became a human blueprint
and construction, morality had to consider what it was, and to become
the inwardly justified morals of conviction.[46] The evidence for ethics
emancipated itself from theology especially; and an autonomous,
natural ethics was evolved.[47] Kant therefore brings about the Copernican revolution, not merely in epistemology, in his *Critique of Pure*

Reason, but also practically (or morally), in his *Critique of Practical Reason*. In the *Groundwork of the Metaphysics of Morals* he lays down the principle of this autonomy: the human will is itself law, independent of any external causes that determine it.[48] Human dignity is founded on this fact. It says that human beings are not the means to an end, but an end in themselves.[49] For Kant, human beings are a law unto themselves and an end in themselves because they are free. Freedom is not a concept based on experience. It is an incomprehensible idea of reason, or a necessary presupposition for reason. It therefore belongs to a different order from the order of nature.[50]

Kant's teaching about the autonomy of morals has often been misunderstood as subjectivism, and by theologians most of all. But the last thing it means is wilful individualism and sovereign self-assertion. On the contrary, Kant's categorical imperative is: 'Act only according to the maxims which you can at the same time will to be universal law.'[51] This principle leads to absolute respect for the dignity of every human being; and it follows that we make neither ourselves nor anyone else a means to an end.[52] This, then, is not a subjectivistic ethic. It is an inter-subjective one. In other words, Kant links morality to the reason shared by all free beings.[53] The human being 'should certainly follow the laws he himself has made, but he should follow them only to the extent in which they can be viewed as general; for otherwise they would not be truly reasonable. This is the meaning of the demand for autonomy in law and morals.'[54]

The theological problem about Kant's autonomous morality is that, since for him morality has its own autonomous justification in human freedom, a theonomous justification is excluded. God does not serve as sanction for laws imposed from outside. He serves the perception that all the duties arising from the free will are divine commandments.[55] Our actions are not binding on us because they are God's commandments. We see them as God's commandments 'because we find them inwardly binding'. True religion has no laws except those which we perceive through pure reason. True religion must serve to promote humanity.[56] 'Everything which a man thinks he can do to please God except good conduct is mere religious delusion and false worship.'[57] But Kant even goes a step beyond Descartes, since he does not merely reverse the justifying structure of morality, in a logical development of Descartes' approach. He also changes the very structure of its meaning.

If human beings are an end in themselves, it follows that morality does not have its end in God either, but is also an end in itself. In Kant's words, its end is the happiness of the human being. This happiness is to be found in the harmony between the moral and the natural order. Since human beings cannot guarantee this harmony, Kant has to introduce the idea of God as a postulate of practical reason.[58] But since the human being is an end in himself, God must not be the meaning and end of morality. Here God rather becomes a means to the end of human beings.

In saying this Kant has not merely changed the justificatory structure of autonomy, as Descartes did. He has changed the structure of its meaning as well. Whereas for Aquinas the ultimate meaning and felicity of men and women is to be found in glorifying God – in the beatific vision – the modern era is concerned to upgrade what is human. It is interested in a happiness which, though it can be achieved only through God, does not subsist in him. For Thomas, God is the supreme happiness of men and women. For Kant he only serves that happiness. Correspondingly, the Christian tradition is concerned with the divinizing of human beings, whereas the modern era is concerned with the humanizing of human beings or human society. For this, the idea of God has a no more than functional importance. The notion is ethicized and subjected to the criterion of practical relevance. And so the traditional relationship between religion and ethics is turned upside down. Morals are no longer based on religion. Religion is based on morals. To put it theologically: dogmatics no longer provide the foundation for ethics. On the contrary, dogmatics are developed in the light of ethics.[59]

Nietzsche's criticism of the moral concept of God can only be understood against the background of the movement of thought initiated by Kant. But when he takes the further step of getting rid of the auxiliary concept 'God' as well, he does this in a yet further development of the modern approach, which he now outdoes; for the latent functionalizing of the idea of God in modern times meant that human beings who were recognized as autonomous were divinized anew. This could happen in two ways. The human being could either be made an aspect of God (Spinoza's view); or God could be made an aspect of the human being (as in Feuerbach).[60] It was only where this latter view was accepted that the modern autonomizing process reached its peak. In tendency, we already meet this final form of the modern interpretation in the young Schelling, and in the early Fichte of the atheism dispute of 1798. In the nineteenth century we find it above all in Feuerbach and Marx. It achieved its classic form in our own century in the postulatory atheism of Nicolai Hartmann, Jean-Paul Sartre, Albert Camus, Maurice Merleau-Ponty and Ernst Bloch. The idea shared by all these very different thinkers is this: if there is to be human freedom, there cannot be an almighty God. The autonomy of the human being, radically understood, excludes all theonomy.[61]

Nietzsche thought the consequences of this emancipatory autonomy stringently through to the end. First of all he radicalized Feuerbach's approach. Like all truth, the idea of God is for him a value judgment, a theoretical sketch, a perspective created by human beings themselves. But the God whom the human being has evolved he can also kill. According to Nietzsche, this death of God is the real completion of human freedom, the leap from what is human to what is superhuman.[62] But what sets Nietzsche above the other modern thinkers is that he has the courage to face up to the most extreme consequences of the notion about the death of God. It is as if the horizon were blotted out. There is no longer any above or below. But Nietzsche does not lament this nihilism, in which the supreme values are devaluated. He proclaims a nihilism of strength.[63] He says 'yes' to life without any reservation or subtraction. He says 'yes' to the fact that human beings are an interim and a downfall.[64] *Amor fati* is his formula for human greatness.[65] Human beings do not find their fulfilment in the world beyond, or merely at the end. They find it in every moment, for every pleasure and gratification longs for deep, deep eternity.[66] So after the death of God many other gods are possible. 'For this is divinity: that there are gods but no God.'[67]

Through Nietzsche, men and women discovered a new human potentiality, a liberty they never knew before. Here God is in no way a necessity any longer, either as justification for human autonomy (as he was for Descartes), or as the completion of its meaning (as he was for Kant). When modern autonomy is thought of in truly autonomous terms, it is no longer a *praeambulum fidei* – a preliminary to faith. It is no longer a substructure, which had first to be justified through God and is completed by him. There are now possibilities for autonomous human fulfilment which no longer require the idea of God at all. And here Nietzsche does not wish, 'like the lowest of human creatures', to reduce the longing of human beings to banal dimensions.[68] On the contrary, the human being cannot merely deny God. He can also choose the counter-possibility to God. To be or not to be is indeed the question here. At this point especially Nietzsche is an uncannily modern thinker, of considerable relevance in today's vacuum of significance and its orientation crisis. And his thinking is probably only on the way to full recognition.

But God could only be denied as radically as this because he had earlier been so radically asserted as the divine God. It was Christian freedom which first discovered the whole abyss of human freedom as freedom in confrontation with God. And in so doing it simultaneously made it possible to turn against God. The emancipated autonomy we encounter in Nietzsche at the end of the modern development of the concept is a Christian idea in distorted – even deranged – form. For the moment that freedom emancipates itself from the only dimension that corresponds to it – the infinite God – it loses its appropriate measure altogether, whether it sees itself in the image of the restlessly striving Prometheus, or as the Dionysius who throws himself hungrily into ecstatic life. But a human being who has made himself absolute and a god is no longer a *human* being. He turns into the arrogant *Herrenmensch*, a superman who strives beyond himself, but can no longer humble himself to serve other people. A man who wants to be man's God (*homo homini deus*) will soon become his wolf (*homo homini lupus*). What he ought to be is a human being for other human beings (*homo homini homo*). A humane humanity of this kind is possible only for the person who lets God be God – the person who recognizes the infinite dimension beyond or above every human being, without claiming it for himself. But if the dialectic between the infinite dimension and infinite human longing on the one hand, and the merely finite realization of that longing on the other hand, is not to end in the melancholy of the unhappy awareness (Hegel's phrase), the dialectic can only be resolved in one way: if God gives himself to human beings and if human beings find their fulfilment in God. It is only theonomy that can justify and fulfil autonomy.

Whereas modern autonomy took over critically a Christian theonomy which had failed to comprehend its true nature, today Christian theonomy has to take over emancipated modern autonomy, so that this may be what German calls '*aufgehoben*' – a word which combines three different meanings: to abolish, to preserve, and to gather into something higher. So theonomy will criticize (*tollere*) autonomy's unchristian presuppositions and conclusions; it will preserve (*conservare*) its latent Christian wealth; and it will integrate it once more into Christian theonomy (*elevare*). The result might be not merely a new definition of the place of theology in the modern world; it could even mean a new definition of the place of the Christian faith itself in the modern world.

3. Theological models for mastering the modern problem of autonomy

(a) The restoration model: autonomy as a defection from theonomy

When we look at the exaggerated form given to the modern autonomy problem in Feuerbach, Marx and above all Nietzsche, we can easily understand why theology for the most part initially thought that it could only save its own skin by way of a decisive 'no' to the modern autonomous claim. People believed that the French Revolution showed that the autonomous standpoint led straight to chaos and nihilism; and thinkers like Edmund Burke, Joseph de Maistre, F. J. Stahl and others were convinced that these consequences could only be nipped in the bud if theonomy were firmly restored. The influence of this restoration philosophy on theology, and on the church's official statements condemning the history of freedom in modern times, was considerable.[69] The result was an integralistic, closed-in concept of the church, a church in a state of siege. The disastrous anti-modernist doctrinal promulgations at the beginning of the century, and the disciplinary measures of the time, were the clearest expression of this mentality; and they profoundly harmed both the outward image of the church and its inward vitality.

Even the renewal movement in the church during the first half of our century was not able to win through to a positive judgment about the modern idea of autonomy. Hardly any book is as characteristic of this new movement as Romano Guardini's *Vom Sinn der Kirche* (English title *The Church and the Catholic*), which was first published in 1922.

It begins with his famous saying about the awakening of the church in souls. Guardini saw this awakening against the wider horizon of an awakening to reality, including metaphysical reality; for him it was therefore part of the surmounting of modern subjectivism and individualism.[70] In his late book *The End of the Modern World* (1950, ET 1957), Guardini takes up these ideas again in order to show that 'autonomism's faith in revolution'[71] is today drawing to a close. The Tübingen dogmatic theologian Karl Adam was no less sharp in his judgment. In his much read book *The Spirit of Catholicism*, first published in Germany in 1924, he describes the modern era as a great apostasy: 'The mark of modern man is his loss of roots . . . The slogan "Away from the church" in the sixteenth century led in the eighteenth with inner cogency to "Away from Christ", and thence, in the nineteenth, to "Away from God". In this way modern spirituality was torn out of its most important, most profound living context, torn from its roots in the absolute, in the substance of being, in the value of values.' 'The autonomous human being, torn away from his national group and community' is for him 'the man devoured by the spirit of "criticism", the man alienated from reality, the man of mere negation'.[72]

Voices like this could easily be multiplied.[73] They are united in seeing modern autonomy as a defection from Christian theonomy. They are largely speaking blind to the Christian roots of the modern era, and its positive Christian potentialities. If we are to make critical use of these potentialities, in order to arrive at an appropriate definition of Christianity's place in today's world, then a mere restoration of mediaeval thinking is excluded, even though it be Aquinas' brilliant synthesis.

(b) The progressive model: autonomy as the realization of theonomy

The Second Vatican Council signified the fulfilment of the reform movement within the church. But it also signified a change in that movement, as the church opened itself for the modern world in a new way. This opening was expressed in the positive reception of the modern notion of autonomy. The ground for the change of thinking was prepared theologically by the critical reception of the modern subjectivity problem in the work of the Belgian Jesuit Joseph Maréchal. His suggestions have proved extremely fruitful for theology, particularly in the shift towards anthropology which we find in the theology of Karl Rahner.[74] In a modern re-reading of the Thomist synthesis, Rahner was able to show that theonomy and autonomy are not antithetical, but condition one another reciprocally.[75]

Following up Rahner's approach, Johann Baptist Metz arrived at a new theology of the world. He summed this up in the thesis: 'The worldliness of the world, which developed in the modern secularizing process and which faces us today in a more acute global form, was not in origin anti-Christian (whatever may be said of its individual historical forms). It came into being through Christianity. It is an originally Christian event, and therefore testifies that the power of "Christ's hour" which rules in history also rules in the situation of the world today.'[76] 'We may therefore say that "Christianizing the world" means in a primal sense "making it worldly" – putting it in possession of its own character and its own property.'[77] These arguments could be understood as a legitimation of the *status quo* of modern, Western bourgeois civilization, and in so far as its theoretical ideologization. But in his later political theology Metz makes it clear that his postulates are related to the future and orientated towards praxis, and that they are therefore an option 'for the ability and need of all men and women to be conscious subjects.'[78] Metz sees Rahner's theonomy-autonomy formula in this context and develops it further: 'The struggle for God and the struggle to allow everyone to be a free subject are not antithetical. They tend in the same direction and are in proportion to one another.'[79]

With these postulates Metz first of all took up the theology of secularization which in Protestant theology was represented particularly by Friedrich Gogarten.[80] There, however, attempts to elucidate modern processes of secularization and liberation appealed, not to Aquinas, but to Luther's doctrine of the two kingdoms and to Protestant kingdom of God theology, thus taking up in new form the postulates of liberal theology and the analyses of Max Weber and Ernst Troeltsch. The most ambitious attempt to understand the modern history of freedom as Christian history has been undertaken by Trutz Rendtorff.[81] He has brought out the real background of the theology of secularization more clearly than anyone else. Hegel's conception and synthesis was pressed into service here, by way of Karl Löwith: the modern era is no apostasy. It is the worldly form taken by Christianity.

The approach of the theology of secularization was developed in detail in double form, the two strands running radically counter to one another. Jürgen Moltmann in particular has developed a consistent theology 'from above', tracing back the modern history of freedom directly to the biblical message of the kingdom of God.[82] The counter-approach 'from below', on the other hand, tries to interpret and integrate the autonomous modern development in a Christian sense, in a process of hindsight, so to speak.[83] In liberation theology (which stems primarily from Latin America), the two converge in a way which is not ultimately fully clarified hermeneutically. The old distinction between the natural and the supernatural spheres, between Christian salvation and social well-being, is cast aside in favour of a new integral viewpoint: redemption is interpreted as liberation and the struggle for liberation is at the same time a struggle for the kingdom of God.[84]

Three questions must be put to this progressive solution to the autonomy problem.

1. Does it not underestimate the emancipating dynamic of the modern autonomizing and liberation process which runs counter to Christian theonomy? Does it not in fact make the dispute too simple?

2. Do the proponents of this view not too rashly assume the irreversibility of the secularization process? And have they not overlooked the dialectic of enlightenment, which Max Horkheimer and Theodor Adorno worked out?[85] This is in continual danger of turning into new irrationalism and of itself becoming a mythology and ideology. P. L. Berger especially has recently pointed out from the sociological standpoint the limitations of the postulate of progressive secularization.[86] Some people believe that today it can be confronted with the thesis about the continued existence of religion.[87]

3. Does this model not ultimately fail to recognize the divinity of God, in its infinite qualitative difference from the world – what scholastic terminology calls God's aseity? But if God no longer means 'something' which is not already 'given' with the modern world, or with the world in general, then the word God has no content. It is null and void. It becomes an empty formula and a pious superstructure.[88] Metz himself makes this point: 'The name of God stands for the fact that "transcending" is not simply a symbolical paraphrase at a higher level, or an impotent reflection of what happens anyway – which is what it would have been, if it were merely a "transcending without transcendence".'[89] But if the word God means 'something', and

something of decisive importance for the world and human beings, then the revelation of God must provide substantial criteria which do not merely confirm and elevate modern autonomy and modern liberation processes, but also help us to evaluate them in a new way.

(c) The correlation and analogy model: autonomy as a parable of theonomy

If we do not want to level down the permanent difference between salvation and well-being, redemption by God and liberation by human beings, theonomy and autonomy, but do not wish either to fall back on the unfruitful antithetical solution offered by the restoration model – then all that remains is for us to define the relationship between theonomy and autonomy in a way that tries to think together their unity and their difference. Here correlation and analogy are modes of thought which suggest themselves.

Paul Tillich tried quite early on to take this path in his correlation method.[90] But the question and answer scheme he chose is unduly harmonizing and does not sufficiently bring out the antagonistic element in the relationship between Christian theonomy and modern autonomy. Karl Barth's teaching about an analogy of relation (an *analogia relationis*) between God and human beings, who are his image and parable, takes us deeper.[91] Later on he developed this doctrine further, teaching that the world and worldly happenings are to be seen as parables of the kingdom of heaven.[92] Eberhard Jüngel has taken up this model and has shown that civil rights and liberties cannot be derived from the liberty conferred by God (otherwise the gospel would become law); but that none the less, by way of an analogy of relation, the freedom for which we have been set free by God (cf. John 8.31; Gal. 5.1) offers criteria for a proper understanding and a proper praxis of human liberty which, taken simply by itself, is ambivalent.[93] Wolfgang Huber and H. E. Tödt have made analogy fruitful as a method of theological interpretation and a way of 'decoding' human rights in our modern era. Their aim here is to bring out both the critically limiting and the constructively inspiring significance of the gospel for the realization of human liberty.[94]

There can be no doubt about the fruitfulness of this balanced, middle-of-the-road position for a Christian legitimation and interpretation of modern human rights and liberties. But the question is whether this approach can be communicated beyond the Christian sector, since it is based on revealed theology or – to draw its boundaries more closely – on christology. At the back of Barth's doctrine about the *analogia relationis* is an explicit dissociation or differentiation from the Catholic doctrine about the *analogia entis* (the analogy of essence) and the possibility of a natural knowledge of God, which depends on this analogy. So in this approach the danger of revelation positivism[95] cannot be rejected out of hand. And that means that this approach threatens to thrust the truth about human beings on to men and women heteronomously. But modern autonomy can hardly be heteronomously legitimated and interpreted. Catholic theology will hardly be able to accept this narrowly Christocentric approach, and will feel bound to seek for a more comprehensive starting point from which to define the relationship between Christian theonomy and modern autonomy.

For Catholic theology, the *analogia entis* and the *analogia fidei* – the analogy of essence and the analogy of faith – belong intrinsically together. This is made plain by the classic axiom: 'Grace presupposes and perfects nature.'[96] In our present context we cannot enter into the many and varying problems which arise today from the relationship between nature and grace. Of course nature and grace are not two separate though parallel spheres, or two separate storeys, one above the other. There is an inner relationship of premise and transcending. For the love of God which communicates itself in Jesus Christ presupposes human beings, who are created for love and open for love. It presupposes the person. If we apply this to our problem, theonomy then presupposes human autonomy, because God's divinity has to be recognized by men and women in responsible freedom, since God desires to be glorified through free created beings. On the other hand human freedom only arrives at completion and fulfilment through theonomy – through the recognition of God and through fellowship with God. For part of human freedom is openness into an infinite mystery. It is only in the context of the infinite that men and women can experience what is finite as finite and contingent; it is only in the context of the infinite that freedom is possible. This gives human freedom an element of restlessness and lack of repose. It does not find its final fulfilment in any encounter within the world; it is of itself unfulfillable. It can arrive at fulfilment only when it encounters a freedom that is infinite, not merely in its formal claim but in its fulfilment too – only in the encounter with God.[97] So theonomy brings autonomy to fulfilment as autonomy. The greater the unity with God, the greater the freedom of the human being.

This reciprocal relationship of premise and transcending can also be described as a reciprocal analogy. In its infinite openness, human autonomy is an anticipatory image, a prefiguration, a shadowy parable, a first sketch, which only arrives at its final implementation and perfection in Jesus Christ. Jesus' 'Abba' relationship with God does not merely finally manifest who God is. It also finally manifests who human beings are: the beings who are finally accepted by God. So as *the* image of God (II Cor. 4.4; Col. 1.15), Jesus Christ also perfects human beings as God's image (Gen. 1.26). As the Son of God he is at the same time the new Adam (Rom. 5.14; I Cor. 15.45). In him the open, equivocal mystery of human beings becomes unequivocal and clear. In him God reveals 'man to himself'.[98] Irenaeus of Lyons offers a classic exposition of the connection here: 'In earlier times it was said that man was created in the image of God, but it was not so shown. For the Word in whose image man had been made was still invisible. That is why man so easily lost his resemblance. But when the Word became flesh, he confirmed both: he showed the true image by becoming what his image was; and he secured the resemblance by making man resemble the invisible Father through the visible Word.'[99] Irenaeus expresses the relationship between God and human beings in a pregnant way: 'For the glory of man is God; the work of God and the vessel of his wisdom and power is man.'[100]

Starting from this analogy between God and human beings, the order of salvation and the order of nature, nature and grace, we shall in closing draw a few conclusions, at least in outline, which may point the way to a solution of the problem posed by modern autonomy. We shall do this first under a more positive aspect and then under a more critical one, although in our present context we can offer no more than a few first indications, which would certainly require a deeper and broader exposition.

First of all, the reciprocal analogy which already determined classic Catholic theology permits us to take up the modern problem of autonomy in a positive sense. It confirms the thesis which we already postulated at the very beginning: the unconditional bond with God as the origin and goal of men and women (which is what theonomy means) does not exclude autonomy. On the contrary, it sets it free.

Consequently, theonomy properly understood is by no means a kind of heteronomy. Where, in the name of autonomy, modern criticism of religion has taken up a stance in opposition to theonomy understood in a heteronomous sense, it must be considered theologically correct. Theonomy, properly understood, justifies autonomy and brings it as autonomy to fulfilment.

But this reciprocal analogy between autonomy and theonomy does not merely make it possible to take up the modern problem of autonomy positively. From this aspect the concept itself can be deepened. The modern subjectivity problem allows us to understand the nature presupposed by grace as freedom, or to understand this more clearly than was the case in tradition. We can hence arrive at a theological recognition of the rights and liberties which the modern era has stressed and which belong intrinsically to human beings as human beings. Vatican II took this step in principle in its declaration on religious liberty, with which it also moved from the rights of truth to the rights of the person – a step which was not a matter of course, in the light of previous tradition.[101] The principle that 'grace presupposes nature' therefore means that 'grace and truth presuppose freedom'.[102] The proclamation and acceptance of the gospel presuppose the intellectual and moral responsibility of the individual, and an order in society in which there is liberty of information and communication. Intervention for the rights and liberties of men and women is therefore an implication of the Christian message itself, and one of its essential elements. There was much confusion in the church's tradition over this point, and here the modern era has helped the church to arrive at a better and more profound perception of its own concern.[103]

The reciprocal analogy between autonomy and theonomy also involves a critical correction in two different ways, or rather: a closer critical definition in two respects of the modern interpretation of autonomy, which can in detail be construed in a number of different senses. If we start from the theonomy of the order of creation or salvation – or, more precisely, from christology – the autonomy which is open and undetermined acquires a particular content.

The theonomy of the order of creation reminds us first of all of the 'given' relations which are constitutive for human existence. It therefore excludes a radically emancipatory understanding of autonomy. What is already given and laid upon human freedom as the condition which makes it possible is what we call nature.[104] Nature is God's creation. It is not made by human beings and cannot be made by them. It therefore has its own dignity. It has to be cultivated by human beings, but it must not be manipulated arbitrarily and at will. This suggests that the idea of natural law ought to be creatively renewed. This is not something for Catholics alone. Even less is it a purely neo-scholastic concern. We already find a basis for it in the philosophy of the ancient world, and traces of it are to be found in the New Testament (Rom. 2.14f.). It was taken up, not only in the patristic and scholastic writings, but in Protestant theology as well. We find it again in a number of different guises in the modern law of reason and liberty, and in the idea of human rights and fundamental values.[105] Ernst Bloch especially has shown that it can also become a part of socialist thinking.[106] It belongs to the foundations of the European cultural heritage and – if I am right – it is the real concern of an autonomous morality in the Christian context – an autonomous morality which in taking up this concern has the whole of tradition behind it.

Second, the theonomy of the order of salvation reminds us that human beings cannot perfect themselves. It therefore prevents any ideology from becoming fixed and final, or from taking possession of men and women. It protects the transcendence of the human person and is a plea for a freedom that is always greater than all possible fulfilments. The order of salvation – or, more precisely, christology[107] – therefore sheds light on the worldly conduct of men and women. The religious and the secular relations of human beings, the ethics of salvation and the ethics of the world, can certainly be distinguished – indeed the distinction between them is essential and indispensable for the things that are Christian. But the two cannot be divorced in principle. This middle way (equivocity) between radical difference and complete likeness (univocity) is called analogy. It does not permit us to deduce from the order of salvation specific standards for worldly be-haviour; for deduction presupposes univocal concepts. But never-theless, Jesus Christ is the prototype of fulfilled Christian freedom, and from him the fundamental attitudes of Christians emerge. The law of Christ (Gal. 6.2) is therefore a law of liberty (James 1.25), a Christian liberty which fulfills itself specifically in the ministry of love. This is the freedom for which Jesus Christ has set us free, and it is here first of all that the essential character of Christian ethics must be sought.

III

The Modern Sense of Freedom and History and the Theological Definition of Human Rights

1. The present discussion

(a) The restoration model

In 1976 the papal commission *Justitia et Pax* issued a working paper on 'The Church and Human Rights', in which we find the following statement: 'We are well aware that the church's attitude to human rights in the last two centuries has all too often been characterized by hesitation, objections and reservations. Any declaration on human rights prompted by the spirit of liberalism and laicism has even on occasion evoked fierce reactions from the Catholic side.' The paper actually goes so far as to talk here about open hostility and condemnation by the popes.[1]

This undoubtedly correct historical judgment also makes the intellectual background of the repudiation clear. The rejection meant a categorical 'no' to the modern notion of autonomy and to the practical — which is to say political — conclusions which the French Revolution drew from it.[2] People believed that the French Revolution showed that the autonomous standpoint led to chaos and nihilism. Thinkers such as Edmund Burke, Joseph de Maistre, F. J. Stahl and others were convinced that these consequences could only be averted by a firm restoration of theonomy and theocracy. The result was an integralistic, closed-in concept of the church, a church in a state of siege.

The first half of our century saw a movement for renewal in the church; but even this was unable to win through to a positive view of the modern notion of autonomy. In his late book *The End of the Modern World* (1950; ET 1957), Romano Guardini was still talking about 'autonomism's faith in revolution'[3]; and we can find equally caustic judgments in Karl Adam, Joseph Lortz, H. E. Hengstenberg and others. All these thinkers had one thing in common: they viewed the modern awareness of freedom and history as an apostasy, a defection from Christianity, a repudiation of the order of being based on theonomy, an alienation, an uprooting and a road to chaos. They were blind to the Christian roots of autonomy, and blinder still to the Christian potentialities of the modern era.

(b) The progressive model

Vatican II signifies the final breakthrough of a new definition of the relationship between the church and the modern history of freedom. The various theological renewal movements of our century had paved the way for this new definition, while Leo XIII prepared the ground where the church's official teaching was concerned. The Pastoral Constitution *Gaudium et spes* then took up the modern idea of autonomy in a positive sense (36; 41; 56). The Declaration on Religious Liberty is more significant still, since it does not merely recognize the autonomy of the various worldly sectors. The Pastoral Constitution does that too. But the Declaration also recognizes the autonomy of the human subject. Up to then only the rights of truth had been accepted. The Declaration on Religious Liberty now makes a transition from the rights of truth to the rights of the person. This laid the foundations for papal policy on human rights from John XXIII onwards.

After the Council, theological development moved far beyond these texts. The modern history of freedom now often came to be interpreted as an implementation of Christian liberty in the world, ideas of Hegel, Max Weber, Ernst Troeltsch and others being pressed into service here. The modern era has ceased to be viewed as an apostasy. It is now seen as the realized form of Christianity in the world.

This first of all provided the foundation for 'the theology of the world' which Johann Baptist Metz developed, largely on the basis of Friedrich Gogarten's ideas. This theology was summed up in the following key assertion: 'We may therefore say that "Christianizing the world" means "making it worldly" in a quite primal sense – putting it in possession of its own character and its own property.'⁴ This thesis could of course easily be misunderstood as a legitimation of modern, Western bourgeois civilization, and as being in this sense its theological ideology. Consequently, in his later theology Metz – largely following Ernst Bloch – developed a viewpoint which was related to the future and orientated towards praxis. Its basic option was 'the ability and need of all men and women to be conscious subjects'. Metz's postulate was now: 'The struggle for God and the struggle to allow everyone to be a free subject are not antithetical. They tend in the same direction and are in proportion to one another.'⁵

In Latin America especially, political theology triggered off liberation theology (although this takes extremely complex and varied forms). Liberation theology sees Christian salvation and the social well-being of human beings together, in a single, integral (which does not mean integralistic) viewpoint. It must be said, however, that this approach has not really been thoroughly clarified, hermeneutically and theologically. Redemption is interpreted as liberation, and the struggle for liberation is at the same time a struggle for the kingdom of God.

In a study by the World Alliance of Reformed Churches entitled 'A Christian Declaration on Human Rights', this trend towards a theological rehabilitation of human rights becomes a direct theological justification of these rights, founded on the message of the kingdom of God. On the basis of a draft made by Jürgen Moltmann, the study says: 'We understand the basic theological contribution of the Christian faith, in these matters, to be the grounding of fundamental human rights in God's right to, that is, his claim on human beings.' This is then immediately explained: 'This is to say that human rights are ultimately grounded not in human nature; nor are they conditioned by individual or collective human achievements in history.'⁶

It must be said that this statement – and especially its final, diametrical reversal of the earlier restoration model – also misses the mark of the modern sense of freedom and history. To deduce autonomy exclusively and directly from theonomy ignores what autonomy is about. By so doing, theology is in danger of becoming an ideology which, in a process of hindsight, really legitimizes the ideas that have already crystallized in the course of modern history, with its increasing awareness of human autonomy; or it may simply ratify the programmatic goals of the various social, cultural or national liberation movements. This attempt to justify autonomy theologically 'from above' ends up in a curious dialectic; for by missing the mark of human and worldly autonomy, it is also unable, logically enough, to preserve its specifically Christian character either. As Metz rightly points out, what is Christian then becomes no more than a symbolic paraphrase at a higher level, and the ultimately impotent reflection, or mirror image, of what happens and is said anyway.[7]

It is evidently only possible to escape this dialectic if we try to find a differentiated definition of the relationship between the biblical message and modern human rights, a definition which holds on to both the inner connection between the two and their difference – a definition, that is, which preserves what is specifically Christian by recognizing the autonomy of human beings and the world. In theological tradition, this problem of identity and difference is discussed under the heading of 'analogy'[8]. The aim of analogy is to mediate between the identity and the difference of separate sectors of reality, by seeing them in a relationship of mutual correspondence. If we apply this to our present problem: Christian freedom belongs to a different level from the moral freedom which is expressed in the modern categories of autonomy and human rights. These two freedoms are not simply the same thing; but they are not irreconcilably opposed to one another either. They are linked in a relationship of mutual correspondence. The one reality can therefore be deciphered by means of the other. Before we consider this thesis in the context of the modern problem, we must first of all look at the notion of analogy in its traditional context. We can of course only do so briefly, which also necessarily means in abridged form.

2. The theological tradition

(a) Biblical tradition

This is not the place to enter into the discussion about analogy which has gone on ever since Heraclitus and Parmenides. The problem played an important part in Plato and Aristotle especially. But here we shall turn directly to the biblical tradition first of all. In this tradition the *concept* of analogy certainly plays a merely marginal role (Wisdom 13.5; Rom. 12.6), but analogy *in itself* is central for the biblical understanding of creation.

To see the world as creation really means seeing it as an image and parable of God. To say this is to say two things. On the one hand the world and human beings are radically dependent on God, and related to him; this belongs to the very nature of their existence. On the other hand, the world and human beings possess a relational independence over against God. By understanding creation as God's free act, the Bible emphasizes the dependency aspect, compared with the cosmologies of its environment; for in these the divine and the worldly, theogony and cosmogony, are intermingled. But just because the world is totally and radically dependent on God, it is at the same time a reality that is radically different from him. Since it is radically dependent on God, the world is radically non-divine. It therefore stands over against God in relational independence. In its very dependence on God, the world is a reality independent of him. It is not a mere seeming, behind which the real divine reality is concealed. According to Karl Rahner, therefore, the basic law determining the relationship between Creator and created being is this: 'The radical dependence and the genuine reality of the existent coming from God vary in direct and not in inverse proportion.'[9]

When mythical 'cosmos' thinking was surmounted by the Christian belief in creation, this meant above all that human beings were freed from the clutches of a cosmos that was sacrally interpreted and stood in a direct relation to God. This becomes clear in the biblical version of the doctrine that human beings are made in the image of God (cf. Gen. 1.26). In the ancient world, the king was God's image and therefore represented the cosmic and metaphysical order. So when the Bible 'democratized' the concept of the image of God, transferring it to every single human being, it was affirming that every man or woman, irrespective of his or her racial, ethnic and religious affiliation, possesses an unconditional dignity over which no one can dispose (cf. Gen. 9.6). Because the human person belongs to God wholly and radically, he is absolutely removed from the grasp of his fellow human beings. In this way the unconditional dignity of human beings, simply *as* human beings, was proclaimed for the first time in religious history and the history of thought.

The dignity of human beings in their direct relationship to God is therefore founded on the idea of creation; and this also explains the universality of the biblical message of salvation. Because human beings are by their very nature completely dependent on God, while being at the same time free in this dependency, the Christian message of salvation is not something alien and heteronomous. Its universal claim is therefore not an authoritarian or totalitarian claim. On the contrary, it is based on the autonomy of human beings which belongs to their creation. The bearing this has on knowledge of God is brought out in Rom. 1.18ff., while its influence on moral requirements is made plain in Rom. 2.14f. In the second of these passages, Paul – taking up Stoic terminology – says that the heathen who do not know the law are 'a law to themselves'. Being a law to oneself is in fact precisely what is meant by moral autonomy.[10] For Paul, accordingly, the human being possesses autonomy, and this is the premise which makes it possible for the faith communicated in salvation history to be accepted in responsible freedom.

We can therefore say that freedom to believe presupposes that there is moral freedom. This is the condition which makes faith possible; while at the same time it is free faith that brings moral freedom to fulfilment. Paul brings out this last aspect when he says that for him Jesus Christ is the likeness of God that brings to fulfilment the human likeness to God given with creation (II Cor. 4.4; Col. 1.15; Heb. 1.3). So the Christ event is therefore universal because Jesus Christ reveals 'man to himself', as Vatican II's Pastoral Constitution *Gaudium et spes* says – because in the mystery of Jesus Christ the mystery of human beings is finally revealed (22).

According to this biblical viewpoint, then, the dignity of human beings lies in their freedom. This is the presupposition of the Christian message of salvation. And it is this human dignity which, on the other hand, is again given its final definition by Jesus Christ. The last Council took up this angle of vision anew and, as we know it was this that provided the sustaining foundation for the view of human rights adopted in the encyclical *Redemptor hominis*.[11] But before we can discuss this in detail, we should look at least briefly at one result of the biblical tradition which had a particularly important effect on Catholic theology. Of course we can only do this in summary form.

(b) The Thomist tradition

Like all great ideas, the idea of the autonomy grounded in creation needed time before it could become part of general opinion. The Western Father, Augustine, above all, maintained a view of humanity aligned wholly towards God. Here the relatively independent values of human beings and the world could not come fully into play. But the independence and inherent autonomy of created reality was already clearly formulated in the theology of the twelfth century;[12] and it was given its classic form a century later by the great mediaeval thinker Thomas Aquinas.

Aquinas' thinking is theocentric. He ponders over the idea that all things issue from God and that all things return to him.[13] But he corrects and modifies this circular mythological pattern, which had played a part in the reflections of the Neoplatonists especially. In the light of creation thinking, Aquinas now introduced the liberty of the human being as a constitutive element in this total process.[14] For Thomas, the human being is the pivot and hinge of this whole movement, which starts from God and returns to him.[15] But it is only because they are free beings that men and women can recognize God as origin and goal, and can trace back reality to him.[16] So in Aquinas, theonomy presupposes human autonomy. Material theocentricism is matched by a formal anthropocentricism. This means that the human being is not – as the Greeks held – merely one link in the cosmos, albeit the supreme link. On the contrary, according to the biblical view he has been appointed lord of the world.[17]

In Aquinas this conception had far-reaching consequences for his view of the way in which human beings arrive at moral norms;[18] for he does not deduce moral norms directly from the *lex aeterna* – the eternal law; nor does he make human reason a purely receptive organ for reading the order of nature. Human insight into the moral order is certainly mediated through the natural order, but it is nevertheless actively creative at the same time. This creatively active insight is possible because, through their reason, human beings participate in the divine reason. The *lex aeterna* is therefore not a principle from which moral standards can be deduced, but it is none the less the enabling metaphysical ground which makes it possible for human beings to arrive at particular norms. Specific moral precepts therefore emerge from this eternal law solely through reflection and reduction, not directly and deductively.[19] As God's image, however, and as participating in the divine archetype, the human being is at the same time above everything that is purely natural. Human beings are pointed beyond themselves too, and are given over to a dynamic which cannot find fulfilment in any finite value, however elevated. This is the starting point for Aquinas' teaching about positive law — especially about the *lex divina* of the new covenant. This *lex evangelica* is not a written law. It is unwritten. It is a law of liberty, which can be understood as law at all only in an analogous sense.[20] It is the inner dynamic of love, given in the Holy Spirit, which points the law perceived by reason towards the consummating goal — the beatific vision of God, which surpasses natural reason and is itself no longer surpassable. So when he is thinking about the discovery of moral norms, Thomas is able to unite in a brilliant synthesis the theonomy that accords with creation and the gospel, and the autonomy for which creation and gospel provide the ground.

Here, therefore, theonomy presupposes autonomy and at the same time brings that autonomy to its fulfilment. This reciprocal relationship is expressed by Thomas (and by the scholastic tradition generally) in the classic axiom: 'Grace presupposes and perfects nature.'[21] We cannot enter here into the complex problems which arise today from the relationship between nature and grace. Of course nature and grace are not two parallel sectors, or two separate storeys, one above the other. There is an inner relationship of premise and transcending. For the love of God which communicates itself in Jesus Christ presupposes human beings who are created for love and are responsive to love. If we apply this to our present problem: theonomy presupposes human autonomy because God's divinity has to be recognized by men and women in responsible freedom, since God desires to be praised and glorified by free created beings. Conversely, however, human freedom is only perfected and fulfilled through theonomy — through the recognition of God, and through fellowship with him. So theonomy brings autonomy to fulfilment *as* autonomy. The greater the unity with God, the greater the liberty of the human being.

Unfortunately this brilliant conception did not come to be accepted in later scholastic theology, not even among the Thomists. On the contrary, in late mediaeval Nominalism a voluntarism carried the day

which strained the Christian idea of theonomy unbearably, and in so
doing profoundly misunderstood its real nature. It was Nominalist
doctrine that, if only he wanted to, God could even command human
beings to do what is untrue, unjust and immoral, and that they would
nevertheless be bound to do what they were commanded, out of pure
obedience. In practice too the liberating impulses of the gospel
remained ineffective in wide areas of life. Slavery and serfdom, as well
as the inferior view of women, continued to be legitimated for many
centuries. Religious freedom and liberty of conscience were denied to
Jews and heretics. The detour via the modern history of freedom was
needed in order to mediate again, even to the Christian churches
themselves, a full awareness of their very own tradition.

When we try today to arrive at a theological definition of human
rights in the context of the modern awareness of liberty and history,
recourse to the Thomist tradition can undoubtedly be helpful. It shows
us that we do not have to choose between theonomy and autonomy. It
also makes it clear that we do not have to justify human rights
deductively 'from above', from a theonomous understanding of
human beings and the world. Indeed it shows that we must not justify
them by this method, if we wish to arrive at a proper understanding,
not merely of autonomy, but of theonomy too. Human rights are
already given with creation. They cannot be historically deduced. But
by a process of reflection they can be reductively integrated into the
theonomy of the Christian order of salvation, as its very own premise;
and the ultimate definition of the meaning of human rights is to be
found within a theonomy that is understood in a Christian sense – that
is, in the light of Jesus Christ.

Yet even though the Thomist tradition is still helpful today, it is not
sufficient for a contemporary theological definition of human rights.
Aquinas' thinking still moves entirely within the mediaeval idea of
ordo, or order. He therefore knew nothing about the modern notion of
a self-justifying human autonomy – an idea which has been current
coin ever since Kant in particular. Moreover – as his attitude to slavery
shows – Aquinas' idea of *ordo* was still less able to accommodate
modern ideas about liberation from conditions of dependency incompatible with human dignity. Consequently, although the renewal of the
Thomist conception is a help, it is still not an adequate theological
answer to the modern problem. Today we have to attempt afresh what

Thomas achieved so brilliantly for his own time. Of course what follows can only be the very first approach to such an attempt. Today we can perhaps best express both our continuity and our discontinuity with previous tradition if we reformulate the axiom we have already quoted, and say: grace – that is, God's free communication of himself to men and women – presupposes human freedom and brings it to its final goal and definition. Let me now try to justify and develop this thesis about an *analogia libertatis*.

3. Systematic reflection

(a) The theological definition of freedom

The starting point and the stimulant of modern thinking is freedom. According to its modern interpretation, freedom is not merely a human characteristic or capacity. It is a transcendental definition of the human being. That is to say, it is the condition of being human *per se*, and marks the real difference between human beings and other living things. Modern anthropology has shown that the human being is open to the world – that is, he does not belong to any one environment, specific to his species. This openness to the world is the negative side, so to speak, of what in positive terms we call freedom: self-determination instead of determination by some outside force, autonomy instead of heteronomy.

Modern philosophy is the philosophy of freedom. Consequently in modern times questions about God and salvation have also had to be considered afresh in the context of freedom. This does not mean that earlier interpretations of God and salvation in the framework of the traditional philosophy of being are simply wrong, but they are empty: they do not interpret modern human experience. In this sense Nietzsche's assertion that God is dead was a valid summing up of the modern criticism of religion in the name of freedom. But this negative assertion must be coupled with a positive one. Transcendental freedom is by nature freedom that transcends itself. And this implies an absolute aspect which throws open a new way of access to the idea of God. Here I can do no more than indicate the broad lines of this approach, following some comments made by Hermann Krings.[22]

The *transcending* nature of freedom is directly given with its *transcendental* nature. This is because finite freedom is not simply undetermined and open. On the contrary, its character is already 'given' to it in a particular way. It is determined physiologically, biologically, psychologically, sociologically, and in other ways. But freedom can itself determine the things that determine it. In each of these acts of freedom we transcend (or go beyond) the specific determinations of our freedom, because this transcending does not merely pass from one finite determination to another. It reaches into the infinite. For we can only recognize the finite as finite (and in so far be free with regard to it) by knowing, at least implicitly, that there is something infinite. The infinity of the horizon is the condition that makes freedom possible. Being open towards the infinite means that freedom is not merely related to one particular sector, or to another. It is related ultimately to the whole of reality. Every act of freedom reaches ahead to the whole of reality. In every act of freedom the whole of reality is present in an anticipatory fashion. Freedom is *Da-sein*. The German word is used to signify 'existence', but its original meaning is 'being there'. And since its nature is *Da-sein*, freedom must never be a means to an end. It must always be an end in itself. Transcendence to the infinite is the reason for its unconditional dignity, the dignity which means that it is not at our disposal.

If we take the transcending character of transcendental freedom seriously, together with the absolute element which is implicit in it, this opens up a new approach to the question about God. Here God is not sweepingly and precipitately identified with the absolute aspect of human freedom. That could only lead to a reduction of theology to anthropology, which is what Ludwig Feuerbach proclaimed. The question about God emerges from the tension between the finite definition of freedom and its infinite openness. Because of its infinite openness, human freedom cannot be fulfilled and satisfied by any finite definition or any finite good, however great. This makes human freedom restless and unquiet. But because of its finite definition, freedom can never confer this fulfilment on itself. If it is ever to arrive at inner fulfilment, it can only be when it encounters a freedom which is infinite – infinite not merely in its formal openness, but in its actual, substantial fulfilled-ness as well. Finite freedom can find fulfilment only in the encounter with infinite freedom. So God would have to be thought of, not as absolute Being, absolute substance, and so forth (as in classic metaphysics), but as perfect freedom. And we should therefore have to understand him as the condition which makes possible the absolute fulfilment of the meaning of human freedom.

Since in spite of all its specific definitions human freedom is at the same time undefinedly open, it has the chance to define itself in very varied ways. If, now, this undefined openness is theologically defined, or determined, in the way we have suggested, this is one way in which human beings arrive at self-determination. Since this self-determination – or self-definition – on the part of the human being is *ipso facto* free, it is impossible to show that it is compellingly necessary. But it can be shown to be a useful possibility of human existence, and one which should be accepted in intellectual responsibility. So before we discuss our previous train of thought in any detail, or develop it further, let us first of all look at the results of this theological definition of human freedom. These results can be considered both negatively and positively.

A negative result of the theological definition of the human being is that all ideologies and utopias will be viewed critically. We use the word ideology when – to put it somewhat simplistically – finite forces and contingent conditions are sanctioned by being assigned unconditional value. In this sense ideology, theologically speaking, means the idolatrous worship of worldly realities, a worship which makes for bondage. The fact that God is God then means the shattering of idols – a judgment on the absolutization of worldly values that makes men and women free. But faith in God does not merely destroy ideology – the semblance of the absolute; it also destroys utopia – the dream of the absolute, if this is a dream that the absolute could ever be created in history through history. If ideology represses human freedom, utopia expects too much of it. Freedom is ultimately deified and hence demonized. Utopian messianism is always and inevitably intolerant and fanatical towards other designs for freedom. God in his divinity frees men and women from this compulsion to redeem themselves which makes for bondage. He relieves human beings of the burden of having to play God. He frees them for a humane humanity.

This brings us to the positive results of the theological definition of human freedom. It does not merely liberate men and women from ideological and utopian compulsions. It also frees them for a new humanity, whose basic attitude may be described as reverence: reverence for human beings and reverence for the world. Anyone who sees human beings and the world in the light of the absolute freedom over which no one can dispose, will never misunderstand freedom as a despotic power over things and people; although this misunderstanding is particularly widespread today. People who see things in the light of absolute freedom will also resist one-sided, often cynical, 'scientific' and technocratic ways of dealing with the world. For them, feast and festival will again become the supreme expressions of human freedom. Finally, wherever human freedom is understood to be an actualizing image of the absolute, freedom will acquire absolute primacy, compared with every other mental and spiritual good, let alone all material benefits. Here all programmes, systems and structures have to be subjected to constant revision, in the light of human dignity.[23] God's transcendence therefore proves to be a protection for the transcendence of the human person as well.[24] We might even say that religious freedom is the most fundamental of human rights, not merely historically but in substance too.

Here we can do no more than offer these brief and incomplete suggestions about the practical results of a theological definition of human freedom. We shall now pick up the logical thread once more, by showing that to think God in the context of freedom means thinking him in the context of history at the same time; or – in theological terms – understanding him in the light of his revelation in salvation history.

(b) Freedom defined in the light of salvation history and christology

Freedom as the transcendental definition or determination of human beings is not something that is factually 'given'. It cannot be objectively established and proved. According to Fichte, the awareness of freedom can come about only through free acts. Freedom is 'possessed' only when it is performed, when it is brought about as a historical event. So every theory about freedom is transmitted – mediated – through the praxis of freedom. It was Hegel especially who discovered that freedom, and thinking about freedom, is mediated through history; and he saw thinking about freedom as the subsequent reconstruction of historical freedom. Dilthey made this notion the fundamental idea behind his hermaneutics: 'What man is, only history shows.'[25] But since being interprets itself in the history of freedom, we shall have to go a step further still and, with Heidegger, talk about a history of being – that is, an interpretation of reality in and through history (an idea, incidentally, which the later Schelling anticipated in his doctrine of potency).

It is not merely freedom which shows itself in and through history. The absolute element which is part of human freedom is also conveyed in and through historical contingency.[26] The history of human rights shows this with particular clarity. The awareness of these rights can be traced back to a variety of historical circumstances, motives and concerns at the beginning of modern times. Christian impulses also played a considerable part here.[27] But of course the question is whether, and how, in the circumstances of today (which have changed considerably), we can preserve and pass on the non-contingent factor which finds expression in human rights. This does not seem to me possible without an active, actualizing recollection of the Christian tradition which is operative in these rights.

For the Christian tradition, the intrinsic link between freedom and history is actually especially important. We cannot objectively prove that God is perfect freedom, any more than we can objectively prove the existence of finite freedom. God can only be perceived as perfect freedom if he shows himself as freedom – that is, if he freely reveals himself. Knowledge of God is therefore mediated through the experience of God in history. This does not simply put an end to Pascal's distinction between the God of the philosophers and the God of Abraham, Isaac and Jacob, but it does give the distinction a fundamentally new definition. The experience of faith can now be interpreted as a qualified experience of freedom, that is to say as the experience that reality is in its ultimate foundation freedom, and that it interprets itself as freedom in history. This means that human freedom is mediated, not merely through history, but through the history of revelation and salvation history as well. But it has to be said – with Kierkegaard and contrary to Hegel – that this mediation is not logically transparent and cannot be reduced to a definition. It can only be adopted by the understanding *in* freedom and *as* freedom – in theological terms: in faith.

In trying to conceive this determining and mediating of human freedom through salvation history, traditional dogmatics have had recourse to the doctrines of original sin and the universal significance of

Christ's saving work. In so doing they have retained the insight that both sin and redemption provide that every human being must first of all perform his own free act, but that they effect personal calamity or personal salvation only by way of the personal decision for sin or for faith. In this way traditional dogmatics already saw the whole of history as dialogue or – to put it theologically – as the history of a covenant between the God who reveals himself in history and the historical decision of the human being to believe or not to believe. So the historicity of salvation embraces both the 'objective' historical 'givenness' of salvation or disaster, and its subjective character as a decision laid upon the individual.[28] It is only when someone, in the act of faith, gives himself up to the encounter with God and his revelation that these make an impact on him, and for him become salvation. On the other hand, since human freedom exists in unfree conditions, freedom presupposes liberation.

This history between God and human beings reached its eschatological completion in the God-man Jesus Christ. Jesus Christ therefore becomes the eschatological determination or definition of human freedom. In him the undefined openness of human freedom is finally and radically defined and fulfilled, through the absolute freedom which is finally and eschatologically communicated in him.[29] Liberation theology is therefore in principle right (even if it is not always correct in its detailed implementation) when it interprets salvation history in our modern context as the history of liberation, and when it sees salvation in Jesus Christ as the freedom for which Christ has set us free (Gal. 5.1; John 8.36). In a similar way, Gisbert Greshake interprets grace as the concrete form of freedom.[30] This also makes it possible to take the specific historical mediations of freedom seriously. For it is only when we think of freedom as liberation that we have arrived at the Christian understanding of what freedom is.

I cannot develop these suggestions in theological detail here. In our present context I must confine myself to indicating some specific conclusions which emerge from the christological definition of human freedom – conclusions which have a bearing on the understanding and praxis of freedom. Here I am venturing upon a subject which is a matter of keen controversy in present-day theological ethics. The dispute is carried on under the heading of the *proprium christianum* – the specific character of the Christian faith. The point at issue is whether the Christian faith contains practical norms for Christian behaviour in the world, or whether it merely brings into the total context of faith standards of conduct which already exist in human society, integrating them, criticizing them and being stimulated by them.[31] Although this question is of direct importance for the theological determination of human rights, ethics is not my particular field. I should therefore prefer not to venture upon the thin ice of this debate, which the experts are now pursuing with considerable differentiation and with subtle nuances. I will rather indulge the hope – perhaps immodestly – that the dialectic of determination or definition which underlies our previous reflections may perhaps offer a way out of the cul-de-sac. For when we talk about a christological definition of men and women and their freedom, we of course do not mean by that merely a formal framework. We mean content as well. But this content does not belong to the level of categorial norms, in the sense of specific practical precepts. It is part of the transcendental determination of the human being. In a similar sense Karl Rahner talked about a supernatural existential.[32] To put it in biblical terms, the law of Christ (Gal. 6.2) is not the letter which kills (II Cor. 3.6) but a law of liberty (James 1.25). Christian freedom – the freedom determined by Jesus Christ – is therefore the real *proprium christianum*.

What does this mean in concrete terms? We can answer this question by showing (1) in what way Christian freedom presupposes human freedom, as the condition that makes it possible; and (2) by showing how Christian freedom brings human freedom to fulfilment. Both questions assume that freedom is by its very nature open to different definitions. Its open and undefined nature must be determined by way of historical self-determination. Faith in Jesus Christ – that is, adopting Jesus' way of existence – claims to be the eschatological determination of men and women. What does it mean specifically? Here we can only elucidate one of the many possible aspects.

1. Human freedom is the premise for Christian freedom, since God presupposes a partner whom he can address in freedom, and who can respond in freedom. But this means that Christian freedom presupposes a freedom that is not understood in purely individualistic terms but is freedom for communication and information.

2. The Christian freedom which perfects human freedom can even less be individualistically interpreted. It is freedom which proves itself

in love (Gal. 5.13), a freedom which does not consist in being-in-itself or being-for-itself, but in being-for-others.[33] Regarded purely in the light of reason, this self-emptying freedom in love is foolishness. It is foolishness which can ultimately be justified only in the light of the foolishness of the cross (I Cor. 1.18, 23). If we take the two things together, we shall have to say that Christian theology will never be able to interpret human rights and liberties simply as individual rights. They will always be social rights as well; and theology will insist that human rights for all can never be achieved without sacrifice and without forgiveness. This attitude is contrary to reason; yet in many historical situations it can prove to be the only reasonable course of action, because often enough sacrifice, forgiveness and reconciliation liberate men and women for a new common freedom.

Again I must leave the matter there, with only these few hints. But, simply in a fleeting glance forward, I should like in closing to develop these last thoughts a little more, by touching on the social and ecclesial mediation of Christian freedom. I do not want to avoid the institutional problem, which presents itself theologically as the problem of the church, since this might give rise to the suspicion that what the theonomous determination of autonomy is secretly aiming at, is once more a clerical theocracy under a fresh label.

(c) The institutional determination of freedom

Ever since the Greeks, freedom has always been a political concept too, because it is only in the *polis* that freedom can be implemented in practical terms. Freedom is fired by the freedom of other people, and it can come into being only where other people allow it a space in which to be free – that is, when it is recognized as freedom. The premise that makes freedom possible is therefore communication with other freedoms; and freedom takes practical form in a free order, that is, an order in which freedom is generally recognized. This was one of Hegel's fundamental ideas, and it seems to me to offer a more fruitful approach to the institutional problem than the corresponding theories of Arnold Gehlen. According to Gehlen, the institution suspends the question of meaning, and therefore suspends the freedom of human beings at the same time. But if we develop Hegel's approach, we can say that freedom and institution are not antithetical terms. They are in fact complementary. This of course also means that an institution can be legitimated only if it is an institution in which freedom is implemented. Consequently its task is not to suspend freedom but to stimulate it, protect it and support it. And whether it fulfils this function is something that must be continually and critically tested.

Against this background the church has to be seen as an institution for Christian freedom.[34] But if we see the church as an institution for Christian freedom, then its function is to intervene on behalf of human rights both inside and outside the church; for human rights are the presupposition for Christian freedom. Intervention on behalf of human rights in the world of today is convincing only if, in its own sector, the church is a model in the way it implements human freedom as the presupposition for Christian freedom. But since the church is concerned with Christian freedom – that is, the freedom defined by Jesus Christ – concern for the integrity of its message about Christ cannot possibly conflict with the concept of the church as an institution embodying Christian freedom. The tension between the two things must be argued out in a way that accords with human and with Christian freedom. That is to say, there ought to be institutions within the church which do not merely stand up for the rights of truth, but stand up for the rights of men and women too. Up to now the spirit of absolutism has put its stamp on canon law. A more modern form, on the lines suggested, would also lend the church's law a more Christian character.

If we start from these premises, the church will have to reformulate the theme of human rights, which is so much discussed at present, and also so much misused.[35] Here we can only point out the urgency of the whole matter. It is urgent because any theory of freedom is useful and convincing only if it reflects a praxis of freedom to which it corresponds. So today, human rights can only be given a theological and Christian definition in the context of the modern sense of freedom and history, if the church too is given a more modern and a freer form – freer in the Christian sense of the word. But of course to develop this in detail would go far beyond the limits of this essay.

Here we must content ourselves with having pursued a little further the discussion about a fundamental definition of the relation between Christian freedom and human freedom. Someone may ask: 'But what practical purpose does this serve?' There would seem to me to be two answers to this question. First, this definition should enable the church (or the churches) to make modern human rights their own concern, and to intervene on their behalf. Second, we certainly cannot assume today that human rights exist as a matter of course. It is not only their practical implementation that is in question. Their interpretation is disputed as well. Indeed because they have been illegitimately appropriated for ideological purposes and because exaggerated demands have been made on them, they are acutely endangered. Theology points to the ultimate foundation of these rights and to their final definition; and it tests the use and misuse of human rights against these things. In this way theology helps to save a vital legacy of Western humanism for a new era of human history.

IV

Christology and Anthropology*

1. An introduction to the problem

(a) The facts of scripture and tradition

One of the fundamental statements of the Christian creed is that Jesus Christ became a human being 'for us men and for our salvation' (*propter nos et propter nostram salutem*). He gave his life 'for us' or 'for many' – that is, for all of us – on the cross.[1] These central and fundamental credal statements of Scripture and tradition mean that *the key signature of the whole of christology is soteriology*. This makes the anthropological significance of christology a central theological theme, a theme that is already treated in the New Testament with the help of the Adam/Christ typology which we come across in Rom. 5. 12–21 and I Cor. 15. 45–49. The New Testament also brings out the connection between christology and anthropology by taking up the Old Testament statement that every human being is created in the image of God (Gen. 1.27), and by calling Jesus Christ *the* image of God (II Cor. 4.4; Col. 1.15), the image in which all reality was created and towards which it tends (I Cor. 8.6; Col. 1.16f.). So, as the Second Vatican Council put it, in Jesus Christ God 'revealed man to himself'.[2]

Modern biblical theology, and the systematic theology which it has influenced, has therefore continually and rightly emphasized that the christological statements of the New Testament are not intended as isolated assertions about Christ's essential Being-in-itself, and his

*This is a slightly shortened version of a paper presented to the International Theological Commission in Rome on 3 October 1981.

divine and human nature. They are concerned with his meaning for salvation. The christological statements in the New Testament, that is to say, belong to the context of salvation history. They are meant *functionally*, to take the word that is often used here.[3]

It has also been pointed out that the development of christological doctrine in the patristic church was also *soteriologically motivated*. This is true above all of the clarification of the unity of substance (ὁμοούσιος) of Jesus Christ, or the Holy Spirit, and the Father.[4] For it is only if Jesus Christ and the Spirit are true God that we are in truth redeemed – that is, have fellowship with God. By saying in their definition that Jesus Christ and the Holy Spirit were of like substance (or nature or essence) with God, the Councils of Nicaea and Constantinople wished to secure the reality of our salvation.

Of course the history of the dogmatic development in the patristic church shows also that *Christ's significance for salvation is to be found in his Being*. Eminent scholars have meanwhile made it clear that this foundational connection already exists in the New Testament. The statement about Christ's nature undoubtedly serves the soteriological idea. But it also provides the foundation for this idea, and is its guarantor.[5]

(b) Two extreme positions

In later theological development, the inward unity of christology and soteriology was for the most part lost – and hence the link between christology and anthropology too. In scholasticism, christology and soteriology developed into two independent dogmatic sectors. Yves Congar comments on the result: 'Perhaps the greatest disaster that has afflicted modern Catholicism was that in doctrine and catechetics it turned to God and religion "as they are in themselves", instead of ceaselessly enquiring at the same time what all this means for men and women. If today we are confronted with human beings and a world without God, this is to some extent a reaction against this kind of God, a God without human beings and without a world. If we wish to obviate the difficulties which are stumbling blocks for our contemporaries on their way to faith, and if we want to combat the challenge of atheism, one of the things we must do is to show ceaselessly how God's world is bound up with our human world.'[6]

Apart from a number of other contributory factors, which we shall be looking at presently, this one-sided development is the background to a no less one-sided reaction. This reduces christology to its anthropological significance, and seeks to counter classic ontological christology with a more modern, functional christology, which purports to be more soundly based on biblical testimony. This position may be seen especially in the Bultmann school, in the wake of the existential interpretation of the New Testament.[7] We find it in extreme form in Herbert Braun, for whom christology is merely one variant of anthropology, which provides the constant.[8] Trends of this kind may also be found with greater or less consistency among Catholic authors as well. The aim is no longer the divinization of human beings. The declared purpose is now their humanization.[9]

It is obvious that once the human being is made the measure of christology in this way, this also affects the understanding of what christology is about, and its anthropological meaning. In fact it affects the interpretation of soteriology itself. For then it is ultimately speaking sufficient if Jesus Christ is above all the true and perfect human being, who reveals God to us as the secret of human beings and the world, and who moves us to the appropriate behaviour. This stands the soteriological argumentation of the Fathers on its head. It is turned into its very opposite. Karl Adam already (in 1933) protested against similar tendencies in liberal theology, objecting that 'it would be an idle game with empty words if we were still to talk about redemption here. If Jesus were simply a man and nothing else, he could give us nothing more than human love – he could in his turn give us only what is human, with all its limitations and all its questionableness. And we should still have to bear the burden of our profoundest misery, the misery of our sin and death.'[10]

(c) The task of mediation

The two extremes we have described are one form of the well-known *identity/relevance dilemma* of modern Christianity.[11] If Christianity strives to be relevant for men and women, it is in danger of becoming so open that it loses its identity; while if it strives to preserve its identity, it threatens to become petrified and to lose all its relevance for human beings.

This dilemma means that mediating between the extremes is a double problem:

1. The first difficulty is the relationship between christology and anthropology. This is a *formal (or essential) and fundamental problem* of christology – a problem of christological hermeneutics, so to speak. In how far are human beings part of the constitution of christology itself? In how far is anthropology the presupposition of christology and its horizon? In how far does anthropology therefore belong, not merely to the *consectaria* of christology – its results – but actually to its *praeambula* – its premises?

2. The second difficulty is the relationship between christology and anthropology, as a *material and categorial problem*. To what extent can the christological concepts 'nature' and 'person', and the fundamental soteriological categories – 'sacrifice', 'satisfaction', 'atonement' and so forth – be expressed in such a way that they have something to say to modern men and women, something that has to do with their experiences and problems, and that has a bearing on their existence? Many people find all these traditional words and concepts of the proclamation difficult to understand today. And a theology which desires to witness to 'God for us' has to take these difficulties seriously. So 'christology and anthropology' – the subject we are considering here – has to do with the problem of how to give the christological and soteriological tradition a new, living, actualized form today.

Behind both these difficulties is ultimately another fundamental problem which is common to them both – perhaps the most fundamental problem of all, in present-day theology: how can the ontological statements about the essential nature of God and Jesus Christ 'in themselves' be related to the functional statements about their meaning 'for us'? To put it in more abstract terms: *what is the relation between metaphysics and history*? In the last resort the relationship between christology and anthropology faces us with the crisis of metaphysics in and outside theology, and the erosion of the theological concept of truth which this crisis involves. And this is probably the deepest root of the present crisis in theology.

2. The relationship between christology
and anthropology as a formal and fundamental problem

(a) *The modern shift towards anthropology*

In line with the thinking of ancient philosophy, classic theological tradition treated the meaning of Jesus Christ for salvation *in a cosmological context*.[12] Justin already tried to show that it was the logos which is at work in a fragmentary way in all reality which now appeared in all its fullness in Jesus Christ.[13] In the fourth century, this link between christology and cosmology led to a severe crisis. Arian christology was conceived in extreme cosmological form, since for Arius Jesus Christ was a kind of cosmological principle or demiurge. Consequently, as a result of the Arian controversy, soteriology was detached from the cosmological context.[14] But the *ordo universi* continued to provide the framework within which an understanding of the nature and meaning of Jesus Christ was developed.[15]

Modern thinking is very different. It is characterized by *a turning towards anthropology*. Now the human being is no longer merely one link in the visible creation, even if the supreme link. He is the starting point and the horizon bounding the understanding of reality as a whole. Kant was building on what Descartes had already said when he gave the principle of modern subjectivity its classic formulation: perception does not depend on the objects of perception; the objects of perception are themselves constituted as such by the perceiving subject.[16] It is by way of this fundamental approach in modern thinking that we have to understand the concept of function, which is so important in present-day christology; for Kant can also give the name of function to the subject's capacity for conferring unity.[17] Neo-Kantianism has taken up this use of the word and has made a strict distinction between substantial and functional concepts.[18] The concept 'function' or 'functional' (when it is used reflectively and not merely superficially) has to do with the meaning of things *for me* and for us, the way in which they appear, as distinct from their being *an sich* – in themselves – which cannot be known by human beings.

The results for christology of this shift to anthropology became clear even in Kant himself. He finds the doctrines of the Trinity and the incarnation uninteresting because from them 'nothing whatsoever can be gained for practical purposes'.[19] This shows that to develop christology in the context of anthropology was bound to lead to conflicts similar to those which arose from the dispute about cosmological thinking in the patristic church. It was only after a laborious process of critical distinction and creative reception that a new form of christology became possible, a christology based on anthropology.

(b) The results for modern theology

The results of the modern turn to anthropology became plain in the theology of the seventeenth and eighteenth centuries. The Socinians had already developed a christology and soteriology that was reduced to anthropology. The concepts of sacrifice, satisfaction and atonement were especially subjected to criticism, because they seemed incompatible with any profound understanding of the human being, his dignity and his irreplaceable uniqueness.[20]

These were material and categorial consequences. But more important still was the fundamental new christological approach which was developed by Friedrich Schleiermacher, and which has continued to exert influence down to the present day. Schleiermacher's approach was followed up by the proponents of liberal theology, especially Albrecht Ritschl and Wilhelm Herrmann. In our present context it is neither possible nor necessary to go into the complicated details of the theological history. The essential point is what H. J. Iwand stressed as being the 'misuse of the *pro me* as methodic principle' – i.e., the dissolution of christology in statements about its meaning or importance.[21] Hand in hand with this went a denunciation of metaphysics; the rejection of natural theology became a new controversial doctrine that had been as yet unknown in the sixteenth century.[22] The strictly christologically founded and centred theology which was then pursued in our own century by Karl Barth in particular, already had its seeds in liberal theology. Similar trends are to be found in 'modernism' (or what was understood as modernism). Dogma was interpreted pragmatically. It was a symbol, whose function was to provide directions for proper religious conduct and for believing action.[23] As we have seen, after the transcendental and Idealist thinking which underlies these approaches had broken down, the same problems cropped up again under different philosophical auspices in the existential theology of the mid-twentieth century.

Acute critics of modern theology – not merely theologians, but also (and not least) their declared critics – pointed out (not without a certain malicious pleasure in many cases) that these approaches, carried to their logical conclusion, would inevitably end up in atheism.[24] For theological statements which are not founded on Being, and are made congruent with significance, are ultimately exposed to the suspicion of projection. This was Feuerbach's criticism of religion, and it was developed further by Marx, Nietzsche, Freud, and others.[25] A theology that is reduced to anthropology and dissolved in significance ultimately abolishes itself.

Of course the problem goes deeper than this, as was shown by Hegel in particular. If the human subject views the world from a merely functional standpoint, and if he demythologizes it and desacralizes it, he makes the world flat and banal to the same degree. But in addition he himself becomes empty of content and hollow. On both sides a yawning gulf of senseless nothingness opens up.[26] So the end of the modern development is nihilism. At the moment Nietzsche seems more contemporary than Marx. As the modern era draws to a close, the feeling many people have about life in many ways resembles the gnosticism of the closing years of the ancient world. There is a sense of alienation, of being lost, of 'thrownness'; and so the human being is installed as God.[27] It was in the discussions of that earlier, gnostic period that classic christology evolved; and the same discussions seem to be repeating themselves today on a different level.

(c) The late acceptance of modern ideas in Catholic theology

Against the background I have briefly described, it is easy to understand why (with a few exceptions) Catholic theology barred itself for so long against a reception of modern thinking in theology, judging and rejecting modern anthropocentricism in highly critical terms as apostasy, a revolt against Christian theocentricism.[28] Neo-scholasticism, with its conservative mentality, was certainly incapable of taking up the positive intention of the modern era in a creative way. A few theologians and schools were more far-sighted. I need only mention Tübingen Catholic theology in the nineteenth century. But at first these were unable to win acceptance.

In our own century, after important preliminary work had been done by Maurice Blondel and Joseph Maréchal, Karl Rahner in particular developed a new approach. For Rahner as for Maréchal – and as for Kant too, incidentally – transcendental philosophy and metaphysics were not antitheses. On the contrary: the transcendental approach must actually lead to a new justification of metaphysics.[29] So when Rahner defined *christology as self-surpassing anthropology, and anthropology as deficient christology,*[30] he was certainly not intending to dissolve christology in anthropology, or to reduce it to its significance for human beings. I cannot here give a detailed account of Rahner's position and critical standpoint, but four points may be picked out – at least in the form of brief headings – which theology turned towards anthropology may in principle claim for itself.

1. The approach of modern thinking cannot simply, or even principally, be judged as an apostasy, a revolt against the theocentricism of the Christian faith. On the contrary, through its faith in creation, and with its stress on the unconditional dignity of every human person, Christianity has made an essential contribution to the liberation of men and women from cosmological structures and perspectives. According to 'the theology of secularization' (as represented especially by Friedrich Gogarten and Johann Baptist Metz), the modern way of thinking is a basically Christian event, and represents what may be called the worldly implementation of the Christian faith. And even if it has not proved possible to substantiate this postulate, either historically or in the light of practical experience, it does contain at least a very considerable grain of truth, inasmuch as the modern era, even in its criticism of Christianity, remains bound to Christian concerns.[31]

2. Theology cannot choose its time. It has to convey the Christian message to the men and women of its own era, and has to give them an account of the Christian hope (I Peter 3.15). A *theologia perennis* – a theology that is in principle timeless – is of no use to anyone, or to any period. This commits theology today to a critical and creative reception of modern thinking.

3. Revelation in salvation history presupposes men and women as 'hearers of the word'. There is no such thing as faith *per se*. There is only faith heard, understood, affirmed and testified to by men and women. So human beings are as human beings the place and

determining subjects of faith, and must enter into the reflections underlying every statement of faith.[32]

4. Human beings as they specifically exist in salvation history are always already in Christ and are created for him (I Cor. 8.6; Col. 1.16f.). This is what Rahner calls the supernatural existential, and it means that the Christian message does not merely touch men and women as an alien outside force. It is at the same time the expectation and interpretation of what is deepest and innermost in human beings themselves. Against this background it is understandable that Rahner, in his later phase, should have developed christology as the correlative of the hope of human beings.[33]

Because of these and similar arguments, the fundamental intention of an anthropologically mediated christology has been favourably taken up in more recent official doctrinal documents. The statements in the Pastoral Constitution *Gaudium et spes* and in the encyclical *Redemptor hominis* are particularly important here. Both documents talk a new language, compared with earlier statements by the church's magisterium. We need think only of Gregory XVI's encyclical *Mirari vos*, the *Syllabus Errorum* of Pius IX, and Pius X. These new statements represent a considerable step towards giving proclamation and theology a contemporary reference. Of course new stresses still exist more or less side by side with, and separate from, the traditional, ontologically determined christology. But a mediation between the two is not a matter for the magisterium. It is the concern of theology, which has only just begun to shoulder the task of this critical mediation.

(d) Critical development

1. A critical development of the anthropological approach in theology, especially in christology, must start *philosophically* from the extension given to the transcendental approach in post-Idealist philosophy. The basic experience in the breakdown of the Idealist system was the realization of human finitude and contingency. Because of his own finitude, the human being can never again deduce the facticity of his transcendentality; he now experiences himself in a way that is conditioned in multifarious ways. But, as Pascal said, the greatness of human beings is their ability to recognize their misery for what it is.[34] We have

therefore to begin from the inward interlacing of transcendentality and facticity. Thinking of this kind starts from the assumption that subject and object are reciprocally related. The subject forms the world and is in his turn moulded by the world, by nature and culture. This kind of thinking may be termed historical.[35]

In our present context, this means specifically that there is no such thing as *the* human being. There are only human beings in highly varied historical modalities. The fundamental principle of anthropology is therefore, according to Dilthey: 'What man is, only history tells us.'[36] So anthropology cannot abstract from, or disregard, the results of ethnology, or the social and economic conditions under which contemporary men and women live.

2. The inward interweaving of transcendentality and history means *theologically* that when we are considering the history of God with human beings, we must begin specifically: that is, with the human being as he appeared in Jesus Christ. It is this concrete realization of humanity that tells us the nature of 'the destiny of man' (Fichte). To put it epigrammatically: a theological anthropology must begin theologically, not anthropologically. This is the legitimate concern of Karl Barth's definition of the relationship between christology and anthropology. His fundamental postulate was that we have to understand. Adam in the light of Christ, not Christ in the light of Adam.[37] But Barth's narrowly concentrated christological approach must be critically modified[38] by the reminder that the christological starting point of course presupposes that men and women as created beings are 'hearers of the word'; as human beings they are therefore fundamentally open to receive their eschatologically final definition from Jesus Christ. Catholic tradition has termed this passive ability *potentia oboedientialis*. It has expressed the *reciprocal presupposition* with the help of the classic axiom *gratia supponit naturam et perficit eam* (grace presupposes and perfects nature).[39] This means that christology presupposes anthropology, surpasses it and perfects it.

It is this reciprocal relationship between christology and anthropology which is also the theme of Rom. 5.12–21.[40] Here Paul takes over an already existing pattern which may be found both in pagan mythology and in Jewish apocalyptic: the mutual correspondence of πρῶτα and ἔσχατα, the first things and the last. Jesus Christ is God's great 'yes' (II Cor. 1.20); in him God has accepted human beings –

every human being. But the anacoluthon – the lack of strict grammatical sequence – with which the passage begins shows that Paul is breaking through this relationship of correspondence.⁴¹ This is because, according to what he says in vv.13f., the law intervenes (Gal. 3.19), convicting people of being sinners and, by demonstrating this breach, excluding all direct continuity between Adam and Christ. Paul therefore stresses both the difference between Adam and Christ (v.15 ἀλλ οὐχ ὡς, 'but not like'; v.16 καὶ οὐ χώς, 'and not like'), as well as the incomparable and surpassing nature of the Christ side compared with the Adam side (cf. the repeated πολλῷ μᾶλλον 'much more', in vv.15 and 17, as well as the double περισσεία or ὑπερπερισσεύειν, 'abundance' or 'to abound' in vv.17 and 20). Similarly, in comparing the first and the second Adam in I Cor. 15.45–47, Paul simultaneously stresses their incomparability (ψυχικός – πνευματικός, 'physical – spiritual', χοϊκός – ἐπουράνιος, 'made of dust – heavenly'). Yet this antithetical correspondence is only possible on the basis of a structural correspondence (Rom. 5.12, 19, 21: ὥσπερ – καὶ οὕτως, 'just as – so'; v.18: ὡς – οὕτως, 'as – thus'). The Adam side is certainly surpassed, but is itself, in its turn, the cognitive reason for this surpassing. By understanding Adam in the light of Jesus Christ, Paul at the same time makes the importance of Jesus Christ clear in the light of Adam.⁴²

The exegesis of Rom. 5.12–21 shows that there is *a threefold relation between christology and anthropology* which – if we pick up the classic doctrine of analogy – may be described as the *via positionis*, the *via negationis* and the *via eminentiae*.⁴³

3. As result we may say the following:

(i) *Christology presupposes anthropology*. Or to be more precise: it presupposes the human being as the free determining subject, capable of hearing and responding. Christology does not wish to convince in any other way than by virtue of the truth which binds and touches men and women through the conscience. The christological definition is therefore not a definition from outside. Theonomy is not heteronomy. On the contrary, theology can and must recognize the autonomy, properly understood, of human beings and the world.⁴⁴ It must therefore stand up for the liberty of human beings and for the historical and substantial root of that liberty – for religious liberty.⁴⁵ The Christian faith therefore proves to be the protection for the transcendence of the human person.⁴⁶

(ii) Christology presupposes that men and women are open beings capable of growth and advancement. Or to be more precise: it presupposes that men and women are beings who have been endowed with freedom, and that *what is undeducibly new belongs intrinsically to their nature.* So christology is not an ideology of what already exists – a kind of pious phraseology designed to give an elevating form to what is already familiar. It is the undeducible and surpassing fulfilment of the hope of men and women. Here the undefined openness of human beings receives its undeducible concrete definition.[47] That means that *while the human being is certainly the determining subject of faith, he is neither its material nor its formal object.* On the contrary, faith opens human beings for God, who is the only possible determination and fulfilment (material object) of the human being's infinite openness, and in this way it simultaneously so lights up the human horizon (*lumen fidei*) that men and women can know and recognize God as God (formal object) and do not, out of their finite capacity for perception, strip him of his potency, demoting him to a finite idol (εἴδωλον), which has merely the ideological function of satisfying human needs. So what faith means is that human beings find their fulfilment simply by recognizing God as God. In this sense the one and only object of theology is God as the salvation of men and women – the one and only object because it comprehends all else.[48]

(iii) The christological determination and completion of human beings is at the same time the crisis of the definition which human beings as sinners have given themselves. The Christian message of grace is therefore indissolubly linked with the message of judgment, and the gospel cannot be separated from the law. But the cross which breaks sinful nature is not the crucifixion of the human being. What exodus and metanoia do is to break down the sin through which human beings have become curved in upon themselves (sin as *incurvatio hominis*). They lay bare man's original *ekstasis* once more, and bring it to fulfilment. To enter into the *pascha domini* is therefore the way to human perfection.[49]

3. The relationship between christology and anthropology as a problem of content

The content of the christological definition of human beings can be developed and specified from a number of widely differing standpoints. Here we are choosing *the division according to Christ's three offices* –

the prophetic office, the priestly office and the pastoral office; but this is really no more than one possible way of systematizing the many and varied christological titles in the Bible. Although this particular scheme is found only sporadically in earlier tradition, and was first taken up as a systematizing principle in Protestant theology, it has meanwhile won general acceptance in Catholic theology as well, and was officially endorsed by Vatican II.[50] This triple division offers a way of more critical development than traditional dogmatics, where Christ's meaning for salvation was almost exclusively expounded under the aspect of his priestly office. But this confined viewpoint was unable to bring out fully the soteriological and anthropological significance of christology.

(a) Christ's prophetic office

In our present context it is not possible to present in any detail the biblical and theological foundation for Christ's prophetic office, or to show how, on the one hand, the prophet christology of the New Testament led without a break to sonship christology;[51] and how, on the other, the fully developed two-natures christology, in the doctrine of Christ's human knowledge and consciousness, implies a revelation christology.[52] Here we must concentrate on the soteriological or anthropological meaning of this doctrine.

What Christ's prophetic office means anthropologically, becomes clear if we remember that the question about truth is one of the fundamental human questions, and that light is one of the fundamental human symbols. Truth and light are not merely extras – something added to the reality of human beings. They are the medium which makes human life possible. It is only when there is light, and when things appear unhidden (ἀ–λήθεια) that human beings can take their bearings and find their way about in the world. That is why light is a symbol for salvation, and darkness is a symbol for disaster and lostness.[53] Error, darkness and blindness are therefore the results of sin and signs of the calamitous situation of human beings.[54] So when scripture, liturgy and theology proclaim that Jesus Christ is the light, they are implicitly claiming that among the many will o' the wisps and illusions found in the world, Christ has shown human beings the truth about themselves and about the world in which they live.

Vatican II expresses this aspect very clearly: 'In reality it is only in the mystery of the Word made flesh that the mystery of man truly becomes clear . . . Christ the new Adam, in the very revelation of the mystery of the Father and of his love, fully reveals man to himself and brings to light his most high calling . . . It is therefore through Christ, and in Christ, that light is thrown on the riddle of suffering and death which, apart from his Gospel, overwhelms us.'[55] In accord with this conciliar statement, Pope John Paul II has continually stressed that Christ is 'the key to the understanding of that great and fundamental reality which human beings are. For human beings cannot ultimately be understood without Christ. Or rather: human beings cannot thoroughly understand themselves without Christ. They can neither understand who they are, nor in what their true dignity consists, nor the nature of their calling and final destiny. Without Christ, men and women find all this incomprehensible.'[56]

These statements can be given specific form in three different ways.

1. Jesus Christ is the truth about human beings in the sense of the *via positionis*. In him the truth and the light which has shone into the world from the beginning, but was kept dim, is made to shine out again in all its fullness (John 1.5–9). Christ again discloses to men and women their creatureliness, and so interprets their existence as indebted existence – existence 'thanks to God' – which therefore finds its meaning, not through its own achievement but in thanksgiving. Christ reveals and interprets the secret of human reality, which men and women could really also discover through their own reason (natural knowledge of God; the natural moral law).[57] The gospel of Jesus Christ interprets 'the signs of the time'.[58] It is a prophetic interpretation of reality.

2. The *via negationis*: as the primal truth, the gospel of Jesus Christ also exposes the human lie, which comes about because human beings do not want to find their truth in God, and consequently live in an inner contradiction. Here the gospel updates the prophetic criticism of idols. So one of its functions is to criticize ideologies. And part of this function is to be critical of society.

3. As well as the *via positionis* and the *via negationis*, there is a third way: the *via eminentiae*. This is expressed in Jesus' parables of the kingdom. In these Jesus teaches his listeners to see the world again as God's parable; and in so doing, he also sets about giving a new creative

description of the world.[59] For the parables quite often contain wholly unexpected and improbable features, which show everything in an entirely new light: the light of the unconditionally forgiving love of God, and the hope for the coming of his kingdom. This opens up a new horizon for men and women. It makes it possible to look at things in the way which theological tradition has called *lumen fidei* – the light of faith – as distinct from *lumen naturale* – the light of nature. Towards the end of our discussion, and in summing up, we shall have to ask about the character of this new comprehensive Christian perspective.

(b) Christ's priestly office

The doctrine about Christ's priestly office cannot be developed in detail here either. We shall therefore presuppose the central and fundamental significance of the representation idea (the ὑπέρ formula), which is already bound up with the notion of sacrifice in the Marcan-Mattheian version of the tradition of the Lord's Supper (Mark 14.24; Matt. 26.28). Again, we cannot look in detail at the biblical foundation and interpretation of sacrifice, atonement and high priestly theology, their development in tradition, and the special form they take in the various theories about redemption. Here we shall confine ourselves to the anthropological importance of these things.

The concept of *life* and *the link between life and love* can provide a positive starting point for an anthropological understanding of Christ's priestly office. Like light, life is a primal word. 'Hardly any word with which philosophical thinking has concerned itself since time immemorial is open to so many interpretations as the word life. Hardly any term eludes so completely any attempt to confine its use to one particular definition without loss of meaning.' For like light, life is not just one thing among others. It is 'the "how" which characterizes all living things as such'. To be alive is happening, self-movement, self-implementation. So being alive is not accessible to objective observation. 'To experience life means experiencing something objective from which the subject is not able to detach himself. . . . One of the fundamental definitions of the meaning of life, as a philosophical concept, is therefore the inherent identification between thought and other, non-thinking things. The concept of life is hence always opposed to the dichotomy of thinking and matter.'[60]

Life is therefore always more than something purely biological. Life includes human beings and their question about life – about real, fulfilled and true life. Life itself points to the direction in which an answer is to be found. For everything that is, is merely a transition to something else. What is alive must go out of itself in order to preserve itself. 'Unless a grain of wheat falls into the earth and dies, it remains alone; but if it dies, it bears much fruit' (John 12.24). So 'whoever would save his life will lose it; and whoever loses his life . . . will save it' (Mark 8.35). Life and love therefore belong together: life fulfils its meaning in self-sacrificing love. So when the claim to happiness and self-fulfilment leads a person to refuse this self-giving and self-sacrificing love, not only is human life drastically curtailed and reduced; the same is true of the Christian life.

Through his sacrificial offering of his life 'for the many' Jesus Christ did not merely disclose anew this meaning of life. He also made it possible in a new way. At the same time he showed that the connection between life and love means that love is only perfected when it goes beyond itself in the direction of God, and is only fully realized in the fellowship of life and love with God. It was in line with this when Aquinas interpreted in the light of God's greater love the words of the proclamation about 'satisfaction' and 'sacrifice' – words which are so hard to understand today.[61] This means that the sacrifice is not merely a ritual act; that is no more than a programmatic expression of the giving of the self to God, so as to arrive at fellowship with him. The external sacrifice is therefore a symbol of the inward sacrificial attitude of mind, which means that the person performing the sacrifice is stepping out of the sphere of sin so as to recognize God as true life, so as to be reconciled with him, and in order to have fellowship with him. The sacrifice is hence a real symbol of praise, acknowledgment, thanksgiving and intercession to God.[62] Hegel was therefore right when he defined sacrifice as the authentic practice in the sphere of religion and faith.[63]

In this sphere particularly, it is very difficult for people today to understand what is meant. The modern autonomistic interpretation of human beings seems hard to reconcile with the message of redemption. It is true that the problem of human alienation has been much discussed ever since Rousseau; but generally speaking the solutions offered have been in purely immanent and autonomous terms.[64]

Whenever men and women have been recognized as contingent and conditioned, responsibility for the situation has been shifted on to circumstances, or the past, or opponents, or nature, or something else; while the phenomenon of personal guilt has for the most part been suppressed.[65] This can reach the point of gnostic and nihilistic interpretations of reality, in which reality as it is is vilified as totally corrupt and absolutely negative. The widespread abandonment and watering down of the doctrine of redemption (particularly ideas about sacrifice and atonement) is not so much a theological problem as an anthropological one.

In this situation the church can only preach the message of redemption in *a triple conflict* with 'average' contemporary anthropology. It must stress the need of men and women for redemption and – contrary to all evolutionary and revolutionary utopias – must insist on the radical nature of the calamitous situation (*via negationis*). On the other hand it must also point out that reality can be redeemed. It must counter the neo-gnostic vilification of the world, and keep the hope for reconciliation alive (*via positionis*). Finally, it must show that redemption does not only mean liberation from alienations of all kinds. Since it is reconciliation with God, redemption also means the healing of human beings, community and friendship with God – indeed participation in God's own life (*via eminentiae*). So in this question the church's proclamation can fulfil the *aggiornamento* enjoined upon it only by reminding people of essential though largely forgotten dimensions of what is human and what is Christian.

(c) Christ's pastoral office

Salvation and redemption do not have to do with the private and personal sphere alone. They also have a social and political dimension, even though they are not in themselves political entities. For the Old Testament, eschatological salvation already included the gathering of the nations and the establishment of the eschatological *shalom*. Jesus Christ is our peace (Eph. 2.14), because as the good shepherd he gathers the scattered sheep and gives his life for them (John 10.11–16).

The shepherd and king symbols used in the Old and New Testaments again pick up one of humanity's primal hopes. For life and salvation are possible only in an order of liberty, peace and justice.

'Kingdom', 'city' and 'country' have never been merely political concepts. They are religious symbols too, and have been so from time immemorial. The king therefore counts as God's representative – even as God's son. He represents the sacral cosmic and political order within which alone salvation is possible. This is how the ideal figure of the εὐεργέτης grew up – the benevolent king who, god-like, rules over his people, as a shepherd pastures his flock.

According to the New Testament, the way in which this human hope is fulfilled is certainly paradoxical. Jesus Christ is not only the Messiah on the cross. He is also the king on the cross (Mark 15.2, 9, 12, 18, 26). This Christian interpretation of royal rule by way of the *titulus crucis* is brought out again in John, in the scene with Pilate. Jesus, derided by the mob and with the crown of thorns on his head, is asked by Pilate: 'Are you the king of the Jews?' In his answer Jesus defines the nature of his kingship in two ways. It is a kingship that is 'not of this world' and its task is 'to bear witness to the truth' (John 18.33–37). Jesus' kingly, pastoral office is therefore implemented in service, in poverty, in powerlessness, suffering and death; it is fulfilled in the powerless and defenceless proclamation of the truth (Matt. 28.18f.), and is given effect in an anticipatory way in liturgical acclamation. In this sense Jesus Christ is 'king of kings and lord of lords' (I Tim. 6.15; Rev. 19.19).

It is therefore significant that in the second century we already find a Christian interpolation to Psalm 96.10: '*Dominus regnavit a ligno*' (The Lord reigned from the tree).[66] The traditional speculative justification of Jesus Christ's royal dignity on the grounds of the hypostatic union[67] therefore requires a staurological interpretation if it is not to be triumphalist. In my view, Augustine shows the positive form this interpretation could take, in his much misunderstood and misinterpreted teaching about the two cities. *Civitas dei* and *civitas terrena*, the city of God and the earthly city, are in conflict with one another, and have been so since the beginning of history. But the two are not simply identical with church and state. The distinction cuts right across church and state. The two cities are intermingled.[68] What defines the two are two modes of love: love of self and love of God.[69] The city of God is therefore to be found everywhere where there is love. This is the sense in which Aquinas answered the question whether Jesus Christ is the head of all human beings, and not merely the head of the church. According to Thomas, Christ is not only the head of all those who acknowledge him in faith. He is also the head of all who, without knowing him, are joined with him in love.[70] The political significance of the message of Jesus Christ – if political is understood in a comprehensive sense – is that through word and deed it works towards a 'civilization of love'.[71]

Whether and how far this approach permits *a political theology* is a complicated question which we can do no more than touch upon here.[72] But the question must at least be mentioned, because here too what is at issue is the anthropological relevance of the christological faith. For on the one hand it is entirely correct to say that salvation is not something inward and private; it also has a political and public dimension. But it must also be said that the phrase 'not of this world' brings out the distinction equally clearly, and forbids a political theology which sees itself, not merely as a political ethic (which has always existed) but as a comprehensive approach to theology, and its total context.

So beyond the alternative of integralistic identity and spiritualistic dualism, all that is left to us is *the analogy* between the two spheres.[73] In Jesus Christ we see, as it were in an image and parable, what freedom, justice and peace are. Statements of faith are therefore never merely a formal horizon for understanding and interpretation, as some trends in moral theology would like to suggest. Yet in the nature of things, no univocal positive norms can be derived from analogous statements. In the context of our question, therefore, the fundamental axiom for the relationship between christology and anthropology which we derived above from the Adam/Christ typology or analogy, can be modified in the following way: love presupposes justice and outbids it. So love does not replace justice. As the unconditional acceptance of the other person, love give him his due. It therefore requires justice and practises it. It confers the proper vision through which to discern the changing requirements of justice in the changing conditions of society (*via positionis*). It perceives unjust conditions, criticizes them, and motivates people to overcome them. Love is the soul of justice, so to speak (*via negationis*). But love also outbids the demands of justice, so it is only love which leads to a truly human order, in which there is friendship, forgiveness, solidarity, and the readiness to help other people (*via eminentiae*).

4. A summing up and a glance forward

We may sum up our conclusions and our forward-looking perspectives in three theses.

1. The premise of christology is a relatively independent anthropology. In this sense theology should adopt a *positive* attitude to the modern turn to anthropology and the modern notion of autonomy. But christology is also *critical* of particular anthropological schemes, whether they be theoretical or practically lived; and it points to the fundamental problem which the anthropological approach leads to. It therefore *outbids* anthropology, by defining the meaning and purpose of human beings as the humanization of men and women through their divinization, which cannot be brought about by human beings themselves. A christologically based anthropology of this kind, and an individual and social ethic based on the Christian viewpoint, is an urgent requirement.

2. The anthropological significance of christology is Christ's 'being for others'; and this is founded on his 'Being in itself'. Jesus' *pro*-existence presupposes his *pre*-existence, just as, conversely, the significance of the acknowledgment of his pre-existence (which means faith in the immanent Trinity) is only comprehensible and – in Newman's sense – realizable, if we discover the meaning of his pre-existence for us. To talk about 'ontological or functional christology' is therefore to pose a false alternative. And this suggests that our task is to integrate christology and soteriology in a new way; and the same may be said of the economic and the immanent doctrine of the Trinity.

3. By way of the *via analogiae*, the trinitarian Being of God revealed in Christ's 'pro'-existence leads to a metaphysics of love; and that means a relational metaphysics, whose centre is not the category of substance (as in ancient philosophy) but the category of person, for whom love is the meaning of being. This relational metaphysics based on the person can take up the legitimate concern of the modern shift towards anthropology. But at the same time it can go critically beyond that concern, so as to arrive at a new total view of reality, from the standpoint of the Christian faith.

It is obvious that these brief theses are really a programme for theological research, not a finished result. As yet Catholic theology has no more than begun to work positively and critically on the fundamental anthropological approach of modern thinking and its consequences. This task was laid upon it by the last Council. But theology can of course only match up to this task *if it remains theology and does not turn into anthropology.* Theology certainly has its essential anthropological dimension. But it is only the recognition of the God-ness of God which leads to the humanization of human beings. That is why the God-man Jesus Christ is the eschatological fullness of humanity (Eph. 4.13).

V

'One of the Trinity . . .'

Re-establishing a Spiritual Christology in the Perspective of
Trinitarian Theology

1. The Chalcedonian dogma under attack

The creed of the Fourth Ecumenical Council held at Chalcedon in 451
is undoubtedly one of the great formulations of Christian belief. This
confession of faith in Jesus Christ, true God and true human being in a
single person, may be considered the comprehensive doctrinal interpretation of the mystery of Christ. Here, in the form of a dogma, we
have the kerygma of Holy Scripture: 'And the Word became flesh'
(John 1.14). The dogma has not infrequently been viewed as being,
beyond that, a comprehensive definition of the essence of Christianity
in general. People talk about a divine-human principle which – starting
from its prototypical realization in Jesus Christ – is reflected, in an
analogous sense, in the mystery of the church. 'In a not insignificant
analogy, [the church] is similar to the mystery of the Word made
flesh'.[1] This dogma therefore expresses the fundamental scandal of the
Christian faith: God in human form, God on the cross (cf. I Cor. 1).

It can therefore come as no surprise to discover that it is the
Chalcedonian dogma above all which has become 'a kind of provocation' (Peter Stockmeier), 'positively like a red rag to a bull' (Gerhard
Ebeling). We find the objection to it already formulated in the Gospel
of John: 'You, being a man, make yourself God' (John 10.33). We
continually hear the echo of this demur in the patristic church – in
Celsus, in Julian the Apostate, in Porphyry. For them, the church's
creed seemed to be an immense backsliding, a retrograde step, away

from the enlightenment of the philosophers and the philosophical victory over the polytheism of simple-minded faith, for which the gods appear in human form.[2] In the different guise appropriate to a different age, we meet a similar criticism today, perhaps from the standpoint of a philosophical belief (Karl Jaspers), which reproaches the Chalcedonian dogma with materializing the God who is of his very nature non-material. In a similar way, John Hick, starting from the standpoint of linguistic philosophy, has only recently talked about 'the myth of God incarnate'.[3]

Even in theology and the church, Chalcedon was a stumbling-block – and still is. In the fifth and sixth centuries the dogma split the Christian faith into Chalcedonian churches and non-Chalcedonian ones (Copts, Jacobites, Armenians and Ethiopians); and contemporary theology splits over Chalcedon in a similar way. It has even been said that present-day theology has put Chalcedon in the dock.[4] Admittedly, the reason is not so much that the dogma is viewed as a provocation. The opposite would be closer to the truth. It is often no longer understood, and is pushed aside as being for people today an irrelevant and incomprehensible speculation. Luther affirmed the dogma in principle. Yet even he asked: 'Christ hath two natures. What is that to me?' What was important for him was not what Jesus Christ was in himself, but what he means for me, and for us.[5] Melanchthon, and even more the Pietists, followed Luther. Liberal theology readily took up the criticism and, from Schleiermacher onwards, concentrated its efforts on censure of metaphysical, essentialist thinking.[6] Adolf von Harnack thought that the bare, negative definitions of the dogma 'lack warm, specific content. For the believer, his faith is the bridge from earth to heaven. The creed makes of this bridge a line finer than the hair on which the professing Moslem once hoped to enter paradise'.[7]

It is not difficult to find many utterances among contemporary theologians, both Protestant and Catholic, which tend in the same direction. Almost everywhere we hear about the *aporia*, the impossible deadlock, presented by the so-called doctrine of the two natures – in Tillich, in Rahner, in Pannenberg, in Schoonenberg, Küng, Wiederkehr and many others.[8]

It must, however, be said that what is considered the real cause of offence today is not so much the teaching about Christ, as the church and its dogma, which claims to be able to say something generally valid and timeless about God in terms that are historically conditioned.[9] And it is certainly true that today, because of intensive historical research, we know more than people did earlier about the human – often all too human – elements, and the factors conditioned by the time, which also played their part in the development of the Chalcedonian dogma: the rivalries between great episcopal sees, between Alexandria and Antioch, but also between Constantinople and Rome; imperial power and the pressure of the imperial commissioners, who had almost to compel the council to formulate a new creed; the disputes between the various schools; the monkish quarrels; and much more beside. And for all that, the compromise arrived at with such difficulty, and after so much resistance, did not last long. It immediately became once again the object of new disputes, and could only be forced through at the next Ecumenical Council in Constantinople (553) in the form of the still disputed, so-called 'neo-Chalcedonian' interpretation – forced through, moreover, under extremely distasteful, indeed shameful, circumstances.

It would therefore seem legitimate to ask: how can anything which has come into being in this way, and was so much at the mercy of its time, set up the claim to infallibility and permanent validity? And speaking generally: how can the absolute ever find expression in history except in a relative and provisional way?

Yet these very queries show that the question behind the dogma of Chalcedon is still in substance our question too, even today, in spite of all the shifts of horizon that have taken place in the meantime. It is the question about the unity and the difference between God and human beings, and about the position and importance of the human element in the Christian faith. It is a question about the final significance for our salvation of Christ's humanity, and the importance of our human historicity for the mediation of salvation. As we know, these questions were also at the heart of the controversies with the Reformers in the sixteenth century.[10]

We can therefore say that although what was under discussion in Chalcedon was an individual question – a question which to many people may seem abstract, remote from life and the Bible – what was really at stake was evidently the proper understanding of the whole of the Christian faith. It is a question of determining the essence of Christian belief, and a question about the human element in Christianity.

Our aim here is not to discuss this fundamental theological question in general and in the abstract. Our purpose is rather to elicit the answer which the Council of Chalcedon gave more than fifteen hundred years ago, and to interpret that answer. Recent research has come up with some interesting findings which could provide the basis for a new contemporary interpretation of Chalcedon.

2. A few lessons provided by modern historical research

As far as the history of theology and dogma is concerned, the problem facing Chalcedon is well known, and it will be enough to sum it up here very briefly. With their creed, the first two General or Ecumenical Councils of Nicaea (325) and Constantinople (381) presented a binding interpretation of the central content of the New Testament kerygma: the eternal Son of God, one substance or essence with the Father, became human in time for our sakes and for our salvation. This liturgical creed has retained its validity down to the present day, and Chalcedon did not have to supplement it. It contained the essentials of the whole Christian faith.[11]

Yet a more precise interpretation had none the less become necessary, because in defining the incarnation, two different theological models stood over against one another. Taken to their extremes, both destroyed the inner significance of the creed, and hence strayed on to the heretical fringe. One of these models was the *Logos-sarx* scheme held by the Alexandrians, which stressed the unity of God and man; the other was the *Logos-anthropos* model of the Antiochenes, which emphasized the distinction between Christ's divinity and his humanity.[12] After this differentiating christology had been brought into disrepute by some utterances made by Nestorius,[13] the Council of Ephesus (431) laid down that 'one and the same' Son of God from eternity and in time became man, so that Mary could rightly be called the mother of God (*theotokos*) (DS 250f.). The union formula of 433, on the other hand, tended rather towards the christology of the Antiochenes, although the Alexandrians agreed to it. It preserved the distinction between the divinity and the humanity in the unity of both (DS 272). It was precisely this distinction in the unity that was now disputed by the devout but theologically naive monk Eutyches. He believed that Jesus' humanity was dissolved in his divinity, like a drop

of milk in the sea. The question was therefore whether Christ only
exists in two natures before the incarnation, or whether he has two
natures after the incarnation as well.

At first the Latin West hardly took any part in this discussion. But the
lack of profundity in speculation was to a certain degree outweighed
by greater clarity in distinguishing terms. For in the West, from
Tertullian onwards, the distinction between *natura* and *persona* was
common coin;[14] Augustine renewed it in his own individual way.[15]
Pope Leo the Great was able to draw on this tradition in his well-
known *Tome*, or *epistola dogmatica*, to the patriarch Flavian, and
could hence arrive at a compromise, on the formulatory level at least.
The starting point was acknowledgment of 'one and the same' Son, our
Lord Jesus Christ; and this acknowledgment of the unity was repeated
in the middle of the text and at the end. But it was added that in this
unity the difference of the two natures is preserved. The two are
without confusion and without change, but also without division and
without separation. Jesus Christ is therefore true God and true man in
one person and hypostasis (DS 301f.).

Until a short while ago, this Chalcedonian formula was seen as a
victory for Western theology, as this was expressed by Leo the Great
especially. Moreover, the Chalcedonian dogma was often viewed as a
kind of dialectical counter-stroke of 'differentiating' christology,
directed against the 'unity' christological position of Ephesus. This
viewpoint would then like to see the Second Council of Constantinople
(533) as a renewed victory for neo-Chalcedonian unity christology.[16]
For it was this Council which for the first time presented the fully
developed doctrine of the hypostatic union, according to which the
human nature of Jesus Christ subsists in the hypostasis of the Logos
(DS 424–430); and it put forward this christology 'from above' in the
bizarre-sounding formulation of the sketic monks: 'One of the Holy
Trinity has suffered in the flesh' (cf. DS 424; 432).[17] But this dialectical
view of the history of the dogma could suggest that Chalcedon
provides the justification for a christology 'from below', which could
then be set over against the church's fully developed doctrine of the
hypostatic union.[18]

Recent research has confounded these hypotheses.[19] The brilliant
investigations of André Halleux especially have put judgments about
the Council of Chalcedon on a new footing. Halleux was able to draw

on earlier research, and his conclusions have meanwhile been accepted both by Catholic scholars (above all Alois Grillmeier) and Protestant ones (e.g., A. M. Ritter and Luise Abramowski).

On the basis of a detailed analysis of the texts and sources, Halleux has shown that the council's definition really contains no more than two word-for-word quotations from Leo's *Tome*. The rest of the text is a mosaic of purely Eastern church formulations, drawn especially from Cyril's Second Letter to Nestorius, and from the union formula of 433, as this was interpreted in Cyril's letter to the patriarch John of Antioch, which put its seal on the union formulation. Even the formula which clearly goes back to Leo (according to which the uniqueness of each nature is preserved in the unity) was subjected to a 'cyrillisation stilistique'. The conclusion from all this is that Chalcedon's christological formula represents a more or less homogeneous Eastern creed – indeed a largely Cyrillic one; though admittedly with what Ritter calls a Leonine 'thorn in the flesh'.

This result shows first of all that the continuity in the church's doctrinal development is much greater than has hitherto been assumed. This is true of the continuity between Ephesus and Chalcedon; and it applies equally to the continuity between Chalcedon and the neo-Chalcedonian interpretation of Constantinople. This means that it is no longer possible to play off Chalcedon against Ephesus and Constantinople, and to interpret it in the sense of a one-sided christology 'from below' – that is, a christology starting from Jesus the human being. Like Nicaea-Constantinople and Ephesus, Chalcedon is concerned with a christology which begins 'above', with the eternal Son of God, who as 'one and the same' became a human being in time.

Second, the starting point in the creed passed down to us, and the triple stress on the unity in Jesus Christ, makes a description of the Chalcedonian dogma as 'the doctrine of the two natures' problematical.[20] But if the doctrine of the two natures is merely a commentary on the creed, this also counters the objection that the abstract Chalcedonian formula lacks any reference to salvation history. For after all, Chalcedon sees itself as an interpretation of Nicaea-Constantinople, with its account of salvation history – and as an interpretation whose explicit meaning is to protect and defend the creed's human and historical dimension. The council therefore neither wished nor needed to expand the salvation-history and eschatological dimension, since all

that was necessary had already been said in the creed. What it wanted
to do, and had to do, was to protect what the creed says against
doctrines which would have eroded its foundations, and robbed it of its
inward value. This places Chalcedonian christology fundamentally
within the creed's trinitarian perspective.[21]

Third, all this certainly does not mean that we are brushing aside as
unimportant the stronger stress on the true humanity of Jesus,
compared with earlier doctrinal statements. On the contrary, this
stress represents a revolutionary break-through, which cuts right
across Hellenistic thinking. For the mingling of divinity and humanity
which Eutyches maintained was in complete accord with the Hellenistic mind, and was in sharp contrast to Christian thinking, with its
stress on the qualitative transcendence between God and human
beings. For the Bible, the fact that the human being is not God (Ezek.
28.1, 9) and that God is not a human being (Num. 23.19; I Sam. 15.29;
Hos. 11.9) is fundamental. Any kind of human-divine hybrid, or
anything between God and human being, is unthinkable, according to
Christian ideas. Consequently Chalcedon, like Nicaea, is stating in the
language of Hellenistic philosophy something that is completely and
utterly non-Hellenistic – indeed anti-Hellenistic. So, with its distinction
between divinity and humanity, Chalcedon is anything but a Hellenization of Christianity; it is its *de*-Hellenization.[22] The council replaces
the Hellenistic symbiosis and synthesis of the natures of God and man,
by the specifically Christian model for defining the relationship.

In substance, Chalcedon solved this task with immense clarity. But
the council was not completely successful with its terminology. At that
time, the terms nature and hypostasis were not as yet by any means
understood in their later technical sense. It was left to others, such as
Boethius and Leontius of Byzantium, to clarify these terms successfully
and finally. The Second Council of Constantinople was able to draw on
this. But at what cost? For does not the doctrine of *enhypostasia* rob
Christ's human nature of its most essential element – its personhood? Is
human nature not thereby positively beheaded? Moreover, is not every
attempt to think together in a single person the true humanity and the
true divinity, not ultimately a contradiction in itself, or at best the
expression of a pure paradox?

At this point a second important finding of recent research takes us
further. Luise Abramowski,[23] picking up earlier hints, has shown with

a wealth of material that the council's formulation about the ἀσύγχυτος ἕνωσις, the 'unconfused unity' or 'union' derives from Neoplatonic philosophy. In Proclus above all, the formula about 'unconfused unity' or 'union' serves to solve the problem of how reality can proceed from the One, can participate in its fullness, and can then return to it; and how in this way the difference of the many over against the One can still be preserved.[24] The fundamental postulate is as follows: every thing caused rests in its cause, but also issues from it, then again to find fulfilment by returning to its origin. Here, therefore, we have a 'unity without confusion' as well as a 'distinction without division'. This pattern of mediation was soon taken up by the Fathers, in order to interpret theologically, not only the unity of body and soul in the human being, but also the nature of the one mediator, Jesus Christ. For he is the mediation between God and the world in the form of a unique unity, which frees humanity for its creative independence and at the same time brings it to its highest possible fulfilment.

The Chalcedonian formula, therefore, is not a mere compromise, concluded *ad hoc*. Nor are these purely negative statements, or simply a paradox. The four much cited negative epithets – without confusion, without change, without division, without separation – express a philosophically thought-through concept in its Christian transformation. Indeed these formulations offer an answer, from the standpoint of Christian faith, to the fundamental philosophical problem *per se*: the relation between unity and diversity, or between identity and difference. Consequently it is perfectly correct to maintain that the doctrine of the *enhypostasia* does not mean any deficiency in Jesus' humanity, but is rather its final perfecting. The highest possible unity with God does not amputate and reduce the humanity. It brings that humanity to its true and complete fulfilment. The result is not a dualism or parallelism of the two natures, but an unconfused unity which starts from God, but which at the same time frees what is human to be itself.

This is the point where we should consider a third finding of research into dogmatic and theological history. It has to do with the Sixth Ecumenical Council, or Third Council of Constantinople (680/1). It was this council which actually concluded the development of christological doctrine, and it is only in the light of that conclusion that Chalcedon is fully comprehensible. And yet up to now the Third Council of Constantinople has generally received shabby treatment in theology, and has been viewed as a kind of Chalcedonian appendage, which produced a more or less scholastic development of the Chalcedonian doctrine of the two natures into the doctrine of Christ's two wills and two natural energies. It was only after we had come to know more about the splendid theology of Maximus Confessor, and his Christian 'personal' metaphysics or cosmology,[25] that Joseph Ratzinger was able to bring to light once more the deeper concern of this Council.[26]

The Council certainly clearly adheres to the two physical wills and energies of Jesus Christ, which spring from his two natures. But equally clearly, it sees his human will as subordinated in obedience to the divine will in such a way that his human, fleshy will is called, and is, the 'own' will of the divine Logos. For this, the Council appeals to John 6.38: 'I have come down from heaven, not to do my own will, but the will of him who sent me.' Here the Logos calls the fleshy will his own; but although the human will is deified, it is not abolished (DS 556). Maximus Confessor distinguished between the two physical wills which belong to the two natures, and the one gnomic will which is a property of the person.[27] This again is not a symmetrical parallelism. What is maintained here is an intermingling in freedom. The assumption of the human will in God's will does not destroy human freedom; it liberates human freedom from its bonds, and makes it truly free.

The real step forward taken by the Third Council of Constantinople, however, is probably that it no longer considers the ontological problem merely in terms of nature, but primarily in terms of freedom and personhood. So, as the ancient world drew to its close, and as the era of the Fathers ended, the path was paved for a modern reception of the patristic christology summed up by this council.

3. Systematic aspects of a christology in trinitarian perspective

With what has just been said, we have already taken the step from historical analysis to a contemporary systematic exposition. In fact what we have said makes this step compellingly necessary. For the Chalcedonian dogma itself is based on the principle of living tradition. It sees itself as the interpretative development of the common faith of the church, as this was decisively formulated in the Nicaeno-

Constantinopolitan creed. This in its turn is the summarizing, binding interpretation of Holy Scripture. But the controversies before Chalcedon and afterwards make it clear that developing interpretation is the condition of true tradition, whereas mere repetition in a different situation lays tradition open to misunderstanding, or even to blank incomprehension. Thus, in its own way, the council acknowledged the principle of living tradition, in which tradition and interpretation form a unity.

Of course that also means that Chalcedon and Constantinople III were not merely an end. They were also the beginning of an on-going discussion. Not because the doctrine of these councils was wrong, but just because it is true, the doctrine has to be seen as an open, self-transcending formula which leads us into always greater and deeper truth.[28] The dogma of the patristic church cannot therefore be used as a yardstick of orthodoxy, in a simplistic, fundamentalist way. Orthodoxy is not a fixed *standpoint* – it is a *way*, the way which the church takes, and which a person takes with the church. We must not deviate today from the path of the early and patristic church; but neither can we stand still on it. We must follow the path further, though certainly *eodem sensu*, in the same sense or direction (cf. DS 3020).

It was the great achievement of the patristic church's doctrine, and especially the Chalcedonian dogma, that in spite of all Hellenistic trends towards divinization, it clung to the scandal of the *logos sarx egeneto* – the Word made flesh – thus preserving Jesus' true humanity and historicity. Our task today is a diametrically opposite one to the task of that earlier time, and it is no less difficult. For us, unlike the people of the patristic era, Jesus' humanity is unquestioned. Our danger is not a false deification, but a one-sided humanization, a picture of Christ reduced more or less to the measure of what is purely human. The question which faces us today is therefore this: in the face of widespread atheism, how can we talk about Jesus Christ in such a way that in him God comes to new and convincing expression? How, that is, can we think the unity of God and human being in contemporary terms?

The modern era no longer asks the question about God in the context of cosmology – if it asks it at all. It asks the question in the context of anthropology. For us, the human being is the starting point from which we ask about the meaning of the whole, and from which we ask the question about Jesus Christ also. That is why, ever since Schleiermacher especially, the 'nature' categories used at Chalcedon were criticized, and why Schleiermacher himself sought out his own, new way of interpretation in the context of modern subjectivity, not in the context of metaphysics. He started, not from Jesus' divine *being*, but from the special power of his divine *consciousness*; for him this was the real Being of God in Jesus.[29] This attempt has always aroused the suspicion of ambiguity. For the starting point in human subjectivity only makes it possible to state the Chalcedonian dogma unambiguously in a new way if it is interpreted, not merely with categories of consciousness, but with categories of being as well. What is required, therefore, is the ontological question in a new form, starting from the standpoint of modern subjectivity.[30]

This mediation of modern subjectivity philosophy and classic ontology can be undertaken particularly well with the help of the concept of person.[31] For on the one hand the human person exists uniquely in himself and for himself, and on the other hand he is open for reality as a whole. Modern anthropology (as represented by Arnold Gehlen, Helmuth Plessner, Max Scheler and others) talks about openness to the world, as the human being's distinctive character. We can also take Heidegger's phraseology, and say that the human being is *Da-sein*, 'being there'. In him being is as such *there*. His always unique consciousness is the 'being alongside itself' of being.[32] This openness constitutes the restlessness and disquiet of the human person. He is always on the move, because in his infinite openness he is unable to find fulfilment in anything finite. Only through the encounter with God, the fullness of all reality, does the undefined openness of human beings find its final definition, its fulfilment and completion. The approach 'from below' therefore leads to a total reversal of thinking, because the question about the human being posed 'from below' can find its final answer only 'from above', from God. The human ex-istence which transcends itself infinitely (Pascal) possesses itself only in owing itself to something beyond itself; it is 'owed' existence – existence 'thanks to' something outside itself.

On the basis of reflections like these, it is understandable, and also legitimate, if in trying to arrive at a new interpretation of Chalcedon many contemporary theologians no longer take as their starting point the question about the relationship of Christ's two natures; they now start instead with what was the centre of Jesus' life and person, according to the testimony of all the Gospels: his personal communication with the Father.[33] It is generally recognized in historical research that Jesus addressed God with wholly unique intensity as 'Abba', and that he retained this personal unity to the point of his obedience unto death (Mark 14.36).[34] The fact that Paul passes down Jesus' form of address in prayer in the original Aramaic (cf. Rom. 8.15; Gal. 4.6), shows that here we have a particularly sacred saying of tradition, and a remembrance of Jesus' most individual language. It is interesting here that in this form of address Jesus never associates himself with his disciples. He always says 'my Father' or 'your Father'. His relationship to the Father is unique and untransferable. He is the Son in a unique sense. We are God's sons and daughters only through him (cf. Matt. 11.27), by partaking in his Spirit (cf. Rom. 8.15; Gal. 4.6).[35]

The later development of christological doctrine can be understood as an interpretation of this centre in Jesus' life and death. For in Jesus' relationship to his Father, Jesus exists wholly from the Father and wholly towards him. He is nothing of himself, but is in everything from the Father. He is 'owed' existence *per se*. He owes himself in a unique way, with everything he is, to the Father.[36] He exists solely because the Father gives him everything which he has and is, namely his deity. So Jesus is on the one hand confronted with the Father in obedience and love, and is hence different from him; but on the other hand he is also God's image, the picture which makes God present, his icon. He speaks and acts in God's stead. In the form of human obedience he is God's *Da-sein*, his existence, his 'being there', in history; the human obedience is at the same time the obedience of God's Son. For in this unity in difference, and difference in unity, he is the eschatological revelation of God, as well as the eschatological fulfilment of human beings. In him is manifested, in eschatological finality in the midst of time, what from all eternity God is: relation, self-giving love between Father and Son, into which human beings through the Spirit are destined from eternity to be accepted, and which is their true bliss.

Our thesis is therefore this: Jesus' personal 'Abba' relationship expresses his sending by the Father in time, a commission which he accepted in obedience. And this manifests the eternal relation of the Son to the Father, and hence indirectly the eternal deity of the Son (his pre-existence), and the trinitarian mystery as a whole. Consequently the whole of the christology and trinitarian doctrine developed after Easter is the interpretation and exposition of what was the centre and foundation of Jesus' life, ministry and death: his unique personal relationship to God, his Father. The misnamed two-nature christology is subject to the personal and ultimately trinitarian relation between the Father and the Son, and belongs within that wider framework. Aquinas grasped this connection between christology and the doctrine of the Trinity supremely well when he termed the temporal sending of the Son through the Father the 'economic' form of his eternal procession from the Father.[37] That is the reason for the (to our ears) somewhat bizarre formula (drawn from the sixth-century theopaschite dispute) that 'One of the Holy Trinity suffered in the flesh'.

In this way the Trinity is gnoseologically (*quoad nos*) a logical conclusion from christology;[38] it is this that is the legitimate concern of christology 'from below', according to which we perceive the invisible in the visible (see the Christmas Preface). But ontologically (*in se*, or in itself) the Trinity is the transcendental, theological premise for christology; and this is the enduringly valid concern of christology 'from above'.[39] The trinitarian unity of Father, Son and Spirit in their relational difference is, as it were, the grammar of the 'differentiated unity' of God and man in Jesus Christ, and the condition that makes it possible. The trinitarian and christological formula says that the greater the difference and independence, the greater the unity; and this is also the fundamental model for the Christian definition of the relationship between God and the world, or God and human beings.[40] Love therefore becomes the meaning of being.

This new interpretation of patristic christology raises many other questions about the being, consciousness and personhood of Jesus – questions into which we cannot enter in our present context.[41] Here we are confining ourselves to one consequence of this interpretation. It has the advantage that it allows us to comprehend once more, in a new way, the soteriological and spiritual dimension of christological dogma. This soteriological concern was of decisive importance in the disputes before and after Chalcedon, and at the council itself. It is quite simply incorrect when Harnack maintains that this dogma is profoundly irreligious.[42] The very opposite is true. In defending the true humanity of Jesus, Leo the Great reverted to the ancient principle according to which that which is not assumed by Jesus Christ cannot be redeemed (*Quod non est assumptum, non est sanatum*).[43] Leo wished to preserve the independence of Jesus' true human nature, in the interests of the full humanity of salvation. But this means that the divinization of human beings – the lofty ideal of Greek philosophy and theology – is their true humanization; and conversely, the full humanity of human beings lies in their divinization. The *sacrum commercium* – the mutual giving of human beings and God – is therefore the centre of the Christian message.[44]

Later on this soteriological and spiritual intention of the Chalcedonian dogma came to be less and less understood. What was a mystery of salvation was increasingly turned into an intellectual mystery; and in trying to solve it people really did often lose themselves in insoluble deadlocks. Here a new interpretation based on the concept of the person can be of help. This tells us that the unity in Jesus Christ is not a symbiosis of different natures. It is the qualitatively unique and greatest possible personal unity and fellowship between God and human beings. This makes it the prototype and profoundest source of our fellowship with God. For through faith and baptism we are made like in form to Jesus Christ and thus 'admitted' into his innermost attitude and disposition, which was his obedience towards the Father, and into his self-giving love for human beings.

A christology of this kind avoids the fatal impression of being a mere speculation. It becomes the foundation for Christian ethics and spirituality, in which contemplation and action are a unity, and in which a restless 'owing everything to oneself' gives way to a humility which wishes to be nothing of itself, to obedience, to poverty of spirit, to patience. We could really name all the fruits of the Spirit (cf. Gal. 5.22f.). The starting point, centre and goal of this spirituality is – as it was for Jesus himself – the prayer which 'in the fellowship of the Holy Spirit' cannot be merely a personal 'Abba', but which has to be the common utterance of 'Our Father'.[45]

A spiritual christology like this is not an evasion of the questions of Christian existence. If in such a christology theonomy and autonomy are not antitheses, but if complete fellowship and friendship with God is the foundation for human and Christian freedom, then christological dogma will become the basis for a new Christian humanism.

At this point the controversies about early Christian dogma become relevant and topical in a completely new way. For all too long the

church's magisterium and Catholic theology, starting from the theonomy of everything that is Christian, have disputed and fought against
modern autonomy.[46] Here, as in many other questions, Vatican II
signals a change of direction. Today, admittedly, the pendulum often
swings too far in the opposite direction. People often strive, not merely
for a christology 'from below', but for an anthropology and ethics
'from below' as well. They make human autonomy their starting point,
and see theonomy more or less as the ultimately, formally permanent
horizon for that autonomy, but not as its concrete form. And then
Christianity has nothing substantial of its own to add to humanism.

The direction in which the patristic church points us is different.
Here it is theonomy which actually liberates autonomy, and which at
the same time defines the content of human autonomy, which is in itself
undefined and open. This is the view of the last Council: 'In reality it is
only in the mystery of the Word made flesh that the mystery of man
truly becomes clear . . . Christ the new Adam, in the very revelation of
the mystery of the Father and of his love, fully reveals man to himself
and brings to light his most high calling' (*Gaudium et spes*, 22; cf. 21;
41). 'Whoever follows Christ the perfect man becomes himself more a
man' (ibid., 41).

The relationship between christology and anthropology can be more
closely defined in three ways: as an affirmation of everything that is
right, true, good and lovely about human beings (*via positionis*); as a
prophetic criticism of all forms of alienation in human beings, and
between human beings (*via negationis*); and finally as the creative
surpassing of everything that is possible in purely human terms, and
thus as the completion and fulfilment of human beings in God (*via
eminentiae*).[47]

This threefold relationship between christology and anthropology
makes plain the specifically Christian contribution to a more humane
world and a civilization of love. For here the christological doctrine
developed in the patristic church, and newly interpreted in the light of
modern scriptural exegesis and a modern world view, has a real
contribution to make. And this contribution is a trinitarian ontology of
the person, and the perfecting of that person in love.

PART TWO

The Church as a Sacrament
of Salvation

VI

The Church as a Universal Sacrament of Salvation

1. The relevance of the question for us today

The question about the place of Christians and the church in the secular world of today is still one of the most vital questions with which contemporary faith is confronted. Many Christians have the impression that the church, its proclamation and its sacraments, are some kind of special sacred enclave, which exists side by side with the secular world. They feel that the church's preaching and its liturgy have little to do with 'life as it is really lived' and with 'actual reality'. It is not the least of the services rendered by Karl Rahner that he should have sought ceaselessly for an answer to this urgent problem. And his service was all the greater because the answer he offers is not the fruit of any short-term, fashionable adaptation to the present situation. It springs from the fundamental idea behind his whole theology. For Rahner, the central and essential concept of Christianity, and in a sense the formula that sums it up, is God's gracious communication of himself to human beings and the world.[1] This means that the whole of reality is always already aligned towards Jesus Christ, and that its final purpose is salvation.[2] According to this conception, the church is the real symbol and the primal sacrament of this self-communication of the threefold God in truth and love.[3] Its sacraments are not some special sector. They are an emblematic manifestation of the liturgy of the world.[4]

In its concern to offer a description of the nature of the church to the people belonging to it and to those outside, the Second Vatican Council took up essential elements in this idea, and summarily defined the church as the universal sacrament of salvation.[5] After the council, however, this important statement came to be forgotten for the most part, and indeed discredited. Some people see it as theological window-dressing, if not actually an ideological self-enhancement of the church as it really and specifically is. For this reason among others, in the post-conciliar phase other conciliar statements about the church were placed in the forefront, above all the description 'the people of God'. Whereas the definition of the church as sacrament largely remained theological jargon, the term 'people of God' became something of a slogan, which then certainly tended to lead to more misunderstanding, rather than to real comprehension. It would therefore seem useful to think about *one* of the council's complementary statements about the church – a statement which, as we shall see, is anything but uncritical.

The topical nature of this subject is also made plain by its ecumenical relevance, although we cannot go into that in detail here, since it would require a discussion of its own.[6] It is generally held that the question of the ministry is the most important point of remaining controversy – indeed that it is the crux of the ecumenical discussion. That judgment is correct if we realize that the question of the ministry brings to a point an even more fundamental problem: the relationship of the visible form of the church to its hidden nature, which can only be grasped in faith. All the churches certainly agree that the church is a complex reality, composed of visible elements and a hidden dimension which can be grasped only in faith. The problem begins only with the enquiry about the more precise relationship between the hidden, spiritual reality and the visible, institutionally constituted church. The question is then: how far does the institutional form of the church belong to the true church – that is, to its essence? As we shall see, the council gave its answer to this question when it defined the church as being essentially a sacrament.

There are therefore at least three topical problems, or problem complexes, all of which suggest the importance of a new discussion about the council's definition of the church as universal sacrament of salvation. These three problem complexes are: the relation of the church to the world of today; the relation of the Catholic Church to the other churches; and relations, or conditions, within the Catholic Church itself. Let us first of all ask what the council meant by its statement, since this has already become strange and alien to many people today.

2. The statements made by Vatican II

The Second Vatican Council talked about the church as a sacrament in many different places. Especially important are the statements in the constitution on the church, *Lumen gentium*, 1, 9 and 48, as well as the more passing reference in 59. To these must be added comments in the Constitution on the Liturgy, *Sacrosanctum concilium* 5 and 26, in the Pastoral Constitution *Gaudium et spes* 42 and 45, and in the Decree on Missions, *Ad gentes* 1 and 5. Naturally enough, it is in *Lumen gentium* that we find the most important utterances on our present subject, and the textual history of the constitution is particularly illuminating when we try to grasp what these statements really mean.[7]

The textual history[8] shows that it was by no means a matter of course from the very outset for the council to define the church as a sacrament. The text of the preparatory commission was largely drawn up by S. Tromp, the main author of Pius XII's encyclical *Mystici corporis* (1943). In this preparatory text nothing is as yet said about a sacramental view of the church. On the contrary, this draft remained completely within the bounds of traditional scholastic theology. In the plenary discussions of December 1962, the draft was subjected to devastating criticism because of its triumphalism, clericalism and legalism. A number of bishops demanded instead a view of the church as *mysterium* or *sacramentum* (Döpfner, Lercaro, Suenens, Volk, König, Montini and others). So the intention in pressing for a sacramental view of the church was anything but a bid for its ideological elevation. On the contrary, the aim was to get away from the encrusted, narrow and one-sided elements of the traditional view held by scholastic theology. This fundamentally critical intention must be borne in mind if we want to understand properly what the council's statements really mean.

How did the council arrive at this statement about the church? Not by rejecting tradition, but by recollecting the full wealth tradition offers, compared with its narrow neo-scholastic interpretation.[9] In the nineteenth century, Romanticism, particularly through the medium of the Tübingen school, already prepared the ground for a renewal of the sacramental view of the church found in the Fathers, this trend being initiated by M. J. Scheeben and J. H. Oswald. In our own century, the viewpoint was developed first of all by French-speaking theologians, especially Henri de Lubac. As early as 1938 de Lubac summed up his conviction as follows: 'If Jesus Christ could be called the sacrament of God, then for us the church is the sacrament of Christ.'[10] This approach was developed in German-speaking and Dutch theology especially. As well as Otto Semmelroth, Karl Rahner, Pierre Smulders and Edward Schillebeeckx deserve special mention, among others. So in central European pre-conciliar theology, the sacramental view of the church was already widely held. It is therefore not surprising that the definition of the church as a sacrament can be found in a number of drafts drawn up after the first period of the council. The most important of these is the draft prepared by German theologians (including Rahner) and approved by the German bishops in December 1962.[11] The Belgian theologian Gérard Philips then included the sacramental definition of the church in the commission's new draft of 1963. And it was retained from that point until the final draft was approved.[12]

Between the German draft and the new draft drawn up by the commission, however, there is one important difference. The German draft runs: 'Ecclesia Christi ab ipso convocata et legitime constituta est et sacramentum universale, visibile et definitivum huius salutiferae unitatis existit.' This draft therefore assumes that the definition of the church as a sacrament is comprehensible without more ado. The commission's draft is in this respect more realistic and more differentiated. For here the term 'sacrament' is preceded by an explanation of what this means: it is *signum et instrumentum*. And the text adds that the church is *veluti sacramentum* – 'as it were a sacrament'. In other words, according to the accustomed terminology of sacramental doctrine, the term sacrament can only be used for the church in an improper sense.

However, it emerges from the Relatio of July and that of October 1964 that not all the fathers found the text comprehensible, even with these explanations. Whereas six fathers, speaking for 130 others, pleaded that the sacramental definition of the church should be retained, three resisted on the ground that this definition could be confused with the word sacrament in its proper sense. None the less, the theological commission clung successfully to its formulation, taking the view that the statement was elucidated by the explanation in the text.[13]

Let us therefore try to interpret the council's statements in the light of the texts themselves. If we do this, the following picture emerges.

1. The definition of the church as a universal sacrament of salvation is one definition among others. The council uses a whole series of other descriptions in addition. The phrase 'people of God' is especially important. But there are other terms or images as well: sheepfold, flock, cultivated field, tillage, building, temple, family of God, bride of Christ and – not least – body of Christ (*Lumen gentium* 6f.). It would therefore be completely wrong if we were to try to tie down post-conciliar Catholic ecclesiology exclusively to the term sacrament. The council describes the church rather as a mystery which cannot be exhausted by any single concept. If we are to approach the mystery of the church, we need a multiplicity of complementary images and terms which mutually interpret and also correct one another.

2. In the Vatican II texts, the definition of the church as a universal sacrament of salvation is always embedded in a strictly christological context. This is already brought out in section 5 of the Constitution on the Liturgy, where Jesus Christ is described as the one mediator between God and humanity, especially through the paschal mystery. 'The wondrous sacrament of the whole church' proceeded from the side of Christ as he died on the cross. The Constitution on the Church develops this viewpoint. It begins right at the beginning of chapter one with the words: *Lumen gentium cum sit Christus* – 'since Christ is the light of humanity . . .' That is why it is explicitly stated that 'in Christ' the church is 'in the nature of' a sacrament – a sign and instrument, that is, of communion with God and of unity among all human beings. *Lumen gentium* 9 is if anything even more definite: Jesus Christ is 'the author of salvation and the principle of unity and peace', whereas the church is the visible sacrament of this unity. Finally, section 48 says that through his Spirit, the risen and exalted Christ has made the church the comprehensive sacrament of salvation, and that through the Spirit he continues to be active in the church.

In these texts, therefore, the church is by no means seen as an autonomous, self-sufficient entity. On the contrary, we may take an image of the early Fathers and say that, just as the moon has no light except the light which comes from the sun, the church has no light except that which emanates from Jesus Christ and shines into the world.[14] So it is surely not by chance that in talking about the church the council did not use the misleading expression 'primal sacrament'. According to patristic and scholastic tradition, and in the thinking of the council itself, Jesus Christ alone is the primal sacrament: the church is a sacrament only 'in Christ'; and that means that it is a sign and an instrument, both of which by definition point beyond themselves. The church is the sign which points beyond itself to Jesus Christ, and it is an instrument in the hand of Jesus Christ, since he is the real author of all saving activity in the church.

To define the church as a sacrament 'in Christ' is therefore not intended to deny Christ's pre-eminence, and his lordship over the church. On the contrary, these things are emphatically stressed. Nor is the definition intended to give credence to the neo-romantic notion of the church as prolongation of the incarnation. On the contrary, the council deliberately contradicted this conception. For the council sees the church merely 'in a not unimportant analogy' to the mystery of God's incarnation. But an analogy means that in spite of all similarity, a difference still remains. This difference is that the Spirit of Christ works through the visible structure of the church in a similar way (that is, not in *the same* way) to the way in which the Logos acts through the human nature he assumed (*Lumen gentium* 8).

3. The definition of the church as a universal sacrament of salvation is always put in an eschatological context. According to the council, the kingdom of God shines out in the word, work and presence of Christ. The church represents 'the seed' and beginning of this kingdom on earth (*Lumen gentium* 5), indeed it is 'the kingdom of Christ already present in mystery' (3). In this way the church is a messianic people, although it often appears as a little flock. It is 'a most sure seed of unity, hope and salvation for the whole human race' (9). The church stands under the sign of the salvation that has already appeared but has not as yet been completed. Through his act of redemption, Jesus Christ has brought about once and for all unity, peace, and reconciliation with God, and unity, peace and reconciliation among human beings. This will become manifest at the end of time. But these things are already present in the church in a provisional and anticipatory way, and through the church, as a sign and instrument, they are intended to be

bestowed on all human beings. This comes about through the ministry of the Word of God (Constitution on Divine Revelation), through the sacramental mediation of salvation (Constitution on the Liturgy), and through mission (Decree on the Church's Missionary Activity), as well as through service for society (Pastoral Constitution). Again, as the emblematic, sacramental anticipation of eschatological salvation, the church is not a force or entity which exists in its own right. On the contrary, it points away from itself, and beyond itself, to the salvation of human beings and the salvation of the world. So precisely because it is a sacrament of salvation, the church must continually go beyond itself, in dialogue, in communication, and in co-operation with all people of good will. This aspect is brought out particularly impressively in the pastoral constitution (*Gaudium et spes*, 42, 43, 45).

It is the eschatological context of the sacramental definition of the church particularly which excludes any kind of ecclesiological triumphalism. The Council says explicitly that the church has the form of a servant, in three ways. 1. It is a church of the poor; 2. It is a church of sinners, being 'at once holy and always in need of purification, [following] constantly the path of penance and renewal'. 3. It is a persecuted church. As a servant in these three ways, the church is the sign of Jesus Christ, who emptied himself and took upon himself the form of a servant (cf. Phil. 2.6–11). So to talk about the church as a sacrament is not to deny the scandal of the church as it actually is. On the contrary, the term is intended to make the scandal clear (cf. also *Gaudium et spes* 45).

4. Now that we have looked at the context of the assertion about the church as a sacramental reality, we have to ask what this statement itself means, according to Vatican II. By saying that in Christ the church is *as it were* a sacrament, the council makes it clear that – as we have already said – the classic concept of sacrament used in Catholic theology, which has been developed since the twelfth century, should not be applied to the church. That is to say, the church is not an eighth sacrament, in addition to the other seven. According to the sacramental concept employed since the twelfth century, the church is a sacrament only in an improper sense. By using the term sacrament in this merely analogous sense, the council is going back to the older sacramental concept of patristic theology. At that time, as we know, *sacramentum* was the Latin word used to translate the biblical term

mysterion. The Relatio to the Constitution on the Church expressly brings out this connection. It says that *mysterium* does not mean something unknowable or abstruse. In the sense in which it is used in Scripture, it means that transcendent, salvific divine reality which reveals itself in a visible way.[15] If we start from this understanding of *mysterium*, it may be said that the inner nature of the church is hidden; but that it reveals itself – even if shadows remain – in the concrete, visible *ecclesia catholica*.

The term sacrament is therefore intended to bring out the many dimensions of the church's structure. It tells us that the church is a complex reality which includes visible elements and hidden ones, what is human and what is divine. There is a mystery in the visible church which can only be grasped in faith (*Lumen gentium* 8). So the term sacrament is intended to help prevent both a spiritualistic view of the church and a naturalistic and purely sociological viewpoint. What is visible about the church is also part of its essential nature. That is to say, it also belongs to the true church. But of course what is visible is essential only as a sign and instrument of the true, proper reality of the church, which can only be grasped in faith. The sacramental structure of the church, accordingly, means that what is visible about it is the actualizing and efficacious sign – that is, the real symbol – of God's eschatological salvation of the world, which has appeared in Jesus Christ.

Summing up, we may therefore say: as the Second Vatican Council used the term sacrament to describe the church, this is one conceptual means among others for overcoming ecclesiological triumphalism, clericalism and legalism. It is one way of bringing out the mystery of the church, which is concealed in its visible form and can only be grasped in faith. The council's aim is to express and interpret the truth that on the one hand the church comes wholly from Christ, and remains permanently related to him; but that on the other hand, as a sign and instrument, it is also wholly there in order to minister to men and women and the world. The term sacrament is well suited to express the differentiating relationship and the distinction between the church's visible structure and its spiritual nature. But of course this still leaves many problems open. We shall try to clarify them further by now leaving aside the interpretation of the council texts themselves. Instead we shall now look at the saying about the church as a universal sacrament of salvation from a more systematic viewpoint, in order to come closer to what is meant.

3. Systematic foundations

Our systematic reflections here are inevitably no more than fragmentary. I can do no more than indicate three theses.

1. *Jesus Christ is the primal sacrament.* In defining the church as a sacrament, Vatican II and modern Catholic theology are not drawing upon the classic concept of sacrament developed in the twelfth century.[16] They are reverting to the fundamental biblical meaning of *mysterion*. As we know, the Old Latin translation of the Bible used *sacramentum* as rendering for this word.[17] But the original meaning of *mysterion* was not directly sacramental. In fact in this respect the biblical findings are initially extremely disappointing for any theology of the sacraments. For when Scripture talks about *mysterion*, it is not talking about sacraments; and when individual sacraments are mentioned (especially baptism and the eucharist), the word *mysterion* is never used.[18] But the term *mysterion* is not primarily ecclesiological either. It is meant first and foremost christologically. So the description 'primal sacrament' should not be applied to the church. It should be reserved for Jesus Christ alone.[19]

This argument can be supported relatively easily if we look at the New Testament findings.[20] In the synoptic tradition, the word *mysterion* is found especially in the parable chapter, Mark 4.11f. par.: 'To you has been given the secret (*mysterion*) of the kingdom of God, but for those outside everything is in parables.' The logion does not answer the question what the secret of the kingdom is. But the answer emerges if we notice that in the Bible the term *mysterion* is shaped and coloured by the apocalyptic use of the word. It is applied to the divine resolve which is hidden from human eyes, is unveiled only through revelation, and will be implemented at the end of time. In this context the logion means that the parables of the kingdom show Jesus' listeners the nature of that kingdom in general terms; but it is only the closer circle of Jesus' disciples whose eyes are opened for the dawn of the messianic era (cf. Matt. 13.16f.). It is they alone who are able to perceive in faith that in Jesus' words and acts the kingdom of God is breaking in. The mystery of the kingdom of God revealed to the disciples is therefore Jesus himself, as the messiah.

A glance at Pauline (and especially deutero-Pauline) usage puts us on the same track. To preach Christ as the one crucified (I Cor. 1.23) means for Paul preaching the testimony (another reading has 'the mystery') of God (I Cor. 2.1). This again means the 'secret of the hidden wisdom of God, which God decreed before the ages for our glorification' (I Cor. 2.7). So the mystery or secret is God's eternal resolve to save (Eph. 1.9; 3.9; Col. 1.26; Rom. 16.25), the resolve which in the fullness of time he consummated in Jesus Christ, so as 'to unite all things in him, things in heaven and things on earth' (Eph. 1.10; Rom. 16.25f.). The Epistle to the Colossians can therefore say directly that the mystery is Christ (2.2), 'Christ among you' (1.27). Indeed the writer can identify the mystery with the mystery of Christ (4.3). The First Epistle to Timothy sums up 'the mystery of our faith' in the same sense: 'He was manifested in the flesh, justified in the Spirit, seen by the angels, preached among the nations, believed on in the world, taken up in glory' (I Tim. 3.16).

It was not least Karl Rahner who systematically brought out this original meaning of *mysterion*, thus breaking down the narrowly intellectualized neo-scholastic concept of mystery.[21] For Rahner, God is the final and authentic answer to the mystery of human beings, both in his eternal trinitarian self-communication and in his historical self-communication in Jesus Christ and the Holy Spirit. This means that theology and anthropology are linked through the mediation of christology. This position was received into the teaching of the Second Vatican Council. According to the Pastoral Constitution *Gaudium et spes*, Jesus Christ is the eschatological final revelation, not of God only, but of human beings too. Jesus Christ, the image of God *per se* (II Cor. 4.4; Col. 1.15; Heb. 1.3) fulfils to an all-surpassing degree the character of all human beings as image of God (Gen. 1.27). So 'in the mystery of the Word made flesh the mystery of man truly becomes clear'; Jesus Christ, as the new Adam, 'in the very revelation of the mystery of the Father and of his love, fully reveals man to himself and brings to light his most high calling' (*Gaudium et spes* 22). As God's primal sacrament, Jesus Christ is at the same time the primal sacrament of the human being and all humanity. We shall come back to the far-reaching consequences of this thesis at the end.

2. *The church as the universal saving sacrament of Jesus Christ.*
After what has been said, this definition of the church would seem to be
more appropriate than the misleading description of the church as the
primal or fundamental sacrament, a definition which ought to be
reserved for Jesus Christ. This does not deny that, according to Eph.
3.10, the saving mystery of God which became a reality in history
through Christ is made known to the world through the church. We
therefore very often meet the word *mysterion* in connection with
expressions of revelation and proclamation (Rom. 16.25; I Cor. 2.7;
Eph. 3.8f.; 6.19; Col. 2.2; 4.3). According to the New Testament, the
apostolic office also belongs to the proclamation of the saving mystery
of God in Jesus Christ (Eph. 3.2; Col. 1.25), and this office sees itself as
minister and steward of God's mysteries (I Cor. 4.1). The much cited
saying about 'the mystery which refers to Christ and the church' (Eph.
5.32) also points to the connection between Jesus Christ, the primal
sacrament, and the church; although the interpretation of the saying is
certainly disputed.

Again, Karl Rahner stressed the inner connection between the
realization of God's saving mystery in Jesus Christ and the church; for
the saving mystery really comes into the world only when it is accepted
in faith and publicly avowed. So the church, the fellowship of believers,
is an essential element in the implementation of the divine will for
salvation. This is when God's communication of himself arrives at its
goal.[22] So the church is simultaneously the fruit of salvation and the
means of salvation; for it is both an actualizing sign of God's salvation
in Jesus Christ, and a sacramental instrument for passing on this
eschatological salvation to all human beings.

Above all, the application of the term 'sacrament' to the church
defines the relationship between the visible and the invisible in the
church in a way that is neither spiritualistic, naturalistic nor sociological. If the church is a fulfilled sign of eschatological salvation, then
the church's visible form (or institution) and the content of its
testimony are a unity, and are yet divergent. It is part of the unity
between the sign and the thing signified, that the church in its actual,
specific form, unlike the synagogue, cannot fundamentally fall away
from God's truth and love. If this were possible, it would not be the
truth of God that finally triumphed; it would be evil and the lie. This
offers the approach for an appropriate discussion of the church's

indefectibility and infallibility, as well as the doctrine of *opus operandum*, according to which the church's sacraments mediate salvation by virtue of their objective operation.[23] Yet in spite of this inherent connection, the visible church is not simply identical with the thing to which it testifies. In extreme cases the outward sign and the inward salvific reality can also be sundered.[24] The outward sign, though retaining its reality, may become empty and unfruitful; and conversely, the saving reality can be conveyed even without the external ecclesial sign.

The possibility of this separation was discussed extensively in scholastic sacramental theology. But there it counts as a special case, not the rule; and no ecclesiology can make a norm out of a special case, or turn this into the paradigm, as it were, for an understanding of the church. Consequently a distinction must be made between the 'ordinary' and the 'extra-ordinary' way of salvation.[25] According to the divinely willed salvific order (which does not necessarily mean in the majority of cases) God's eschatological salvation is mediated through the sacramental signs of the church.

This has consequences for a proper understanding of what is perhaps Rahner's best known, and also most disputed, theory: his postulate about the anonymous Christian.[26] This theory can only be understood theologically if the church is interpreted as the universal sacrament of salvation. That is to say, we must not think in the opposite direction, interpreting the concept of the church in the light of this theory, and then practically relativizing the actual, given salvific order in a reductionist way.[27] The theory of anonymous Christians – or what this misleading term actually means – has to do with the *extra-ordinary* (in the sense of 'abnormal') way in which the church is the universal sacrament of the salvation which God in Jesus Christ desires for all human beings (cf. *Lumen gentium* 16). Again, this suggests a number of conclusions about the relationship between the church and the world. We shall have to come back to these at the end.

3. *The individual sacraments as an unfolding of the sacramental structure of the church.* As we have seen, according to the testimony of Scripture, the mystery of God in Jesus Christ is made present first and foremost through the Word. The difficulty that Scripture never describes any individual sacramental act as a *mysterion* or *sacramentum* can be solved, however, if we notice that Scripture calls at least one

sacramental act a visible Word: the celebration of the Lord's Supper. In I Cor. 11.26 Paul says: 'For as often as you eat this bread and drink the cup, you proclaim the Lord's death until he comes.' The performance of the sacramental act is therefore a form of proclamation. Augustine especially taught that the sacraments were to be understood in this sense as 'a visible word' (*verbum visible*),[28] whereas Aquinas talks about signs of faith.[29] So if the sacraments are embodied Word, and signs of faith, this provides the justification for seeing sacramental acts as an integral part of the actualization of God's saving mystery in Jesus Christ.[30]

This holistic viewpoint has been more or less maintained in the Orthodox Church down to the present day, in spite of a partial reception of Western scholastic development.[31] In the Western church, on the other hand, analytical and dialectical thinking increasingly carried the day after mediaeval times. People ceased to ask primarily about the sacramental saving reality. They enquired about the structure of the sacramental signs, about the means of their efficacy, their effect and their validity.[32] In this way a general concept of sacrament was developed, so that the sacraments came to be distinguished from the other acts of the church.[33] This distinction between sacramental and non-sacramental reality was in itself quite justifiable. But the result was that the sacraments were to some extent cut off from their liturgical and ecclesial context, and even more from everyday life. At this point the definition of the church as universal sacrament of salvation again proves its strength. It again fits the seven sacraments more clearly into the totality of the church's life, and allows them to be understood in their interaction and their cohesion as a structured totality.[34]

Karl Rahner made this integral viewpoint fruitful in considering the thorny problem of Christ's institution of the sacraments. The difficulty of proving this institution in the case of each individual sacrament already emerged in the disputes with the Reformers; and these difficulties increased in the light of modern biblical exegesis and historical criticism. Rahner now saw the sacramental concept of the church as a way of leaving behind the tortuous apologetics in which theology had therefore become entangled. His theory is that it is enough to prove that Christ willed the church as a historical sacramental sign of eschatological salvation. Sacraments are then always given wherever the church commits itself in a final and ultimate way.[35]

Of course Rahner does not think that with the aid of this principle the seven sacraments can be deduced *a priori* from the nature of the church. His intention is to offer a way of explaining *a posteriori* the historical development of dogma and theology. All the same, it may perhaps be asked whether he takes sufficiently seriously the fact that, especially if the church is understood sacramentally, it can never be understood for itself, in an autonomous and autarchical sense, nor can what it does issue from itself either. Rahner's theory certainly comes to the aid of a dogmatics under attack by historical criticism, and provides it with an argumentative defence. But since Jesus Christ alone is the primal sacrament (the church being a sacrament only 'in Christ') it is impossible to dispense entirely with the laborious task of biblical theology and tradition history, as it traces back the sacraments, not necessarily to the earthly Jesus, but certainly to the saving work of Jesus Christ as a whole, which embraces both the earthly Jesus and the Lord in his Easter transfiguration. None the less, Rahner's more speculative argumentation retains its importance here as a subsequent theological reflection which makes the historical development comprehensible in the light of the inner nature of the concept, and which at the same time stresses that the real context is the whole economy of salvation. In this sense we can best show that the individual sacraments have their foundation in the primal sacrament if we use a converging argument, which works with both historical and speculative methods.[36]

Another aspect is more important still, however. The explicit crystallization of the seven sacraments must be seen in the context of the investiture dispute, among other things. Once it had been determined that royal investiture was not to be put on the same level as episcopal consecration, kingdom and empire were desacralized. Or to put it more generally: the early mediaeval sacral understanding of the world was then surmounted, and church and world were differentiated.[37] The development of the seven sacraments is therefore connected with the growth of a secular understanding of the world, in which the autonomy of the church (which was what the dispute was really about at the time) and the autonomy of the world mutually conditioned one another.

This historical development must as a whole be judged positively. Yet it also led in actual fact to the progressive mutual alienation of church and world, the church becoming a special sacramental world of its own. To define the church as universal sacrament of the world's salvation could indicate a new, differentiated view about the unity of the two spheres, a unity which preserves the autonomy of both world and church. This would go beyond the unitarian viewpoint of the early Middle Ages, and also beyond the dualist modern definition of the relationship between church and world.

This brings us for the third time to the same fundamental question. The council touches on it, but without providing any conclusive answer. And to this question we must now, in closing, turn our attention.

4. Further perspectives

At this point, where the council was content with hints, Rahner courageously thought further. He saw the existential difficulties which the average Christian, living in a secular world, has with the sacraments; and saw too that to define the church as a sacrament therefore necessarily presented a problem too. For average Christians, the world of the sacraments seems to be a special 'religious' world, parallel to secular reality.

After the council, in order to meet this discomfort, Rahner tried to bring about a complete reversal in the interpretation of the sacraments.[38] Instead of starting primarily with the mental and spiritual reality of the sacramental event, and from there proceeding to its 'worldly' effect, he wanted to effect a movement of the spirit leading from the world to the sacrament. From this viewpoint, the sacraments (and so ultimately the church as well) are no longer 'point-like' divine interventions in the world from outside. On the contrary, the world itself, in its inmost nature, in its very root, from the innermost personal centre of those who are its thinking subjects, is always and lastingly held fast by grace, sustained and moved by God's communication of himself. This innermost dynamism of normal, human, 'secular' life always and everywhere, has found its clearest manifestation in Jesus Christ. In this light, the sacraments reveal the holiness and the redeemedness of human beings and the world in their very secularity.

Sacraments are an emblematic manifestation of the liturgy of the world. What happens in them is not something which does not exist in the world in any other way. But they bring to reflective manifestation, and celebrate in cultic form, what takes place as God's saving act in the world and in the liberty of humanity.

The immediate objection which can easily be made to a conception of this kind is that the sacraments are not merely emblems of a reality which exists without them. They are efficacious signs which actually effect what they signify. But Rahner does not deny this postulate (which is really a matter of course in the framework of a Catholic doctrine of the sacraments). On the contrary, he explicitly brings out its force. For he claims that the emblematic, 'embodied' utterance of what is already given in a person's fundamental attitude has itself, in its turn, a retroactive effect on that attitude. Indeed the fundamental attitude is not real unless it is expressed in 'embodied' terms. So the sacraments are not merely a subsequent manifestation of what in the profoundest sense holds the world together; on the contrary, they are real symbols, in which the thing signified comes about, and implements its own history. As sacrament of the world, the church is at the same time the event of salvation for the world.[39]

The problem about Rahner's revolutionary change in the doctrine of the sacraments lies deeper (and I am taking this doctrine as representative of his whole theology). The difficulty is to be found in his thesis that the relationship between world and church is not the relationship between what is godless and what is holy – between Flood and ark. It is like the relationship between something hidden and existing on the one hand, which is still seeking its full historical self-utterance; and, on the other hand, the complete historical palpability in which the hidden quantity (really existent in the world, for all its hiddenness) is fulfilled and expressed in history, thus arriving at the mode of existence for which it has been destined from the beginning, or towards which it has been aligned.[40]

The justifiable aim of this viewpoint cannot be disputed, from the angle of biblical theology either. For if, as Scripture says, God desires the salvation of all human beings (I Tim. 2.4), then he desires this in an efficacious way – that is, in a way which first determines the existential situation of men and women so that it is aligned towards their decision, and which lends the history of the world a dynamic directed towards

Jesus Christ, for whom everything has been created (Col. 1.16f.). The salvific purpose of all reality (which Rahner calls the supernatural existential)[41] therefore cannot be denied, from the standpoint of biblical theology either. The matter only becomes problematical when it is given absolute status, and is declared to be the only view taken by Scripture. For Scripture does not confine itself to this universal and cosmic viewpoint. It also includes the apocalyptic vision which starts from a continual struggle between the kingdom of God and the kingdom of the world, a conflict which does *not* gradually come to an end with the progress of history, but which, on the contrary, reaches a climax and is intensified as history draws to a close.

This apocalyptic view was taken up by Augustine especially, in his doctrine about the two cities. It undoubtedly corresponds to an experience of contemporary men and women, and for this reason too must not simply be left out of consideration. It is only if we continually keep in mind the negative existential as well as the positive one that we can apprehend the whole drama of history, in which the church is the universal sacrament of salvation;[42] and this negative existential is the lordship of sin, which is more than the sum of individual sinful acts, and which bars the way to alignment towards God and his grace.[43] But it is only in this way too that we can be properly aware of the dramatic element within the church; for the church, Augustine tells us, in its very character as sacramental reality, has a share in both cities and treads its path through the middle of the conflict.[44]

Finally, Scripture has yet a third viewpoint. The new Adam, Jesus Christ, is not merely the clearest manifestation of the innermost dynamic of normal 'secular' human life. He at the same time absolutely excels it. It is not for nothing that in the two passages in which Paul describes the relationship between the first and the second Adam, he several times uses the concept of superfluity and surplus (Rom. 5.15, 17; I Cor. 15.13). Irenaeus of Lyons grasped this viewpoint very well when he wrote that Christ 'has brought everything new by bringing himself, as he was promised. For this is what was proclaimed: that the new should come in order to renew men and make them live'.[45]

None of this controverts Rahner's fascinating unified survey. But his *via positionis* has to be supplemented by the *via negationis* and the *via eminentiae*.[46] For this is the only way in which the church can be kept from becoming in practice ultimately no more than the mere affirmation of what *is*, and what exists in principle, even without the church. If it were to be seen in this way, the church would become a religiously solemn elevation of the world, and hence its ideology. It is only by including the two other aspects that we can retain the critically liberating function of the gospel, and at the same time its value as something wholly new, to which the church has to witness in word, sacrament and ministry. Only in this way can the church be a sign of hope for the 'wholly new thing' of grace and mercy, in the midst of a merciless world, with its unsolvable contradictions.

So we neither must nor can dispute Rahner's insight as such, which he expresses in his theory about anonymous Christians. But we must integrate it into the whole Christian definition of the relationship between salvation history and world history. By doing this, we shall arrive at a full understanding of the conciliar doctrine of the church as a universal sacrament of salvation. In this question at least, theology is only at the beginning in its reception of Vatican II.

Rahner deserves our gratitude, not merely for the answers and solutions which he has given theology in so generous a measure, but also for the questions and problems which he set theology, and which he has left behind him.

VII

The Church as the Place of Truth

1. The problem: truth – a lost dimension

In Romano Guardini's autobiographical notes, there is an impressive account of how, when he was a student, his faith slipped away from him almost imperceptibly, and how he found it again, step by step.[1] The final decision was made in the little attic room in his parents' house in the Gonsenheimer Straße in Mainz. The surprising thing about this account is that for Guardini, two separate decisions were involved in his decision for faith, and these were indissolubly linked. The decision for the truth of Jesus Christ was one. This decision crystallized in the sentence: 'He who holds fast to his soul will lose it; but he who surrenders it will save it.' It is only the person who delivers himself up solely to the truth who will arrive at his own self. But Guardini sensed that this decision for Christ was not enough in itself. For 'who protects this truth from me myself?' he asked. 'Who safeguards it from my cunning in reinterpreting it to suit my wants and needs, or according to my previous understanding, and my personal interests?' For in fact, in the modern quest for the historical Jesus, it is not infrequently the minds of the enquirers themselves which we find reflected in Jesus, or in what purports to be the purely objective results of research into Jesus. So if truth is to make its absolute claim, and if the human being is to be drawn out of the last secret corner of his self-assertion, the truth of Jesus Christ has to have an objective form. Guardini found this in the Catholic Church. For him, therefore, the foundation of his faith was not – as it is for many people today – subjective experience (which can often be highly deceptive). It was the common experience of the 'we' of the church, as this has been passed down by tradition.

For Guardini, the insight that Jesus Christ and the church belong together was evidently a kind of key experience or turning point. He did not make his decision because he found himself confronted with the concept of God. He did not make it even because he had come face to face with the figure of Christ. He made it because of what he saw in the church. Again, when he decided to become a priest, his resolve was essentially the fruit of his recognition that faith in the church is the step into the true order, and that obedience to the church is the principle of true freedom. Even when he was dying, when one of his friends asked him why he had kept his faith all his life, he answered: 'Because I promised my bishop that I would, when I was ordained priest.'[2]

To us today – at least at first sight – Guardini's answer seems inconceivably naive for so subtle and universal a mind, whose questions kept him continually on the move to the end of his life. Far from being attracted by the church's claim to truth, many people today are put off by it – and by its claim to infallible truth even more. They link this claim with a whole series of ideas which are loaded with negative associations: the duty to believe, and oppression of conscience, even Inquisition; intolerance and the breakdown of communication between people; the rigidity of an unhistorical and unalterable doctrinal system; dogmatic formulas to which one may pay due respect, but which are remote from life and reality; while the endless elucidations of these formulas are, if anything, a hindrance to a living faith. Instead of ministering to unity, they are the occasion for conflict, sanctioning divisions and serving to legitimate the church's claim to power and absolute truth.

This catalogue of negatives could be extended at will. It is understandable, if we remember that in modern times the church was certainly often, and for long enough, closed to new scientific insights. Indeed it fought against them, and came to accept them only hesitantly. The negative judgments we have listed are therefore not merely momentary voices and moods. They also reflect the result of modern developments. For the modern mind grew up in a movement of emancipation, away from any 'given' dogmatic authorities. Emancipation and liberation have been the guiding concepts of the modern era. Seeing for yourself, thinking for yourself, judging for yourself, and having the courage to use your own reason: all this is part of the fundamental attitude of enlightened modern men and women. Against this background, obedience towards an institution called the church, with its claim to absolute truth, was bound to seem profoundly alien, indeed no longer conceivable.

In our own century this critical attitude was taken up and even intensified by two powerful trends. One of them was existential philosophy. This philosophy is focused on the human being, who is in every case unique, and on his biography, which is also in every case unique. According to this philosophy, an objective, generally valid truth does not accord with the just claims of this always unique human person. It misses the mark of the human person, not only in his uniqueness, but also in his transcendence, which is never finally definable. Consequently dogma is held to be repressive. It is contrary to the subjective self-realization of human beings, and it puts an end to the dialogue and communication between one person and another.

Then on the other side we have the supporters of critical rationalism. They take as their model the scientific method of arriving at truth, which proceeds by 'trial and error'. According to critical rationalism, truth can never be more than approximately attained; it can never be asserted with final certainty. Truth is a regulative guiding idea for the never-ending process of arriving at knowledge. But if truth is dogmatically asserted, not only is a certain position immunized against criticism and further investigation. The very foundations of an open society are infringed in the process.

Today theories of this kind are more or less part of the underlying attitude of modern men and women. And as a result, many of our contemporaries are perhaps inclined to ask sceptically, with Pilate: 'What is truth?' Is there any such thing as a general truth, binding on everyone? If there is, can I know it with any certainty? If I can, can I make it comprehensible to other people, let alone binding on them? Finally, can anyone claim *the* truth for himself, and define it – at least within certain limits – as religious dogma claims to do? Is there any purpose in doing so, in the religiously, philosophically, culturally and politically pluralist world of today? Is it even possible? Must we not inevitably select, in our modern pluralist society? Is there not here a positive compulsion towards heresy?[3]

The place occupied in earlier thinking by the question of truth has not remained vacant. In the final chapter of his early work, *Vom Geist der Liturgie* (1918; ET *The Spirit of the Liturgy*) – the book which first made him known to a wider public – Guardini already pointed to the momentous change in modern thinking, compared with that of the high middle ages. Where truth once took precedence over praxis, now praxis takes precedence over truth; or, as Guardini himself put it, the primacy of logos has given way to the primacy of ethics, the primacy of knowledge to the primacy of will, the primacy of the contemplative life to the primacy of the active life. To put it in yet other terms: the worth of truth now comes second to life that is worth living; and the fundamental standpoint is often purely utilitarian. Guardini wrote: 'Goethe put his finger on the ultimate point at issue when he made the doubting Faust write, not "in the beginning was the Word" but "in the beginning was the deed".'[4]

These questions and developments did not leave theology unscathed. In the eighteenth and nineteenth centuries Protestant theology was already rocked by the tremors resulting from the modern trend. It is true that Luther still emphatically defended dogmatic language in the church against the (real or supposed) scepticism of Erasmus. But by denying infallibility to the church's teaching office, he none the less undermined the dogmatic principle, and changed the church's understanding of truth. So when Pietism developed, with its criticism of rigid, dogmatic doctrinal formulas, and its demand for an 'experiential' faith of the heart, it was able to establish the preconditions which made it possible for an 'enlightened' criticism of dogma to find an entry. This process ended up in the demand for a radical dedogmatization of Christianity, and for a Christian faith which was undogmatic, ethically interpreted and practical.

Catholic theology was able to keep clear of such influences for a long time. Indeed, in the dispute with Protestantism and rationalism, it actually strengthened the dogmatic principle, compared with patristic and mediaeval theology. On the Catholic side, the term 'dogma' became a positive battle cry, a challenge to the spirit of the modern age. But the Second Vatican Council deliberately threw open the door to today's world, and since then modern problems have found an entry into the Catholic Church as well. The questions which had hitherto been to some extent repressed, now made themselves heard in no uncertain terms. What was demanded was not an undogmatic theology; but it was certainly a meta-dogmatic theology, and a critical dogmatics.

The questions involved were discussed first of all in the debate on infallibility triggered off by Hans Küng.[5] In a different way, and with greater explosive power politically, they are at the centre of the discussion with liberation theology, in its various forms. Here what is at issue is not primarily the problem of revolutionary violence, but – much more fundamentally – a new conception of theology in general. Liberation theology no longer sees itself as an interpretation of the church's traditional doctrine of faith (as theology did earlier), but as a reflection of praxis, and its critical accompaniment.[6] Praxis, it is said, takes precedence over theory. This can very well be understood in a correct sense, and may be quite legitimate, if praxis is understood as the praxis of faith, that is, as a praxis inspired and guided by the truth of the gospel. Many supporters of liberation theology – especially the ones better known to us here – see the matter in this light. Their concern is to fetch theology out of the academic ivory tower in which it is shut up for the most part, among us, and once more to make its *Sitz im Leben* – the situation to which it belongs – the practically lived life of the church.

We European theologians have every reason to pay serious attention to this criticism of our intellectually inbred theology, pursued in academic ghettos. On the other hand, in our world today, where only what is scientifically demonstrable is considered valid, there is good reason for not neglecting the theoretical discussion, and for giving an account of our Christian hope (I Peter 3.15). Without intellectual effort, and if we do not wish to act out of short-sighted, irrational enthusiasm, we cannot – least of all today – communicate the universal claim of the Christian faith. And that also means its universal practical relevance in the various spheres of secular life.

What is ultimately at stake here is an extremely fundamental problem: the place and importance of the question about truth. Remembering the development of modern thought, we are bound to establish that the basic problem facing us today is not primarily the relationship between truth and the church. That question is merely a subordinate aspect of a much more comprehensive problem, which is the loss of the whole dimension of truth. At present we are concerned as a rule merely with the question about life and survival, or with the question about a better life, in the material sense. We no longer ask the old philosophical and biblical question about true life. Guardini was undoubtedly right: this is the real source of the predicament of our time. So before we consider the connection between the church and truth, we must interpose another train of thought, and try to discover for ourselves a new way of access to the question about truth.

2. A transitional reflection: what is truth?

What is truth? In everyday life the question about the truth is anything but theoretical. It is highly practical. In order to equip ourselves properly, for instance, we have to know whether it is raining or snowing, or whether the sun is shining. Only the truth helps us to behave in the way that reality enjoins, and lets us find our bearings in the conditions which make up our lives. In this sense, truth is the light without which we grope our way in the dark, knock up against things, and wander about lost, not knowing where we are.

It is therefore understandable that the question of truth should have occupied Western thinking from the very start. The distinction between true Being and mere seeming stands at the beginning of Western philosophy. Yet as early as the fifth century BC, the enquiry about true reality was shaken. It was the age of Pericles, the age when the civilization of the city states enjoyed its finest flowering. Life had become more complicated and more differentiated, and the validity of the views and canons of behaviour of ancient belief became a problem. The learned men of the time, the Sophists, no longer saw themselves as sages. They were orators, who wanted to convince other people about their view of things, and persuade them to adopt it. According to the Sophists, objective truth is an impossibility. If it exists no one can know what it is; and if he can know what it is, he cannot communicate it. In the Sophist view, the yardstick is not the 'objective' truth of reality. It is the human being. As Protagoras said, 'Man is the measure of all things.' But men and women are complex beings. Everyone has his own perspective. So there is only one answer: the victory of the strong, the conflict of interests, and the will to power.

This makes one thing evident. Once thinking has lost its reference to reality and its objectivity, what counts is no longer insight into the truth of anything. It is now only a matter of public acclaim, propaganda, publicity and entertainment. The idea of truth was thus forced into the service of alien purposes, and ultimately destroyed. And of course rational communication between people was destroyed at the same time. It was replaced by the rights of the strongest, and the conflict of interests.

Socrates, Plato and Aristotle recognized the danger. Josef Pieper has shown the way in which they again stressed the objectivity of thought and its relation to reality, over against the rootless, emancipated thinking of the Sophists.[7] It is only if thought takes its bearings from reality that it can be generally valid, and this is the only condition that makes true communication within a community of free people possible. If the truth of reality is not the point of orientation, there can only be a law of the strongest, violence and tyranny. So according to Plato, truth is the common and supreme concern of human beings. It is their most precious possession. And ever since Plato, this profoundly humane insight has been part of the basic stock of Western tradition. It is one of the foundations of Western humanism.

It was only much later, in the thirteenth century, that Thomas Aquinas formulated in summary form the understanding of truth that had been established by the Greeks and essentially deepened by Christian revelation. Again, Pieper has shown this in a convincing study.[8] According to Aquinas, truth is essentially the being-true of reality itself. It is only because reality is true that our minds can perceive it. It is only because reality displays structures of meaning that we can perceive laws in reality. For Thomas, this truth in reality is ultimately based on the Christian understanding of creation. Because God has created everything according to his eternal ideas, everything that exists is profoundly true, and therefore accessible to our perception. So in defending Christian ideas about God and reality, theology also defends the rationality of reality as well. For the Christian, the world is not a rubbish heap of fortuitous phenomena. It is illuminated – and also illuminable – by mind and spirit. But this light which shines in reality, and is the foundation for the truth of reality, comes to itself only in human thought. Formally, therefore, according to Thomas, truth consists of the creative reconstruction of reality in human perception. In this sense, as Rahner and others have shown, we already find in Thomas the first hints of the modern shift towards anthropology. The human being is not merely the highest created being in visible reality. He is its hinge and pivot. So according to Thomas, truth is the self-manifestation of reality itself. In our own century Heidegger especially has brought out this point, defining truth as the disclosedness, the manifest character, of Being.[9]

Behind this splendid conception of Aquinas' is undoubtedly his awareness of the unique dignity of the human being. But here the human being is not simply the measure of all things. He must take his own measure from the boundaries of the reality with which he is already presented, and must in so far remain 'within bounds'. He finds the way to true existence and true life only if he acts in accord with reality, by cohering with God's coherent order. Behind this understanding of reality and truth is creaturely humility.

This brings out the profound difference – indeed the cleft – which divides this understanding of reality and truth from the modern preeminence of praxis. For Thomas, everything real, inasmuch as it *is* real, is also true. In modern times this is no longer accepted. What is true is what human beings have designed and made. *Verum quia factum* (Vico). The human being no longer sees himself as part of the total cohesion and order of reality. Instead he makes himself reality's lord and creator. Human praxis no longer takes truth as its yardstick. Now truth is the expression and outcome of human praxis. It is a human blueprint, a human construction, a human perspective. In extreme cases the truth is a mere superstructure, an ideological reflection of existing conditions, in any given case. The belief in the primacy of truth held in the ancient and mediaeval world was ultimately based on the conviction that God is the absolute reality and truth, which human beings must acknowledge, in reverence, humility and obedience. The modern view about the primacy of praxis, on the other hand, is based on the notion that human beings are the absolute masters of themselves and their reality. Where this conviction is dominant, it means the end of reverence for what is, the end of responsibility towards God, and ultimately speaking the end of reverence and responsibility for other people as well.

The consequences of this literally boundless magnification of praxis are just beginning to dawn on us, as we see the results of this irreverent and unbridled intervention in reality. But the answer to the resulting crisis cannot be a romantic flight into a seemingly unscathed nature. The proper answer is not escape from reality, but a new responsible recognition of the truth of reality. The humane survival of humanity in an environment which accords with human dignity depends on new insight into the determining character of this truth, which provides the appropriate measure for what we do. So we have every reason to turn our minds once more to this question.

3. The fundamental postulate: truth and the church

This intervening reflection about the nature and importance of truth now brings us back to our main subject: the church as the place of truth. The interpretation of truth we have just developed is largely philosophical; but it is not as alien to biblical tradition as is often claimed. Particularly since the liberal theology of the nineteenth century and the dialectical theology of the twentieth, the differences (which undoubtedly exist) have often been stressed in an extremely one-sided way. In actual fact the Old Testament draws very largely on the Wisdom tradition of Israel's neighbours. In his late book *Wisdom in Israel*,[10] Gerhard von Rad especially once again made plain the deeper significance of the Old Testament's long-neglected Wisdom tradition and literature. Israel's sages also started from the conviction that there is an order in things; only a fool, to his own detriment, exempts himself from observing the orders which sustain life. But for the Bible, knowledge of the world is not enough. All knowledge and all wisdom begins with the knowledge of God. The fear of the Lord is the beginning of all knowledge and all wisdom (Ps. 111.10; Prov. 1.7, 9, 10; Ecclus. 19.20). For ultimately it is God's wisdom that is reflected in the orders of the world, and it is only in the light of the knowledge of God that knowledge of the world becomes wholly real, and at the same time mysterious.

What is special about the biblical understanding of truth and wisdom is that the Bible thinks in quite specific historical terms. The biblical God is a God of human beings, who wishes to be present in their midst in a human way. So the Bible asks about the actual place where we can encounter the wisdom of God in practical terms in the world and history. Of course this can be always and everywhere. To that extent the Bible does not deny the wisdom of the other peoples. But it is more aware still of the perversions and perils of wisdom, the human rejection of wisdom because of the foolishness of the human heart – its self-conceit, its closed-in egoism, and its malice. According to the Bible, in order to counter this human foolishness which perverts the truth, God has prepared a particular place for wisdom. He has let it dwell in a particular way in one people and one country. He has prepared for it a resting place in Israel, and allowed it to dwell in Jerusalem, on Mount Zion. Only Israel can boast of enjoying the fullness of the gifts of wisdom. So in Ecclus. 24 especially, wisdom is identified with the Torah. This identification shows that the God of the Bible commits himself specifically, in concrete terms, to the world. He is power in history, and the trend of his Being is incarnation.

The New Testament takes up this Old Testament approach and brings it to fulfilment. For the New Testament, Jesus Christ is the wisdom of God in person (I Cor. 2.24). 'In him are hid all the treasures of wisdom and knowledge' (Col. 2.3). It is the Gospel of John above all which in its Prologue picks up the Old Testament's wisdom tradition, with the help of the term Logos, Word. Just as the Old Testament talks about the Wisdom which was beside God even before creation, the Prologue (John 1) says that the Word was already beside God at the beginning – indeed that the Word is God, and that in the Word and through the Word everything has come into being, so that from the very beginning the Word is the life and light of all reality. In the fullness of time the eternal word became flesh in Jesus Christ and lived among human beings 'full of grace and truth' (John 1.1–4, 14). Because in Jesus the truth and wisdom of the Logos has itself appeared, Jesus can say in the Gospel of John: 'I am the way, the truth and the life' (John 14.6).

This statement is inconceivably new compared with the Old Testament, and even more so compared with Greek philosophy. What is new compared with the Old Testament is that Jesus Christ is not only the promise of final truth. He is also the final fulfilment of this promise. What is new compared with Greek philosophy is that Jesus Christ does not merely reveal the truth. As the incarnate, earthly, and indeed crucified Christ he is the truth in person. This quite earthly and specific divine wisdom was bound to appear as foolishness to the Greeks (cf. I Cor. 1.22–25).

The way in which this understanding of truth reaches its climax in salvation history and christology is of decisive importance for our subject, and for a justification of the thesis that the church is the actual, specific place of truth – a thesis which for many people is no less foolish and scandalous. God has turned to the world once and for all in Jesus

Christ. This divine commitment does not reach its end with Christ. On the contrary, in and through him it is an enduring presence in the world. If it were not accepted and confessed in faith, the truth of God would not have come into the world once and for all, but would have evaporated, as it were. The witness of faith in the community of believers – that is, in the church – is therefore an essential element in revelation itself. Only in and through the church does the revelation in Christ arrive at its goal. Only in and through the church does it attain persistence and efficacy in the world. Without the church and its testimony we should know nothing of Jesus Christ. Without the church there would be no Holy Scripture. Scripture came into being in the church and for the church. It was gathered, preserved and passed down by the church. So the truth of Jesus Christ is made present and communicated in a human and historical way, not merely through the church's ministry of proclamation, but through its whole life and activity.

Scripture itself testifies emphatically that it is through the proclamation of the apostles and the church that the truth and wisdom of God, realized in history through Jesus Christ, is revealed (Eph. 3.5–11, and frequently elsewhere). According to the Epistle to the Ephesians, it is through the church that the divine wisdom in its many forms is manifested in the world and history (Eph. 3.10). According to I Tim. 3.15, the church can therefore be called the pillar and bulwark of truth. The early Fathers energetically defended this scriptural testimony against gnosticism and its subjectivistic interpretation of Scripture. According to Irenaeus of Lyons,[11] the church is the precious vessel into which the Holy Spirit has poured the truth in all its youthful freshness, and the place where that freshness is preserved. 'Where the church is, there is the Spirit of God; and where the Spirit of God is, there is the church and all grace. But the Spirit is truth.' 'The true gnosis is the teaching of the apostles and the ancient doctrines of the church for the whole world.'[12] So according to the Fathers, the church's proclamation is 'the rule of truth' (Irenaeus, Tertullian, Origen, Augustine and others).

It would be interesting to trace this idea through the later history of theology. It acquired topical relevance once more through the dispute with the Reformers and their scriptural theology. The Council of Trent confronted them with the thesis that the gospel proclaimed in the church is the one and only source of all saving truth. In the language of the last council, we can say: the church is the universal sacrament, that is, the sign and instrument of truth. It is the house and tabernacle of truth, the place, emblem and instrument of God's truth and wisdom in the world.

If the church is the sacrament of God's dialogue with men and women, then it is itself a dialogistic sacrament. Then the ministry of truth laid upon it cannot be performed as a monologue, but only in dialogue. For the truth of God entrusted to the church in all its fullness, and in its final concrete form, is ultimately no other truth than the truth which is to be found everywhere in the world, in trace and fragmentarily, in the wisdom and religions of the nations, as well as in human art and science. So in dialogue with the truth, wisdom and science of the world, the church can and must understand its own truth more profoundly, and articulate it in a way more in accordance with the times. On the other hand, by viewing the truth, wisdom and science of the world against the horizon of the eternal truth which has appeared in concrete form and in all its fullness in Christ, the church must give this truth, wisdom and science a deeper perspective, aligning it towards the ultimate meaning and final goal of human life.

What the world and human beings need – above all in our world, where truth has been forgotten – is a spiritual orientation and perspective of this kind. Today, when we are flooded with information, we more than ever need wise men and women who have a feeling for human essentials. It is only in this way that we can protect ourselves from lending ideologically absolute form to particular aspects and limited sectors of reality; and only so can we preserve our freedom for the truth, which is always greater than these. So in its very function as advocate of the divine truth, the church is at the same time the advocate of human freedom, in confrontation with totalitarian ideologies. The gospel tells us that it is truth that makes us really free (cf. John 8.22). It is therefore a wrong and over-hasty reaction to play off a theology concerned with the truth against a theology of liberation; for it is orientation towards the truth that is the true liberation theology.

We can therefore sum the matter up by saying that the truth of reality which finally appeared in all its fullness in Jesus Christ, and which is enduringly present in the church, continually presents itself afresh in its inexhaustible novelty through the dialogue between the church and the world. And it is upon this dialogue about the truth of reality incarnate in Jesus Christ that the salvation of the world depends.

4. Some specific problems today

I have tried to explain and justify in principle the claim that the church is the house of truth and, as the house of truth, also the universal sacrament of salvation. We must now finally turn our attention to some specific questions. But before doing so, we must look again at some of the objections made to our postulate.

These objections spring for the most part from the modern principle of subjectivity. This principle maintains that the human thinking subject is the point of departure and the point of reference for all knowledge of the world and reality. We can therefore never 'possess' truth 'in itself', but only as it appears at any given moment in the medium of a particular human subjectivity. This modern principle of subjectivity must not be confused with the subjectivism which gives absolute importance to single, individual needs, concerns, perspectives, and so forth, thus making these the measure of all things. The principle of subjectivity makes no such particularist claim. Its claim is an entirely universal one. It postulates that in any given (and ultimately unique) subjective decision, *the* truth is at stake.

This modern approach has consequences both for relations within the church, and for the church's relations with those outside it. Let us look first of all at the results within the church itself. When the thinking subject takes the centre of the stage, there is a danger that any objective truth – and even more a dogmatic truth of general validity – will seem to many people to be beyond their reach. For them, therefore, the centre is not the faith of the church but their own religious experience. The church with its dogma will rather be understood as the 'outer limit', if not actually as a limitation to personal faith. It will tend not to be seen as *Lebensraum* – a space in which to live. In 1922 Guardini could write: 'A religious process of incalculable importance has begun: the church is awakening in souls of men.'[13] Today we are unfortunately bound to say that in the souls of many believers the church is dying. These believers still probably live *in* the church, but they are less and less *living the church* and its faith. If we were to assign absolute validity to the principle of subjectivity, the ultimate conclusion would be the sinful closedness of men and women to the already given truth of God.

But of course this approach also has considerable potentialities, in the positive sense. These must be taken equally seriously. To sum it up in a single sentence: our situation contains the potential for a more conscious and more personally implemented faith. For faith always has two aspects: the 'objective' content of faith (*fides quae creditur*) and the 'subjective' act and implementation of faith, which is not merely theoretical but belongs quite essentially to practical life (*fides qua creditur*). So there 'is' no such thing as faith 'in itself'. There is only faith vitally believed and put into living practice. This means that to communicate faith can never be a matter of merely passing on information about faith, let alone indoctrination. It is first and foremost introduction, inauguration and initiation into the faith practised in the community of the church.

In order to stress that faith has to be subjectively 'adopted' in this way, the last council reminded us that through baptism and confirmation all Christians are qualified and commissioned to testify to the truth of Jesus Christ. They are not merely recipients of faith. They are actually involved in the witness of faith.[14] Twenty years after the council, there are already renewed signs of certain forms of monopoly on the part of the magisterium; so it is important to draw attention once more to the council's statements, and to stress again the importance of 'consulting the faithful in matters of doctrine' (a formulation of Newman's), and the teaching about the sense of faith in believers (*sensus fidelium*).[15] This sense of faith in believers is especially necessary when secular dimensions of living are concerned, or the consequences of faith in the secular world – that is, in questions where faith and life touch and interpenetrate. Here lay people should bring into the church their experience in the world, where this experience is permeated by faith, and should make this experience fruitful for developing a deeper understanding of the truth with which the church has been entrusted.

This does not mean that the magisterium would become nothing more than a kind of superior church notary. The church's teaching office is not there merely to register and confirm the outcome of a consensus 'from below'. The truth of faith has to be proclaimed and addressed to men and women with full authority; that belongs to its nature. So the magisterium should also initiate and stimulate the formulation of a consensus, accompanying the process critically, and above all continually pointing to the unique foundation and permanent criterion, the truth of God in Jesus Christ. In the final analysis, the Christian truth would not have a specific historical form if it did not have a specific mouthpiece and a specific voice – that is to say, if there were no authentic witnesses to the truth. It is only through the voice of its teaching office that the church can speak in definite, precise and binding terms.

Since the witness of the laity is not a pure reflection of the church's magisterium, and since the magisterium is not a mere notary for registering the formation of opinion 'from below', there is only one possible conclusion: the process of arriving at truth in the church must take the form of dialogue. As dialogistic sacrament of God with the world, the church has itself a dialogistic constitution. Today there is no other way in which truth can be received, or in which a consensus about the truth can be reached. This is the point where active congregations, discussion and study groups are important, and this is the chance for adult catechetics and further education in the church.

But modern problems do not only crop up inside the church. They also make themselves felt – and felt much more strongly – in the dialogue with the world, and with other Christian churches and groups. The modern 'subjectivity' standpoint means that wherever we look, we see a multiplicity of views and perspectives which are quite simply irreconcilable. Pluralism is an essential characteristic of our present era. The world in which we live is like a huge department store, offering a bewildering variety of wares. For good or ill, we have to choose. The sociologist P. L. Berger talked about a compulsion towards heresy, that is, towards selection. P. M. Zulehner has spoken of eclectic Christianity.[16] Pluralism like this really comes down to a secularized form of polytheism. That was the way Max Weber, the famous sociologist, saw it. He wrote: 'The many gods of old, divested of their magic and now in the form of impersonal forces, are rising from their graves. They are striving for mastery over our lives, and are again beginning their eternal struggle with one another.'[17] So today, though the preconditions are different, Christianity is really in the same situation as at the beginning, when it confronted heathen polytheism with the monotheism of the Bible.

If the pluralism of standpoints and perspectives is given absolute validity, there is no meaning to be found in the world. Nor are liberty and reconciliation attainable. So the dogma about the one and only God who has revealed himself once and for all in Jesus Christ is not merely an abstract dogmatic truth. It is a truth of universal importance for the whole of life. For the one God provides the foundation for the unity of mankind, and the unity of reality. But how are we to bring about this unity in truth in practical terms, without forcibly reducing everything to a single, and ultimately boring, common denominator?

In this question too we should not see only the destructive tendencies. We should also grasp the positive potentialities, in order to arrive at a constructive solution of the problems involved. This solution can only be: unity in variety. Here we have to distinguish variety from mere multiplicity, and pluriformity from a pluralism of opposing and therefore irreconcilable standpoints. The pluralism of opposing and irreconcilable standpoints is a sign of disintegration, meaninglessness and the incapacity for synthesis. But variety is an expression of richness, and the abundance which is so immense that it cannot be reduced to any single concept, or uttered in any single statement. In his brilliant early book *Die Einheit der Kirche* ('The Unity of the Church'), J. A. Möhler showed that the secret of all true life is to be found in the mutual interpenetration of opposites.[18] All true life moves in tension. Where tension ends there is death. And above all when it is a question of God – the absolute truth and the fullness of life – only a pluriformity of complementary positions is possible. For the dissimilarity of each one of our assertions about him is always greater than the similarity.

This recognition has become important for present-day ecumenical theology, which is striving to arrive at greater unity among all Christians in the one truth, Jesus Christ. There can be no such unity in truth as long as one church condemns as contrary to the gospel the faith which another church confesses – as long, that is, as the anathema formulas stand between the churches, as they in fact still do today. But this does not mean that there could not be a plurality of theologies, spiritualities, church orders, and even credal formulas, on the foundation of the one Holy Scripture and the one creed of the ancient church, which all share and which is binding on us all. The concept of unity in truth does not necessarily mean that the other churches have to adopt all the credal *formulas* of the Catholic Church. A positive acceptance of this kind cannot reasonably be expected, if a certain credal formula has grown out of a historical tradition which the other church does not share; for then the outcome of that tradition, however legitimate, cannot really be assented to from within. In cases of this kind, it would be enough if there were mutual recognition that the other church's confessions are possible, on the common ground of the one truth of the gospel, and are in so far fundamentally legitimate.[19]

Admittedly, I do not believe that in our relationship with our Protestant brothers and sisters we have as yet reached the point today when we can proceed in this way. But two ecumenical happenings on the highest level show that this conception is not a vague utopia, although unfortunately the fundamental importance of these events has been quite insufficiently appreciated among us. I mean the declaration of consensus between Pope Paul VI (in the one case) and Pope John Paul II (in the other) and two ancient oriental churches – churches which already refuse to recognize the Fourth Ecumenical Council in Chalcedon (451), and even more all succeeding councils, and which have therefore been separated ever since the fifth century both from Rome and the Orthodox churches.[20] These declarations now preserve the full content of the Chalcedonian confession, but without using Chalcedon's terminology. That is, they do not talk about the two natures of Jesus Christ in his one person, for in the past this formula was the occasion of separation. So what we have in these consensus declarations is evidently unity in the truth of faith, although the one church does not force its own *formula* of faith on the other. Would it not therefore be possible to arrive at a similar agreement with the Orthodox churches about the Filioque? Or to acknowledge in common with Protestant Christians the true and real presence of Jesus Christ in the eucharist, without declaring as binding the doctrinal formulation rejected by the Reformers, which drew on the doctrine of transubstantiation? The answer must in principle be 'yes', even if we are aware that a long and difficult path has to be trodden, and that both sides will have to rise above themselves and exercise much generous self-denial. But for that very reason, the result could also be an enrichment through the always greater truth, whose fullness and wealth can never be exhausted in history.

This attempt to think about the process of arriving at the truth in dialogue, implies an understanding of truth which sees a close connection between truth and communication. This interpretation starts from the assumption that the truth of reality discloses itself in and through communication between people. We cannot go into this in detail here. It must suffice, in closing, to point to the deeper theological reason behind this understanding of truth. Aquinas indicated this in his exegesis of II Thess. 3.16: 'Now may the Lord of peace himself give you peace.' Thomas explains that peace – which for the Bible means salvation – consists of two things: peace with oneself, and peace with other people. According to Thomas, neither is possible without God. For God is what all have most in common. So the truth of God does not divide; it is that which binds everyone together. It is therefore *the* force which makes universal peace and communication possible.

This viewpoint was later splendidly developed by Nicholas of Cusa in his work *De pace fidei*. According to Nicholas, all religions, churches and philosophies partake in their different ways of the one truth. If they do not give exclusive and total validity to the part of the truth given to them, but if they pass beyond it to the whole, then they must also recognize the truth seen by the other, or others, and so find the way to peace and fellowship in God, who is all-comprehending, absolute truth.

If truth is understood in this way, it is not divisive in character. On the contrary, it confers peace and reconciliation. Indeed it is only the truth which God in Jesus Christ *is*, that confers real peace, because it creates inward concord, beyond outward co-existence. So truth and love are in their innermost being interlocked, and it is pure lack of reflection if we sacrifice the one to the other. Truth without love becomes chauvinistic, intolerant and totalitarian. But love without truth is blind and dumb, and beneath the dignity of human beings. It pretends common ground outwardly which does not inwardly exist. Only the love which drives people to search for truth is genuine and lasting, and only the truth which is sought for out of love, and is realized in love, makes us free.

This is the deeper meaning of the biblical saying *aletheuein en agape* (cf. Eph. 4.15). It can mean both 'do the truth in love', i.e., perform the truth in love, or 'seek truth, driven on by love'. In the second sense, love does not weaken the demand for truth. On the contrary it fulfils itself above all in the truth which binds and reconciles. This inner solidarity between truth and love is the profoundest reason why the fellowship of the church is the place of truth. And just because it is the place of truth, the church is a prophetic sign and instrument of unity, peace and reconciliation in the world.

VIII

The Church as Communion
Reflections on the Guiding Ecclesiological Idea of the Second Vatican Council

1. The call for *communio*

Community – fellowship – communion – is a fundamental reality and a fundamental human longing. On the very first pages of the Bible we read: 'It is not good that the man should be alone' (Gen. 2.18). Out of the same insight, ancient philosophy termed the human being *zöon politikon*, a social being, who is dependent on others materially and physically, as well as spiritually and culturally. Only in the *polis* – in community with other people – can a man or woman find fulfilled humanity.

Today modern knowledge and the mass media have brought people closer together than ever before, outwardly. And yet perhaps the danger of isolation, and the misery of loneliness, has never been as great as it is today, in our modern mass society. This society is a gigantic accumulation of single individuals, but it is not an organically developed whole. Collectivism certainly offers no solution to the problems of modern individualism. Individualism and collectivism are two opposing extremes which are alike in that they both leave the individual alone. Both of them fail to grasp the essence of the human person, who can only find happiness and peace in ties of affection, in shared judgments and common purposes, in mutual sharing, and in concern for personal values.

It is therefore understandable that when the bourgeois world and its individualism collapsed with the First World War, it was not merely totalitarian, collectivist systems which came into being. Among the younger generation especially, during those years, there was also a call for new community. The institutions which made up society seemed to be external utilitarian complexes, over against which the best people of the time set the ideal of personal community or fellowship. Today, under different preconditions, we are experiencing a similar movement among young people. Participation, solidarity, the small group (often called a basic community), as distinct from the – real or alleged – rigid and fossilized institutions of society: these ideas sometimes exert an almost magic fascination. On the other hand all large-scale institutions are subject to very considerable scepticism and fail to carry conviction. This also applies to the church, understood as an institution. That is why many people prefer to talk about 'congregation' or 'basic community', rather than to use the word 'church'.

Of course much about this youth movement is 'half-baked' or immature. What else could it be? And unfortunately ideas of this kind are easily seduced by ideologies and can be misused for ideological purposes. In 1933 the youth movement in Germany was forced to learn this lesson the hard way. But can we deny that behind this movement is a question, and indeed a yearning? A longing for a genuine, more pristine form of human existence, and a hope for a better social order, a hope unsatisfied by all the consumer offers of our modern society?

In the first youth movement after the First World War, there were notable pastors and theologians who knew how to take up the younger generation's longing for community, and to make it fruitful in a renewed sense of the church. These pastors and theologians knew how to stress that, as a community in faith and sacraments, the church was the answer to the question of the time. It was in those years that Guardini wrote: 'A religious process of incalculable importance has begun: the church is awakening in the souls of men.'[1]

Together with the biblical, liturgical, patristic and pastoral revival which took place in the first half of the century, this awakening of the idea of the church provided the historical precondition for the Second Vatican Council, and for its ecclesiological renewal.[2] One of the guiding ideas of the last council – perhaps *the* guiding idea – was therefore *communio* – communion.[3] By taking this as a leitmotif, the council succeeded in uncovering one of the deepest questions of the time, refining it in the light of the gospel, and answering it in a way that took it beyond a purely human questioning and seeking. So the council's *communio* ecclesiology was willingly taken up, and new forms of common responsibility have come into being on all levels of the church's life. The idea of *actuosa participatio* (active participation) has proved a fruitful one, far beyond the bounds of the liturgy. The church has come to be experienced as a communion in a new way. There is a deepened awareness that we are *all* the church.

Today, twenty years after the end of the council, the enthusiasm of that time has largely evaporated. Disillusionment, disappointment, even occasionally bitterness, are widespread. For one person, the council went too far. For another, not far enough. Some people are afraid of restoration. Others hope for it. I can neither join the prophets on the left nor those on the right. For the church, there is only one way into the future: the way pointed by the council, the full implementation of the council and its communion ecclesiology. This is the way which God's Spirit has shown us.

We should have to be blind and deaf not to notice that the great question which moves many young people today – indeed the best of them – is in substance the very same question that arose between the two world wars. Concealed beneath a great deal of astringent criticism of the church, there is also a secret longing (which one may perhaps see as injured love) for an ideal which the church – since it is a church of sinners – can certainly never completely fulfil, but to which it is permanently committed. So the conciliar texts and their communion-based ecclesiology have by no means been superseded. It is even possible to maintain that today the true reception of the council is only beginning – or at least ought to begin. Strictly speaking, there is at present only one alternative: either the communion of Christians as a surpassing fulfilment of humanity, given us in grace; or evolutionary communism, which strives for a communion based on performance.[4] It would therefore seem to be high time to think back to the council, under the heading of communion. This could bring back a greater sense of perspective into church life, and with it greater confidence.

2. Fellowship with God as the fundamental meaning of *communio*

If we look through the many Vatican II documents under the heading *communio*,[5] we get a number of surprises. First of all we discover that, although the *concept* of communion is central to the council's texts, the word used to express this concept is by no means strictly fixed. Apart from the word *communio*, we meet a whole series of similar terms – *communitas*, *societas*, and so forth. Moreover the term *communio* itself has various levels of meaning, in the texts. So in the conciliar documents we have to do with a concept which is only in the process of development. This linguistic finding is an indication that the council found itself up against a substantial problem which it was unable to follow through completely, and which it in fact passed on to us.

A second surprise is more important still. When the council talks about *communio*, it is not talking primarily about the subject that caused so much excitement in the sometimes turbulent post-conciliar discussion. The term *communio* does not initially have anything to do with questions about the church's structure. The word points rather to 'the real thing' (*res*) from which the church comes and for which it lives. *Communio* is not a description of the church's structure. It describes its nature or, as the council puts it, its 'mystery'. For the council's *aggiornamento* consisted in the fact that it again moved into the foreground the mystery of the church, which can only be grasped in faith, over against the one-sided concentration on the visible and hierarchical form of the church, which had held sway during the previous three centuries. So the first part of the Constitution on the Church is deliberately headed *De ecclesiae mysterio* – 'The mystery of the church'.

This heading evidently seemed as strange to some of the conciliar fathers as it again does to many people today. So the theological commission found it necessary to explain expressly that 'mystery' does not mean something unknowable or abstruse, but is a fundamental biblical concept.[6] It means a transcendent saving reality which is revealed and manifested in a visible way. Ultimately, as the Constitution on the Church, *Lumen gentium*, says in its first section, the glory of God is reflected in the face of the church and in its proclamation of the gospel. This understanding of the mystery of the church is completely and utterly Pauline, and in the Constitution on the Church this mystery is described as the mystery of *communio*, under three aspects.

First of all *Lumen gentium* 2, taking up the language of the Bible, says: the eternal Father has created us in accordance with his eternal design and has called us to share (*ad participandam*) in his divine life.

The Constitution on Revelation calls this participation fellowship, personal community (*societas*; *Dei verbum* 1 and 2), whereas the decree on missionary activity describes the same thing as 'peace and communion' (*pax* and *communio*, *Ad gentes* 3). The Pastoral Constitution adds that the dignity of human beings and the truth of their humanity rests in a special way on this communion with God (*Gaudium et spes* 19).

Second, the Constitution on the Church says that the communion which is the purpose of the whole of salvation history is realized in a unique way in history in Jesus Christ (*Lumen gentium* 2f.). Jesus Christ is the one mediator between God and human beings. Through him, God assumed human nature so that we might become sharers in the divine nature (*Ad gentes* 3). So by his incarnation the Son of God has in a certain way united himself with every human being (*Gaudium et spes* 22) – a statement which Pope John Paul II quoted several times in the encyclical *Redemptor hominis*. Jesus Christ is therefore the quintessence of all communion between God and human beings.

Finally we come to the third statement: what took place in Jesus Christ once and for all, is continued by the Holy Spirit (*Lumen gentium* 48), who dwells in the church and in the hearts of believers (4). That is, it is realized from within and spread throughout the world (*Ad gentes* 4). According to the council, the fellowship with God realized through the Spirit provides the foundation for the fellowship of the church. For it is the Spirit who unites the church in communion and ministry (*in communione et ministratione*; *Lumen gentium* 4; *Ad gentes* 4). Through the Spirit, the church is a unity of communion with God and among its own members.

We can therefore sum up by saying that, according to the council, the mystery of the church means that in the Spirit we have access through Christ to the Father, so that in this way we may share in the divine nature. The communion of the church is prefigured, made possible and sustained by the communion of the Trinity. Ultimately, as the council says, echoing Cyprian, the martyr bishop, it is participation in the trinitarian communion itself (*Lumen gentium* 4; *Unitatis redintegratio* 2).[7] The church is, as it were, the icon of the trinitarian fellowship of Father, Son and Holy Spirit.

These fundamental conciliar statements seem at first sight to be a long way away from the human questions about community with which we started. But this only seems to be the case. For what the council is really saying is this: it is not the church which is the answer to the human longing for community. That longing is in fact a striving for something which can be everything for a person, something which surpasses everything human, and which finds its fulfilment only in God's communication of himself, in communion and friendship with God. The longing of the human heart is so immense and so profound that only God is great enough to fulfil it. God alone is the final answer to the question which the human being himself is (*Gaudium et spes* 21). So the question about the church is subordinate to the question about 3God.

But this brings the question about the church up against what is perhaps the most serious problem in our Western world: the atheism of the masses, the attempt to find a foundation for human happiness and human community without God (*Gaudium et spes* 19). Every ecclesiology which seeks to be abreast of the times must face up to this challenge. So questions about the church's structure are not an end in themselves. They are merely a means to an end. In this era of ours, characterized as it is by atheism, they must help the church to be more clearly a sacrament – that is a sign and instrument – of fellowship with God and fellowship among human beings (*Lumen gentium* 1, and frequently).

So twenty years after the council, the fundamental perspective for the church is the renewal of its spiritual dimension, the dimension of mystery. The degree to which a full reception of the council is still lacking in this respect is shown even by the new *Codex Juris Canonici*, which – contrary to *Lumen gentium* 14 – in describing the full *communio* with the church, manages to get by without mentioning the Holy Spirit at all, confining itself to institutional criteria.[8] This shows with sufficient clarity that we are only at the beginning of a reception of the council.

3. *Communio* as participation in the life of God through word and sacrament

Up to now we have looked at the council's *communio* theology exclusively under an initial, though certainly fundamental, aspect. We must now pass on to the main meaning of *communio* as found in Scripture and tradition, a significance which is also strongly echoed in the documents of the Second Vatican Council.

Here too, what is under discussion is not as yet the fellowship of Christians or local congregations with one another. For the Greek word *koinonia* (Latin *communio*) does not originally mean 'community' at all. It means participation, and more particularly, participation in the good things of salvation conferred by God: participation in the Holy Spirit, in new life, in love, in the gospel, but above all participation in the eucharist.[9] This also suggests the original meaning of the article of faith about the 'communion of saints' (*communio sanctorum*), which we already find from the fourth century onwards, in the Apostles' Creed.[10] This usage still exerts its influence today. It is not for nothing that the most usual expression for receiving the eucharist is 'communion'. The word is also used in this sense in the Constitution on the Liturgy (*Sacrosanctum concilium* 55). The Decree on Ecumenism also talks about the *communio eucharistica* (*Unitatis redintegratio* 22), meaning by this not merely the reception of the eucharist, but also the community of those partaking, which springs from the eucharist itself.

This meaning of *communio* goes back to the apostle Paul. In I Cor. 10.16f. we read: 'The cup of blessing which we bless, is it not a participation in the blood of Christ? The bread which we break, is it not a participation in the body of Christ? Because there is one bread, we who are many are one body, for we all partake of the one bread.' Along the same lines, Augustine called the eucharist a 'sign of unity and a bond of love'.[11] The last council took up this saying of Augustine's and based the communion of the church on the eucharistic communion. *Lumen gentium* 7 says explicitly: 'Really sharing in the body of the Lord in the breaking of the eucharistic bread, we are taken up into communion with him and with one another' (cf. *Lumen gentium* 3; *Unitatis redintegratio* 2; *Apostolicam actuositatem* 8; *Presbyterorum ordinis* 6). Consequently the eucharist is the climax of the communion of the church (*Lumen gentium* 11; *Ad gentes* 9).

But the eucharist can only be a climax if it is not the only form of the church's communion. All sacraments in principle build up the body of Christ (*Sacrosanctum concilium* 59; *Lumen gentium* 11). Baptism is of fundamental importance, since it is the gateway to the communion of the church, and its foundation. In addition the council talks about word and sacrament (*Ad gentes* 9; *Apostolicam actuositatem* 6; *Presbyterorum ordinis* 4; *Unitatis redintegratio* 2), or about the two tables, the table of the eucharist and the table of the word (*Sacrosanc-tum concilium* 51; *Dei verbum* 21). With this phraseology, the council, in the spirit of earlier tradition, has taken up an essentially Protestant concern, and has in its own way defined the church as *creatura verbi* – 'creature of the word' (*Lumen gentium* 2, 9; *Dei verbum* 21–26).[12] Pope Paul VI's Apostolic Letter *Evangelii nuntiandi* (1975) developed and considerably deepened this viewpoint.

By linking up in this way with the earlier biblical and patristic tradition, the council breaks through the disastrously contracted viewpoints of later development.[13] For as a result of the second eucharistic dispute, which took place in the eleventh century, euchar-istic ecclesiology came to be largely forgotten, just as the disputes with the Reformers in the sixteenth century meant that the theology of the word also for the most part sank into oblivion. In this way the church came to be understood primarily as a social, hierarchical structure. It was only the biblical and liturgical revival of the first half of our own century that again made people more vividly aware of what the church lives from: the communion of word and sacrament, and particularly the eucharist, in which the preaching of the word and the sacramental feast form a single liturgical act (*Sacrosanctum concilium* 56).

It may therefore be said that, just as the trinitarian confession of the creed is the summing up and the identifying mark of the whole Christian faith, so the eucharist is the sacramental and symbolic actualization of the whole mystery of salvation.[14] As eucharistic communion, the church is not merely the reflection of the trinitarian communion; it also makes that communion present. It is not merely the sign and means of salvation, but also its fruit.[15] As eucharistic communion, it is the all-surpassing response to the fundamental human cry for fellowship.

This biblical and liturgical renewal on the part of the council bore rich fruit afterwards in the life of the church. We cannot be grateful enough for what has grown up since the council in this respect. We therefore have no reason at all for arriving at any one-sided, negative judgment about the development of the last twenty years.

Yet this does not mean that we should shut our eyes to the problems and the hindrances which at present still stand in the way of a full reception of the council's *communio* ecclesiology. For, contrary to the original intention, the biblical and liturgical renewal has often been detached from its context in the communion of the church. The movement aimed to overcome the modern individualism and subjectivism of the West; but this very individualism and subjectivism has subsequently taken possession of the movement itself, and in some respects has robbed it of its fruits. In expounding the word of God, the subjective interpretation has often been put above the church's interpretation, or opposed to it. This has triggered off a fundamental crisis about methods in theology, which (together with many other factors) has often led to a lack of confidence in preaching and in faith. The liturgy has often been understood as a celebration of the fellowship of the church – i.e., as the meeting and gathering of the congregation – instead of a being brought together through common participation in the one body of Christ. It is often the feast of Christians, rather than the Lord's Supper. This has frequently led to neglect of the attitude of worship, and to a loss of the sacrificial dimension – in the ecumenical context, to a detachment of the eucharistic community from the community of the churches. These problems are well known. I mention them here only to show once more that we are still only at the beginning in our reception of the council. Discovering and putting into practice the communion of the church is a task in which there is still much to be done.

We may therefore formulate the second important perspective for the church today in the following way. We must again recollect more clearly the sources from which the church lives: God's word and the church's sacraments. The communion of the church does not come about 'from below'. It is grace and gift, common participation in the one truth, in the one life, and in the one love which God communicates to us in word and sacrament through Jesus Christ, in the Holy Spirit.

4. The church as a unity in communion

The fellowship with God communicated through word and sacrament leads to fellowship between Christians. It finds concrete expression in the communion of the local congregations, which has its foundation in the eucharist. This brings us to the word *communio* as a technical term.

The council was aware that with this interpretation of *communio* as the fellowship of local congregations, founded on the eucharist, it was taking up one of the fundamental concepts and fundamental realities of the ancient church.[16] This meaning is reverenced in the Eastern churches down to the present day (*Nota praevia* 2). Consequently this interpretation of *communio* plays a special part in the Decree on the Eastern Churches (*Orientalium ecclesiarum* 13) and in the Decree on Ecumenism (*Unitatis redintegratio* 14f.). Indeed the interpretation of the church's unity as a *communio* unity, provided the council with the real key for the ecumenical opening it brought about. For by understanding the church's unity as *communio*, it was possible to distinguish between full communion in the Catholic church and imperfect communion with the other churches and Christian groups. But apart from this, the term *communio* as it is used in the conciliar texts is of great importance within the Catholic Church itself. The council lays particular weight on the communion between the old and the young churches (*Ad gentes* 19f., 37f.). Basically, what the council says is that the Catholic church exists in local churches and consists of local churches (*Lumen gentium* 23).

This formula, more than any other, shows how much the revival of the ancient church's concept of *communio* represents a turning point of the first order in the history of theology and the church. For a return to the *communio* ecclesiology of the first ten centuries means departing from the one-sided 'unity' ecclesiology of the second millennium of the church, which was, and still is, one of the essential reasons for the separation of the Eastern churches from the Latin church of the West.[17] The interpretation of the church's unity as a unity in communion again leaves room for a legitimate variety of local churches within the greater unity in the one faith, the same sacraments and the same ministries. This points the way forward, as the church moves into its third millennium.

This renewed communion ecclesiology is the background for one of the doctrines which was most discussed and most disputed at the council and afterwards: the doctrine about the collegiality of the episcopate.[18] Collegiality is, so to speak, the official, outward aspect (though one might also say that it is the inward aspect for the church) of the sacramental unity in communion. We neither must nor can at this point take up the whole debate about collegiality which was carried on at the council. Here we shall only pick out the aspect which touches directly on the unity in communion: the phrase about the *communio hierarchica*. What does this difficult term mean?

In order to explain it, we must go back a little.[19] As we know, the council taught that episcopal consecration is sacramental in character (*Lumen gentium* 21). It therefore rooted pastoral power/authority in the church (*iurisdictio*) once more on the power/authority of sacramental ordination (*ordo*). *Lumen gentium* 21 now adds, however, that the functions (*munera*) conferred through episcopal consecration can be exercised only in hierarchical communion with the head and members of the college, or episcopal body (cf. *Lumen gentium* 22; *Christus Dominus* 4). What this means is more precisely explained in the famous *Nota praevia*.[20] It distinguishes between functions (*munera*) and powers (*potestates*). The functions are conferred through consecration, but they can be exercised precisely as powers (*potestates*) only on the basis of juridical determination through the assignment of subordinate roles. The concrete exercise of the functions conferred through sacramental episcopal ordination is therefore bound to the hierarchical *communio* with the pope and the whole episcopate. By analogy, the phrase *communio hierarchica* is also applied to the relationship of priest to bishop and to other priests (*Presbyterorum ordinis* 7, 15).

With the help of the term *communio hierarchica*, therefore, the episcopal office is incorporated in the universal church or, more specifically, into the communion with the pope and the college or body of bishops. This incorporation is of such a kind that the old distinction between *ordo* and *iurisdictio* is preserved in a new way. *Communio hierarchica* is therefore a typical compromise formulation, which points to a juxtaposition of sacramental *communio* ecclesiology and juristic unity ecclesiology. It has consequently been said that the Vatican II texts contain two ecclesiologies.[21] The compromise proved useful at the council, since it made it possible for the minority to agree to the Constitution on the Church. But just to say this is not entirely satisfactory. The compromise indicates a deeper problem. For the Catholic principle about living tradition makes it impossible simply to eliminate the tradition of the second millennium. The continuity of tradition demands a creative synthesis of the traditions of the first millennium and the second.[22] The synthesis brought about by the last council was highly superficial, and in no way satisfactory. But then it is not the function of councils to draw up theological syntheses. A council presents the indispensable 'frame of reference'. The synthesis is then a matter for the theology that comes afterwards.

So with the term *communio hierarchica*, the council presents us with a problem which up to now can certainly not be regarded as solved. The solution will have important practical results for the realization of collegiality, in its relation to primacy, for the position of the episcopal conference, and for pluralism in the church in general. Twenty years after the council, all these questions are still controversial in many respects.

A solution to this problem is only possible if we think more deeply about the nature of unity in communion, and the precise relationship between unity and communion. For *communio* ecclesiology is a term which can mean several different things. It is used in quite different ways in the eucharistic ecclesiology of the Orthodox churches, in the Anglican interpretation of community, in the congregationalist model of unity, and in the ideas about the conciliar unity of the churches held by the World Council of Churches.[23] So what is Catholic *communio* ecclesiology?

According to the testimony of Scripture, and the church's tradition of faith, which interprets Scripture, unity is a fundamental definition of the nature of the church. The church is essentially the one, holy, catholic and apostolic church, in which all differences of nation, culture, race, class and sex are ultimately speaking *aufgehoben*, to use a German word: that is, they are abolished in the sense of being gathered up and preserved in something higher. All dividing topographical, sociological, cultural and other natural factors can play no really decisive role in this unity, since it is established through the one God, the one mediator Jesus Christ, in the one Holy Spirit; is mediated through the one faith and the one baptism; and is shown and made present in the one eucharist.[24] This unity is the foundation of the universality and catholicity which we have every reason to stress, today above all. The peace of the world today requires us to emphasize, not merely cultural individuality (although this is undoubtedly something to be treasured), but even more the trans-cultural equality and unity of all human beings. It is therefore strange that today people in the church are more enthusiastic about human socio-cultural differences than about unity; and that this is made a reason for self-isolation, for conflicts, and for fruitless tensions, in which we occasionally hear unmistakably nationalistic overtones, or phraseology more appropriate to the class struggle. A new particularism is spreading, which often finds a vent in anti-Roman emotions.[25]

The justifiable concerns of these centrifugal tendencies must of course be justly appreciated. The unity and universality of the church is not a bloodless, abstract, uniform and ultimately totalitarian system. God does not redeem anthropological abstractions, which would always be the same. He redeems men and women made of flesh and blood.[26] The one church takes concrete form, and takes root in particular cultures – we might say that it becomes incarnate in space and time. This is the only way in which the church can be a unity in plenitude. Consequently the universal church exists only in individual churches, and is made up of individual churches (*Lumen gentium* 23). In these individual churches the church universal is active and present (*Christus Dominus* 11).

This means that although the universal church certainly does not come into being through any subsequent union, addition and confederation of individual churches, yet the individual churches are, with equal certainty, never merely a subsequent administrative partition of the universal church into individual provinces and departments. The universal church and the individual church are mutually inclusive. They dwell within one another mutually.[27] That is why it is part of the essential structure of the church to have two focuses, like the two focuses of an ellipse: *iure divino*, it is both papal and episcopal. Neither of the two poles can be traced back to the other. This unity in tension is the foundation of the union in communion. The communion which is both episcopal and papal is the essential organic expression of the essential structure of the church, its unity in catholicity, and its catholicity in unity.

If we take seriously the statement that the church is a reflection of the Trinity, then this statement can even be deepened. In the Trinity, the threeness of the persons neither abolishes nor constitutes the unity of their natures, but is their specific mode of being, so that one divine nature exists only in the relation between Father, Son and Spirit. Analogously, the one church exists only in local churches and is formed from these. Just as the trinitarian creed is the concrete form of Christian monotheism,[28] so the communion of the individual churches is the concrete form and realization of the one universal church. So it is precisely as communion that the church is an icon of the Trinity.[29] Variety in unity and unity in variety is a concept that is better fitted for the trinitarian understanding of unity than a monolithic model of unity.

Of course it is impossible in this context even to outline the results of this approach for the relationship between primacy and episcopacy, the authority of orders and the authority of jurisdiction, and for the interpretation and the realization of collegiality. I will confine myself to saying that this approach makes it possible to distinguish in principle between a plurality, which means wealth and fullness, and a pluralism which dissolves and destroys unity. From this a third perspective emerges: more collegiality, more say in things and more co-responsibility, greater permeability of information, and more transparency in the decision process than we have at present in our church. In this respect not all legitimate expectations have been fulfilled since Vatican II. Once again: we are only at the beginning, in our reception of the council.

5. The communion of the faithful as the participation and co-responsibility of all

It has often been said that Vatican II itself is no more than a beginning. Karl Rahner even talks about the beginning of a beginning. This becomes especially clear when we turn to a fourth dimension of communion, to the communion of the faithful (*communio fidelium*; *Lumen gentium* 13; *Unitatis redintegratio* 2; *Apostolicam actuositatem* 18). This fourth meaning fits organically into what has already been said. For we already saw that the communion of the churches and the collegiality of the bishops is based on the more fundamental communion which is the church, the people of God itself.

It is only at a few points that this is explicitly talked about in the conciliar texts. But substantially speaking, this meaning of *communio* is fundamentally part of the doctrine about the common priesthood of all the baptized, which was revived by the council (*Lumen gentium* 10), and the *actuosa participatio* of the whole people of God, which is based on that common priesthood (*Sacrosanctum concilium* 14 and frequently). This does not apply merely to the liturgy. It affects the whole life of the church. Of especial importance here is the doctrine about the *sensus fidei* or *sensus fidelium* (*Lumen gentium* 13, 35; *Gaudium et spes* 43; *Apostolicam actuositatem* 2f.). Unfortunately the new *Codex Juris Canonici* has passed over this final aspect in complete silence.[30] With this aspect of *communio* ecclesiology, the idea about the church as an 'unequal society' has in principle been surmounted. It means that the common existence of the people of God precedes all differences of functions, charismata and ministries.

In hardly any sector since the council have things moved so much as here. In the meantime, stimulated by the council, bodies of common responsibility have come into being on all levels of the church's life: parish councils, diocesan councils, diocesan synods, episcopal synods. Lay interest, and the preparedness of lay people to take a share of responsibility, is perhaps the most valuable and most important contribution of the post-conciliar period. It was not for nothing that in *Evangelii nuntiandi* (58), Pope Paul VI termed the true basic communities of the church a hope for the church universal; for communion ecclesiology means that there cannot be active members on the one side, and passive ones on the other. This ecclesiology puts an end to the pattern of a welfare church for looking after people. It tends to the subjectivity of the church and all who belong to it.[31]

But *corruptio optimi pessima!* The corruption of the best is the worst of all. There was, and is, hardly any aspect of conciliar doctrine which was, and is still, so fundamentally misunderstood as this one. First of all, the people of God (*laos tou theou*) was misunderstood in the sense of being a political association of people (*demos*). This led correspondingly to a demand for a democratization of the church. Then the word 'people' was interpreted to mean the 'ordinary, simple people', as distinct from the establishment. But as the council uses the phrase, the people of God does not mean the laity, for example, or the rank and file, as distinct from 'the official church', let alone in contrast to it. It means the organic and structured whole of the church, the people gathered round their bishop, and attached to their shepherd, as Cyprian put it. The faith of believers and the doctrine of the church must therefore be understood in a strictly correlative sense.

But which of us is not aware of the tensions, even conflicts, that exist at this point? And the expressions of dissension are not the worst of it. They at least represent one form of dialogue and communication, even if not the best. But the lack of communication, the mutual disregard, the disinterest and the drifting apart: all these things are much worse. This is the phenomenon with which we are often confronted today. It often feels like taking part in a dialogue between the deaf. And anyone who has taken part more than once, already knows in advance what the one side is going to say to the arguments of the other, the response coming with the regularity of a prayer wheel. The paradox of the situation is that the groups and movements which condemn the church's doctrine (at least in certain points), or simply ignore it, showing very little interest in what it is about, none the less want to remain in the church, and have no desire for a breach. This can also be a sign of hope. It is at least an opening for a responsible pastorate.

At present it is obvious that something has gone very wrong with Vatican II's great idea, the *communio fidelium*. In this situation, the first task of the church's ministry and its service for unity seems to me to be to restore dialogue and communication, and to introduce the binding doctrine of the church, as far as possible by means of reasoned argument, into the process of communication within the church, in order in this way to build up once more a full and undivided *communio* and *communicatio fidelium* – communion and communication among the faithful. The ideal of this communion is not harmony without tension. All life moves in tension, as J. A. Möhler showed; where tension ends there is death.[32] And we have no desire for a dead church. We want a living one! But a distinction must be made between genuine tensions, where the poles are related to one another in a complementary way, and unconnected, indeed irreconcilable differences, which shut themselves off mutually and exclude one another, both in logic and in attitude. As Möhler again showed, in the communion of the church neither one nor all can be everything. 'Only everyone together can be everything, and the unity of all can only be a whole. That is the idea of the Catholic Church.'[33] In this sense the building up of living and truly ecclesial congregations and communities of lay people and priests is a fourth perspective.

6. The communion of the church as a sacrament for the world

The church does not exist for its own sake. Consequently something must be said in closing, at least briefly and in outline, about a final dimension of the term *communio*. In doing so we are coming back to what we said at the beginning about the fundamental human question and the fundamental human longing for community.

We said that the church, as sacramentally founded communion, was the surpassing answer to this human question. It follows from this that the communion which the church is, represents the type, model or pattern for the community of people and nations (*Ad gentes* 11, 23; *Gaudium et spes* 39; *Nostra aetate* 1) – and also for the community *between* men and women, poor and rich. According to the splendid idea of Irenaeus of Lyons, through the communion of the church God wishes to renew everything in Christ (*Lumen gentium* 2), and so to prepare his final kingdom, in which he will be 'all in all' (I Cor. 15.28). In this way the church can and must be a sacrament – that is, a sign and instrument of unity and peace in the world. For we cannot share the eucharistic bread without sharing our daily bread as well. The effort for justice, peace and liberty among people and nations, and the striving for a new civilization of love, is therefore a fundamental perspective for the church today. Just because it is a unity in communion, a unity in reconciled difference, the church is a messianic people, a universal sign of salvation (*Lumen gentium* 9).

In this context, it is true, the conciliar texts do not generally talk about *communio*. They speak of *societas*, *communitas* and so forth. The term *communio* is generally used in the strict theological sense. For the communion which the church confers, and which it itself is, surpasses everything that purely human community can be. Death, at latest, is the inescapable frontier to human community. The loftiest utopian dreams about a kingdom of freedom and justice can never undo the injustice done to those who are already dead, the tortured and murdered of the past. So purely human utopias cannot provide a basis for a truly universal hope.[34] But the communion of the church is communion even beyond death. This alone can satisfy the longing of the human heart. The communion of saints – the fellowship between the earthly and the heavenly church (*Lumen gentium* 50f.) – is therefore the only final answer to the question about everlasting life and the unbreakable bond of love.

To understand the church in a new way as a communion, to live it better, and to realize it more profoundly is therefore more than a programme for church reform. The church as a communion is a message and a promise for the people and world of today. This was laid on us by the last council, and it is a task for today above all. We are by no means at the end of the task. We are only at the beginning. With the council, Pope John XXIII wanted to take a leap forward. Up to now only the first beginnings have been successful. A great deal still has to be done – perhaps the most important things of all – if we are to arrive at a renewal from the depths and from the sources, which will be at the same time a response to the signs of the time.

We cannot go back to the era before the council. Even if the leaders of the church wished, they could not do so. And in reality they have no such desire. But today there is not yet any way which leads fundamentally beyond the council, in the direction of a Vatican III or – as others say – a Jerusalem II. It is not only that we do not have the presuppositions and the preliminary work. We have not as yet nearly exhausted the potentialities of the last council. So the only possible way is to penetrate more deeply into that council, so that with its help, inspired by its letter and its spirit, we may venture the leap forward into the third millennium of the church's history.

IX

The Continuing Challenge of the Second Vatican Council

The Hermeneutics of the Conciliar Statements

1. The three phases of development after the council

For many people at the time, the Second Vatican Council was a positively breathtaking spiritual event. Today, twenty years later, many find the conciliar texts completely alien, if they are familiar with them at all. The interest and hope which the council awakened has often turned into disappointment – indeed into a fear that the renewal which the council began is not going to be maintained and will come to nothing.

In the meantime, a discussion about the importance, interpretation and consequences of Vatican II has flared up again. The impetus for this discussion was provided by some highly pointed remarks made by the prefect of the Congregation for the Doctrine of the Faith, and more especially by the convening of an extraordinary synod of bishops devoted to the reception and interpretation of the last council. The resulting debate has taken us into a third phase of post-conciliar development – a phase which will probably decide what the future is going to be.

The first phase in the reception was what H. J. Pottmeyer called 'the phase of exuberance'. This was dominated by the immediate impression that the council was a liberating event. For many people Vatican II seemed to be a complete new beginning and the starting point for an ongoing conciliar drive. It was as if a fuse had been lit. This soon made the conciliar texts themselves appear superseded. Even the official liturgical renewal, for example, sometimes went beyond what the council had explicitly said – for instance in the extent to which the vernacular is used. The theological discussion, even more, soon left the council's texts behind. Even as balanced a theologian as Yves Congar (who was himself very considerably involved in drawing up *Lumen gentium*, the Constitution on the Church) could write: 'The positions of the Second Vatican Council now seem to have been superseded in some respects.' 'The spirit of the council' was frequently invoked, and there were warnings about a 'conciliar scholasticism', tied to the conciliar texts.

Almost inevitably, this first phase was replaced by a phase of disappointment. This disappointment had many reasons. There is no doubt that all legitimate expectations were not fulfilled. This is particularly true of collegiality, and the view of the church as *communio*. But it was not only in the church that there was a radical change of climate at the end of the sixties and the beginning of the seventies. The climate of society as a whole changed as well. Moreover, the dynamic of what was new was often unsupported by the necessary religious and spiritual power. The crisis showed itself, for example, in the dramatic decline in priestly and religious vocations, in a widespread breakdown of penitential practice (particularly the sacrament of penance) and, not least, in a marked decline in church attendance – contrary to what had been expected with the liturgical renewal. The council had thrown open the door to the world of today, and to the other churches and religions; but this often led to a diffusion of what was specifically Catholic, and to an identity crisis. The progressive reformers now complained about the inertia of the church as an institution. The conservatives talked about signs of dissolution. Protest and contention developed on the one side, attempts at restoration on the other. Both finally led to a paralysing stalemate and to a fruitless kind of trench warfare.

The official initiative in setting a new round of discussions going brings movement into the church again, and must therefore in principle be welcomed. At all events, it shows that the last council is still very much on the agenda. Its reception and implementation is by no means finished. In some ways it is only beginning.

2. The need for a hermeneutic of the conciliar statements

Where is this new phase going to take us? We hear not only about expectations, but about grave misgivings as well. We can distinguish three main trends. First, there is a desire to go beyond the resolutions of the council. Second, there is an attempt to stop the movement which got under way with the council, because of a fear that Roman Catholic identity is in danger. The third trend urges a strict application of the council, under the motto: 'Only the council, but the whole council!'

If we are to arrive at a satisfactory answer, two things must be borne in mind. On the one hand, it is a fundamental conviction of faith that councils are an event brought about by the divine Spirit who guides the church. Consequently the results are a guiding principle which is binding on the church. This obligation exists even though the Second Vatican Council deliberately promulgated no infallible – i.e. fully binding – decisions. It would be quite wrong if we tried to play off the council's pastoral intention and language against its doctrinal significance (which was frequently explicitly formulated and continually emphasized), and overlooked the fact that its texts imply 'a serious claim on the conscience of the Catholic Christian' (Joseph Ratzinger's words). The church can therefore only move into the future on the basis of the last council's resolutions, and by implementing them conscientiously. A restoration in the sense of a return to conditions as they were before the council would contradict the very principles of that pre-conciliar period itself, according to which councils are the supreme authority in the church. Any such restoration would plunge the church into a foundational crisis compared with which the present state of affairs is a trifle.

On the other hand one must be realistic enough to see that not all valid councils in the history of the church were fruitful ones. Here people continually draw attention to the Fifth Lateran Council, which met in 1512–1517, just before the beginning of the Reformation, without being able to make any effective contribution to reform which would have prevented the approaching catastrophe. The divine Spirit works through human beings, and they can frustrate his workings. So the last word has not yet been spoken about the historical importance of the Second Vatican Council either. Whether this council will count in the end as one of the highlights of church history will depend on the people who translate its words into terms of real life.

What is at issue for Catholic theology, therefore, is not the council in itself. What is in question is the interpretation and reception of the council. The dispute is about this and this alone. For opinions differ about the reception of the council hitherto, and about the events of post-conciliar development. Where one person talks about renewal, another sees only breakdown, crisis and loss of identity. As long as the dispute is pursued within the limits set by Christian truth and love, a dispute of this kind is part of the church's life which, like all life, exists in tension. In the previous history of the church as well, almost all councils led to crisis and upheaval. So the present situation is by no means unique. It is to some degree normal.

The problem can be solved only if we come to an agreement about the principles which are to determine the interpretation and implementation of the council. As we saw, a third phase in the council's reception is beginning. After the first, wholly positive, exuberant phase, this third phase must be one of authentic, integral interpretation and implementation of the council and its work of renewal. The task with which theology is thereby presented is to work out a hermeneutic for the Second Vatican Council.

3. The difficulties of a conciliar hermeneutic

A hermeneutic of the Second Vatican Council initially comes up against considerable difficulties. One of the main reasons for this is that, in the case of this particular council, at least one important principle for interpreting conciliar texts is denied us. Where the previous councils were concerned, the principle was that its statements had to be understood in the context of the errors condemned, and with this condemnation in mind. But Vatican II deliberately avoided any new condemnation. Its intentionally positive presentation of the truth distinguishes this council especially from the narrow anti-modernist mentality of the beginning of our century. So in this case, the principle that the council has to be understood in the light of the opposite position, falls to the ground.

This, in its turn, gives rise to a second difficulty. Pope John XXIII expicitly gave the council a pastoral purpose and direction. The council did not renounce anything in previous dogmatic tradition. On the contrary, it took up and renewed the doctrine of the church as it had been passed down. In addition, it gave some new doctrinal stresses and made some important binding statements: the sacramentality and collegiality of the episcopal office, the universality of salvation, and others. But it did not issue any new interpretation of dogma in the sense of an ultimately binding dogmatic definition. Following the opening address of Pope John XXIII, which caused such a stir, the council also made a clear distinction between the underlying foundation of faith, which is permanently binding, and its mode of expression. This pastoral language is to some extent a novelty, compared with previous councils. In the case of earlier councils we are familiar with either dogmatic or disciplinary (i.e., canon law) provisions. In both these fields there are generally recognized principles of interpretation among experts. But when the pastoral character is in question, there is not as yet any agreement even as to what should be understood by this, in any detailed sense; even less is there any consensus about an appropriate hermeneutic.

Then there is a third difficulty. It has frequently been pointed out that in the Vatican II texts 'conservative' and 'progressive' statements are often found side by side, with no attempt at reconciliation. People talk about purely formal compromises. For example, Vatican I's doctrine about the primacy and infallibility of the pope is not merely retained. It is reiterated several times, and is in this way emphasized and endorsed. But it is integrated into the doctrine about the church as a whole, and the responsibility of all believers, as well as into the doctrine about the collegiality of the bishops. Yet how this integration is supposed to be conceived and practised in individual cases is by no means clarified in the conciliar texts. So some people have talked about a juxtaposition, a double viewpoint, a dialectic, if nót actualy a contradiction between two ecclesiologies, in the conciliar texts – a traditional hierarchical ecclesiology and a new, better *communio* ecclesiology, renewed in the spirit of the ancient church. So both conservatives and progressives can find support in individual conciliar statements. And this lends all the more urgency to the question about generally applicable rules of interpretation.

4. The hermeneutics of the doctrinal statements

The solution of these difficulties emerges, at least for the council's doctrinal statements, if we do not merely quote individual statements as such, but look at the conciliar process out of which they emerged – that is, if we study the textual history of the last council. If we make this effort, we shall discover quite quickly that to ask whether the council should be interpreted in a 'conservative' or a 'progressive' sense is to ask the wrong question. The council's *aggiornamento* had its roots in what preceded it, a renewal from the biblical, patristic and scholastic sources. The 'progressives' at the council were in reality the representatives of the greater and wider tradition, as distinct from its neoscholastic levelling and simplification. The concern of the 'conservative' minority at the council, on the other hand, was to see to it that recent tradition (represented especially by Vatican I) was not passed over and forgotten, in the course of this renewal from the earlier sources. This is a fundamentally legitimate concern, according to the Catholic view of tradition; and in the end the majority quite rightly accepted it. Admittedly, the harmonization between earlier and later tradition is often not completely successful; for – like most previous councils – Vatican II solved its task, not with the help of a comprehensive theory, but by pegging out the limits of the church's position. In this sense it was completely in the conciliar tradition for a juxtaposition to remain. As in the case of every council, the theoretical mediation of these positions is a task for the theology that comes afterwards.

This suggests a second insight. The council itself, like all other councils, wished to preserve tradition. Otherwise it would have lost its *raison d'être*. But – again like all other previous councils – it did not wish simply to reiterate tradition. It wished to actualize it and give it a living interpretation, in the light of the changed situation of the time. It did not intend to develop any new doctrine, but it did wish to renew the old. The theological language is aimed at and related to men and women in the situation of today, and may be termed pastoral. The word pastoral is therefore used in contrast to a rigid dogmatism, but it is not an antithesis to 'dogmatic'. On the contrary: 'pastoral' means bringing out the enduring relevance of dogma. Just because a dogma is true, it must and can be continually given a new and living impact, and has to be interpreted pastorally.

These reflections show that the methods and language of the last council are not in every respect new, compared with previous councils. That is important for the question of how far its statements are binding, as well as for their interpretation. The general rules of conciliar hermeneutics can therefore quite well be applied to this council also, by analogy. But there are also a number of more particular principles for the hermeneutics of this council's doctrinal statements.

We may formulate the first of these principles as follows: the texts of the Second Vatican Council must be understood and put into practice as a whole. It will not do simply to stress certain statements or aspects only, in isolation. It is precisely the tension existing between individual statements which brings out the pastoral point of the council.

This links up with a second interpretative principle: the letter and the spirit of the council must be understood as a unity. This is in fact a simple rule of every hermeneutics, and is generally termed the hermeneutical circle. Every individual statement can ultimately only be understood in the light of the spirit of the whole, just as, conversely, the spirit of the whole only emerges from a conscientious interpretation of individual texts. We can therefore neither make a legalistically literal exegesis of the conciliar texts without allowing ourselves to be moved by their spirit; nor must we enthusiastically play off 'the spirit of the council' against its actual texts. So faithfulness to the texts which stops at that, is never sufficient. On the contrary, it leads into a cul-de-sac, because one can all too often confront one text with another. The spirit of the whole, and hence the meaning of an individual text, can only be discovered by pursuing the textual history in detail, and from this extracting the council's intention. And this intention was the renewal of *the whole* tradition, and that means the renewal, for our time, of the whole of what is Catholic.

From this a third principle of interpretation emerges. According to its own intention, the Second Vatican Council must be understood, like every other council, in the light of the wider tradition of the church. It is therefore absurd to distinguish between the pre-conciliar and the post-conciliar church in such a way to suggest that the post-conciliar church is a new church; or as if, after a long, dark age in church history, the last council had at long last rediscovered the original gospel. On the contrary, Vatican II itself belongs within the tradition of all previous councils, and it is this tradition which it wished to renew. The council must therefore be interpreted in the context of that tradition, particularly the trinitarian and christological confessions of the ancient church.

Finally, we must mention a fourth interpretative principle: the continuity of what is Catholic is understood by the last council as a unity between tradition and a living, relevant interpretation in the light of the current situation. This principle was already at work in previous councils (even if only implicitly), when these councils lent tradition a precise, articulated form, in the light of some specific error. But what then took place in particular cases, was thought about explicitly by the last council, and was given a universal reference: for the council talks about a relation to the 'signs of the time'. This means: historical origins must be adopted responsibly today against the horizon of the future.

5. The hermeneutics of the pastoral statements

The interpretation of the last council's pastoral statements is more difficult than the interpretation of its statements about doctrine. It is true that, basically, everything the council says, including its doctrinal utterances, are meant pastorally. But there are also pastoral statements in the narrower and more specialized sense. We find these particularly in *Gaudium et spes*, which bears the name 'Pastoral Constitution'.

The very genre 'Pastoral Constitution' is a novelty in conciliar history. The degree to which it is binding, its method, and its interpretation are therefore controversial in a particular way, and are not yet fully clarified in every respect. On the other hand, this constitution was not prepared by any pre-conciliar commissions. It therefore grew out of the conciliar process itself more than any of the other constitutions. It expresses the 'spirit' of the last council particularly clearly. The council also deliberately gave it the solemn character of a constitution and did not reduce it to the rank of a mere message or declaration, as was suggested. This meant that this constitution has had a correspondingly profound effect since the council, an influence which also made itself felt in liberation theology. And rightly so. For what use is all our orthodoxy if it does not bear fruit in practical life? If we were to speak with the tongues of men and of angels, but had not love, we should be sounding brass and tinkling cymbals.

The last council therefore rightly adhered to the doctrine of the Council of Trent and Vatican I, saying that in questions of faith and morals it is both possible and necessary for the church to speak in binding form. In addition, it also maintained that it was its task to explain authoritatively, and to endorse, the principles of the moral order, which spring from the nature of human beings themselves. This is the fundamental claim of the church: and on its basis the council deliberately intended to make binding doctrinal statements in the Pastoral Constitution also. This is clearly demonstrated by the textual history.

But where practical morality is concerned, general principles are not enough. Clear directives are necessary. And yet the particular situation is never merely a special case within, or subordinate to, a general rule. The specific situation also contains something additional – a surplus – compared with the general rule. So traditional doctrine also says that practical directives cannot simply be deduced in the abstract from general principles. They presuppose an evaluation of the particular situation into which the general principles have to be translated. This is where the difficulties begin. And it is these difficulties with which moral theology especially (but pastoral theology too) is having to struggle at present. For in evaluating the particular personal, cultural, social or political situation, the church has no particular spiritual authority and competence. Here it is dependent on human experience, human judgment and the relevant human sciences.

The council took this fact into account, and decided that in judging practical situations within the limits of the common faith, different political, social and cultural options are open to Catholics.

These principles, confirmed by the council itself, have consequences for the interpretation of the pastoral statements (taken in the narrower sense) of the council. In these pastoral statements a clear distinction has to be made between the different levels of a statement and their varying degree of obligation. To be more precise: a distinction has to be made between the generally binding, doctrinal foundation, the description of the situation, and the application of the general principles to the pastoral situation described. In the description of the situation, the council had to fall back on recognitions of a secular kind, for which it possessed no special ecclesiastical teaching authority. The binding nature of these situational definitions is therefore dependent on the validity of the arguments which are brought into play. Their authority is therefore essentially different and, above all, less than the authority of the doctrinal statements themselves. This in its turn has consequences for the application of generally binding statements about faith and morals to the specific situation. The obedience required here cannot be simply the obedience of faith, in the sense of *fides divina et catholica*. And yet this does not by any means relegate such statements to the sector of what is not obligatory at all, and a matter of pure choice. Nor are they solely disciplinary. Catholics are required to enter into such statements with a religiously motivated inner assent, and to go along with them. But this assent and response includes co-responsibility, spiritually and morally. The possibility that here the individual Christian, after a mature examination of conscience, may arrive at a different judgment from that of the church's magisterium, is in line with the best theological tradition.

It was Karl Rahner in particular who demanded an existential hermeneutics of this kind, a hermeneutics which in no way excludes what is generally essential, but which puts this into practice existentially – which means in a way that is unique in every case. The challenge of the last council still exists, as we can see from a glance at the present discussion in moral theology. In the Pastoral Constitution especially, the council has left us a rich inheritance, although admittedly this is certainly still awaiting its full development.

6. New challenges

In the last twenty years the challenge of the council has if anything increased. For in the meantime the external and internal circumstances of its reception have changed profoundly, and have become considerably more difficult. Changes in the third world and in the young churches are the most striking. The church's centre of gravity is increasingly shifting away from Europe to the churches in the southern hemisphere. In the face of the enormous social problems of these regions, the option for a church of the poor is moving more and more clearly into the foreground – and rightly so. A hermeneutics of the conciliar statements which will meet this situation is an urgent requirement rightly put forward by liberation theology, even though this requirement has not yet been satisfactorily met.

In Western Europe and North America (and I shall confine myself to these regions, for reasons of competence) there was a kind of cultural revolution soon after the council. This led to a serious breach with tradition, and to a re-ideologization of Western society, above all among the intellectuals and in the modern mass media. It became obvious that material superfluity was largely matched by spiritual emptiness. New social and economic problems (especially mass unemployment), which were unknown in the prosperous years of the council, contributed to the situation. The result is a widespread indifference towards questions of faith, a profound lack of confidence about fundamental anthropological values, and – in the ethical sector – a lack of orientation to which we may even give the name of crisis.

These shocks and tremors found their way with surprising rapidity into the church as well, and led to a crisis of Catholic identity. The contours of what is Catholic have largely speaking become blurred. The situation in the churches of Western Europe and North America has meanwhile begun to stabilize again; but in spite of that, the more profound problems involved in this post-conciliar upheaval and erosion have by no means been dealt with. In spite of many encouraging new beginnings and movements in the spiritual field, there is a general lack of drive, perspective and hope. Of impatient and hectic activism we have more than enough; but this is no substitute for genuine new vigour. It is more of a hindrance.

The subject to which theology and the church have to devote themselves in this situation is above all the human presuppositions for faith (*praeambula fidei*), and the ways of arriving at faith. Ultimately, what is at stake is the question of God. In the Pastoral Constitution *Gaudium et spes*, the council said some essential things here, and also some new ones. But all the same, as a whole the council's interest was too much confined to the church. It paid less attention to the real foundation and content of faith, which is God, than it did to the church's mediation of faith. In this respect especially, Vatican II is a challenge. It challenges us, in complete faithfulness to the tradition to which the council testified, to go beyond the actual conciliar texts themselves and – in the face of modern atheism – to develop anew the message about the triune God, the God of Jesus, in its meaning for the salvation of men and women and the world.

Ultimately speaking, the whole labour of the council, the post-conciliar reforms and the dispute about them, will have been worth while only if more faith, hope and love grows out of them. This and this alone is the final criterion for every conciliar hermeneutics. For this alone meets the pastoral concern of this council, properly understood. At the moment, down-to-earth observers of the church's life may have serious and well-founded doubts as to whether the council really achieved this goal. But I myself have no doubt that the council's hour is still to come, and that its seed will spring up and bear rich fruit in the field of history.

X

Aspects of the Eucharist in Their Unity and Variety

On the Recent Discussion about the Fundamental Form and Meaning of the Eucharist

1. The eucharist as Jesus' testament

'On the evening before he suffered', 'on the night when he was betrayed' – with this dating the church, in celebrating the eucharist, gives the historical and factual reason for what it does. It traces back the eucharist to Jesus' own act of institution on the evening before his death, seeing the wish that impelled him not merely as the unique historical starting point of the eucharist celebration, but as its enduring factual norm as well.

In examining the four accounts of the Last Supper in the New Testament, historical criticism often disputed this historical and factual legitimation, therefore allowing a gulf to open up between Jesus and the church, the Last Supper and the eucharist.[1] Scholars then saw Jesus (as some do still) in the tradition of the prophetic criticism of the cult, and interpreted 'the breaking of bread' in the early church as a common meal without any cultic significance, and without any special relationship to Jesus' Last Supper. It was only in Hellenistic Christianity, these scholars maintain, that these meals were remoulded into the sacramental Supper of the Lord, under the influence of the heathen cultic mysteries.[2] But at this point there was no way of proceeding beyond general analogies; for the double gesture which characterizes the accounts of the Last Supper – the breaking and distribution of the bread, and the drinking from the one cup – cannot in fact be explained by anything in the mystery religions. On the other hand these gestures can be fitted without any trouble into the rite of the festal Jewish meal (or passover supper).[3] This is true above all of the element which very early on already gave the name of eucharist to the whole ceremony. For the name eucharist goes back to the words of praise or blessing (*berakah, eulogia, eucharistia*) which the head of the family spoke over the third cup of wine, the cup of blessing (cf. I Cor. 10.16).[4]

If we look more closely, however, we shall find that at the Last Supper Jesus did not merely take over already existing Jewish table customs. He altered them as well, giving them a new emphasis in two ways. Departing from Jewish custom, Jesus passed the head of the family's cup to all those at table, so that they could drink from it; and he accompanied the offering of the bread and the cup with interpretative words.[5] So ultimately speaking, Jesus' Last Supper is without analogy. It is *sui generis*, and breaks through all the known categories.[6]

The different versions which we find in the four New Testament accounts, however, show that in these we do not necessarily have to do with Jesus' very own words. We encounter what Jesus said and did rather through the medium of faith and the liturgy of the early church. Paul explicitly calls his account of the Lord's Supper a tradition which he had 'received from the Lord' (I Cor. 11.23).[7] Since in all the texts earlier elements of the tradition have been passed down in different ways, the tradition's original form can hardly be reconstructed, or at most extremely hypothetically; and even less can we be sure of the original wording of Jesus' words of interpretation and institution.[8] This does not jeopardize the authenticity of the accounts of the Last Supper. For they all agree in reporting the unique event, which is without analogy, and which even from a purely historical standpoint can find an adequate foundation and explanation only in Jesus himself.

This is all the more certain because the words and gestures of Jesus passed down to us are demonstrably entirely in accord with his message and behaviour. Their inner logic can be comprehended only against the background of Jesus' life.[9] For Jesus' proclamation is characterized, not merely by the message of the imminent coming of God's *basileia*, but also by the way this message is linked with his own coming and his own person. Another characteristic point is that Jesus sees the coming of the *basileia* in the image of the meal, and that he celebrates it in anticipation in meals. His last meal too, as its eschatological outlook shows, belongs within the perspective and drive of the *basileia* which is thrusting its way into the world (Mark 14.25). The same *logion* also shows that Jesus holds fast to this message of his in the face of his rejection and impending death. God's faithfulness proves itself even in human faithlessness, and there most of all. God now links his salvation more closely than ever to Jesus' person, and appoints him the Servant of God who gives his life vicariously 'for the many' (Mark 14.24; I Cor. 11.24, following Isa. 53.10ff.). So through his death as representative 'for the many', he institutes the new covenant in his blood (Luke 22.10; I Cor. 11.25, following Jer. 31.31).[10] At the Last Supper Jesus proclaims this new saving reality; at the same time he shows the new community of salvation symbolically in the emblematic acts of distributing bread and wine; finally he explicitly identifies himself with the gifts of bread and wine offered in the meal, thus making it clear that, in the giving of his own person, he himself is the new covenant, the eschatological reality of salvation.

Jesus' words and gestures at his Last Supper are therefore the summing up of his whole life. And they are at the same time the anticipatory interpretation of his death. They are guaranteed, as it were, by his life and above all by his death. Without his life and his death they would be a valueless currency, so to speak.[11] In the context of his life and death, they are his 'last will and testament', through which his work is to go on living and operating beyond his death. More: this bequest is his bequest of himself, through which he himself wishes to remain present with, and for, those who belong to him. Jesus' bequest of himself as an enduring presence is therefore *the starting point and the foundation of the eucharist.*[12]

In taking this last will and testament of Jesus as their starting point, the Catholic doctrine of the eucharist and the Protestant doctrine of the Lord's Supper are completely at one. Luther interpreted the Lord's Supper entirely in the light of this last will of Jesus, seeing it as the summing up of his incarnation and death. But by interpreting the *testamentum* in a one-sided way as an endorsement of the promise of the forgiveness of sins, he was bound to lay an equally one-sided stress on passive reception in faith, and to play off this element against the aspect of giving and self-giving. So he makes a sharp distinction between the *sacramentum*, which is received passively, and the *sacrificium*, which is performed actively, and which he condemns in sharpest form. His doctrine of the Lord's Supper is based on a christology 'from above'. It is entirely katabatic: the movement is only from above to below. The other, anabatic element – the movement from below upwards – is excluded.[13]

But of course if we consider Jesus' own legacy of himself, it is not difficult to perceive two dimensions. For in the words of institution, Jesus interprets his sacrifice of his own life by way of the passives of the body given and the blood shed. These Semitic forms, with their reverently veiled language, express God's act, to which Jesus conforms through his act of obedience. Because he owes himself wholly to God the Father – that is, sees himself, literally, as 'thanks to God' – the anticipatory making-present of the new saving reality in the Supper takes place in praise and thanksgiving. This thanksgiving is the verbal expression of an act of sacrificial surrender of his own person to the Father's will. So the sacrificial terminology about the shed blood of the covenant which we find in Matthew's version (Matt. 26.28, following Ex. 24.8) is not fortuitous. It is necessary, because it is true to fact.[14] Jesus' self-expending surrender of himself 'for the many' is the other side of his sacrificial self-surrender to the Father. So it is precisely in his giving of himself to the Father that in the Lord's Supper he makes himself the gift of salvation for men and women.

Jesus' Last Supper therefore discloses in summary form, not only his commission, but also his profoundest nature. He is Being from God and for God, and in this he is at the same time Being for human beings. He is in person *eucharistia* and *eulogia*, thanksgiving and blessing. In this all-embracing sense, the person of Jesus is the pivot of the whole, and christology is the background of the eucharist and the approach from which to understand it. As far as the present discussion is concerned, this means that any approach to an understanding of the eucharist which is purely functional, or purely existential, falls short from the very outset.[15]

2. The eucharist as a memorial (*anamnesis*)

If, in considering the foundations of the eucharist, we begin radically with christology, as we have tried to do here, then the eucharistic celebration cannot be an addition, let alone a complement to the Christ event, especially the event of the cross. But neither must it be understood as the prolongation or repetition of that event. The eucharist is subject to the decree that the Christ event and the event of the cross were once and for all. The relation between the eucharist on the one hand, and the Christ event and event of the cross on the other, can therefore be described only with the help of the biblical category of memorial (*zikkaron*; *anamnesis*; *memoria*) – the remembrance that makes the thing remembered actually present.

The Pauline and Lucan accounts of the Last Supper already include the formula: 'Do this in remembrance of me' (Luke 22.19; I Cor. 11.24, 25). The origin of this command for repetition is disputed.[16] Now that a derivation from the Hellenistic meal in remembrance of the dead has (rightly) been abandoned, and since a derivation from the mystery religions by way of a mystery theology has also proved highly problematical historically speaking, interest is now concentrated on a derivation from the Old Testament and Judaism.[17] Memorial in the biblical sense is at all events never a merely subjective remembrance. It is a liturgical, sacramental memorial celebration in which a past salvific act is made objectively present by means of a true symbol. This applies to the Feast of Tabernacles, for example (Lev. 23.33ff.), and above all to the Passover, as a day for remembering the liberation from Egyptian slavery (Ex. 12.14). By way of this remembrance, in each generation, everyone is in duty bound 'to look upon himself as if he had come out of Egypt'.[18] Through the liturgical actualization, the past act of salvation is supposed to be laid before God, and is pleaded before him, so that he may remember it and bring it to eschatological fulfilment. The recollecting glance back by way of an actualization in the present is therefore linked with an eschatological glance forward to future fulfilment. So in the biblical memorial, all three temporal dimensions are brought together in an accelerated, quick-motion process.

Quite early on, the Fathers of the church used biblical typological thinking to help them to develop the idea of objective, sacramental actualization. Later, in order to make the eucharist comprehensible, they drew on the Platonic notion of the true symbol.[19] In Thomas Aquinas, the eucharist is still – like every sacrament – the actualizing *signum rememorativum* of the salvific act which took place once and for all, a *signum demonstrativum* of the salvation which takes place in the present, and a *signum prognosticum* – an anticipation of the eschatological banquet in the kingdom of God.[20] The familiar antiphon to the Magnificat at the feast of Corpus Christi brings out this triple dimension in poetical language: 'recolitur memoria passionis eius, mens impletur gratia et futurae gloriae nobis pignus datur.' ('The memorial of his passion is renewed, the mind is filled with grace, and a pledge of future glory is given to us.') In this comprehensive sense, the eucharistic liturgy, immediately after the words of institution, goes on to speak about the remembrance of Jesus Christ, his death, resurrection and exaltation, as well as his coming again.

Unfortunately, in the course of the Middle Ages this grandiose unified vision was lost. After the second eucharistic dispute in the eleventh century, there came to be a cleavage between archetype and reflection, type, symbol and *figura* on the one hand, and *veritas* on the other. Originally a symbol had been viewed as something which in a certain sense *is* what it signifies; but it now came to be understood as something which *is not really* that which it signifies.[21] In order to bar the way to pure symbolism, and to preserve the reality of Jesus' presence in the eucharist, the Real Presence of Jesus Christ's flesh and blood came to be separated from the anamnetic, symbolic actualization of the sacrifice on the cross. In this way the presence of the saving person and the fruit of salvation could be explained, but no longer the presence of the salvific event itself; and the sacrament and sacrifice of the eucharist had to be separated from one another. Because the eucharist could no longer be understood as a true sacramental symbol of Christ's passion, the sacrificial character of the eucharist and its relationship to the sacrifice on the cross was bound to become a completely insoluble problem.[22]

It is only against this background that the disputes of the Reformation period about the sacrifice of the mass are fully comprehensible. In actual fact, in the sixteenth century both sides lacked adequate categories for solving the question. With the aid of the categories *repraesentatio, memoria* and *applicatio*, the Council of Trent succeeded in finding a felicitous conceptual formulation,[23] with the help of which it was able to parry the Protestant reproach of an idolatrous addition to the sacrifice on the cross through the independent sacrifice of the mass. But in the post-Tridentine era, the many theories about the sacrifice of the mass show how little this dogmatic explanation succeeded in achieving an adequate theological clarification of the *repraesentatio passionis*.

It was the biblical, liturgical and patristic revival of our own century which for the first time brought about a new situation, and with it new possibilities for ecumenical dialogue also.[24] In Catholic theology, the basic substantial concern of Odo Casel's mystery theology came to be generally accepted (a concern which must be distinguished from the historical justification and the detailed theological explication). According to this interpretation, the saving act which took place once and for all is made present through true symbols. This view was finally officially accepted by the Second Vatican Council.[25]

The revival of the theology of the Word of God proved to be no less important, and even more helpful ecumenically, as a way of understanding the objective presence of the sacrifice on the cross, which took place once and for all. For Paul, to celebrate the Lord's supper was to proclaim the Lord's death 'until he comes' (I Cor. 11.26). The celebration of the eucharist is accordingly embodied word, a public and solemn proclamation of the unique historical happening which through this utterance becomes present, or discloses its presence, thus becoming a public reality, something that is both promise and claim for the individual and for the congregation.[26] Just as the Jewish prayer over bread and wine was an *anamnesis* of God's saving acts, so the eucharist is an *anamnesis* in word and act, in which Jesus' death and resurrection are actually made present; and this *anamnesis* is joined with the prayer for his coming: *maranatha* (I Cor. 16.22).

We may therefore sum up by saying that while Jesus' institution is the starting point and foundation of the eucharist, the *anamnesis* of Christ provides *the inward unity of its different aspects*. Through this memorial, the death and resurrection of Jesus Christ are made sacramentally present in the feast in the form of bread and wine, the Lord who is present is extolled, and his final coming implored; and thus the fellowship (*communio*) with the Lord is communicated. The presence of Christ's person and work, sacramentally mediated through remembrance in word and act, is therefore the inward unifying ground for the different aspects of the eucharist.[27]

3. The eucharist as thanksgiving and sacrifice

Jesus' institution was accompanied by thanksgiving, and it is in thanksgiving that the living remembrance of his saving act is celebrated still. Gratitude and indebtedness is the fundamental creaturely attitude of human beings before God. In salvation history, thanksgiving expresses most clearly the attitude of pure receptiveness in accepting the deeds and gifts of salvation. Praise and thanksgiving (*berakah*) are therefore one element – indeed the fundamental element – in the Jewish grace at table, and especially in the passover liturgy. Eulogy and eucharist are also constitutive elements in Jesus' institution of the Lord's Supper (Mark 14.22, 23; I Cor. 11.24).[28] So, very early on, the word eucharist could be used to describe the whole ceremony of the Lord's Supper.[29] Since earliest times, down to the present day, the central part of the eucharistic celebration begins with the invitation: 'gratias agamus', 'let us give thanks to the Lord our God', and then goes on to proclaim and commemorate in thanksgiving God's saving acts.[30] The Lord's Supper may therefore be characterized as memorial in praise; and this has rightly been seen as the basic form of the eucharistic celebration.[31]

Thanksgiving was already associated with the idea of sacrifice from an early period. The Old Testament already talks about the sacrifice of praise (*todah*), in which bread and wine evidently played an important part,[32] as well as the *hostia laudis*, the sacrifice of thanksgiving (Ps. 50. 14, 23; cf. 116.17; 119.108). The Epistle to the Hebrews takes up this term (Heb. 13.15), and from there it passed into the Roman canon. In this way Scripture personalizes the idea of sacrifice (cf. Ps. 40.7; 51.18f.; Heb. 10.5–10). The Suffering Servant's vicarious sacrifice of his life, above all (Isa. 53.4f., 10ff.), is understood, not as a cultic sacrifice in the technical sense, but as a martyrdom, as the total sacrifice of the person.[33] Philo spiritualized Old Testament sacrificial ideas, and through his mediation it was possible very early on for the Fathers to interpret the eucharist as sacrifice.[34] In Irenaeus, the gifts of bread and wine are then put in the foreground, in antithesis to the gnostic contempt for the material; they are as it were the expression in true symbolic form of the sacrificial attitude which expresses itself personally in thanksgiving. It is therefore no great step from 'gratias agamus' to the *office*, the *oblatio* (*prosphora*, *anaphora*) – even to the *sacrificium* (*thysia*). So if the *oblatio* is increasingly emphasized in the concept of the *eucharistia*, this need be seen as nothing more than a development of what was present from the very beginning.[35]

A development of this kind is unexceptionable, indeed fruitful, as long as it does not isolate a single element from the whole, and as long as the proportions of the whole are preserved. But in the course of the Middle Ages this unified whole was lost.[36] Once the offering of the gifts in thanksgiving ceased to be seen as the sacramental form in which the one sacrifice of Jesus Christ is made present in remembrance, there was a danger that the sacrifice of the mass would acquire independence – would become something on its own. It was against this that the Reformers protested. They could now understand the eucharist only as a *mere* thank-offering for the forgiveness of sins received, but no longer as an efficacious sacrament through which the sacrifice on the cross is made present.[37] To the degree in which today the sacramental meaning of the eucharist is being rediscovered (which means that the eucharist is understood as a sacramental form which has as its content the one sacrifice of Jesus Christ) the way is slowly being prepared, though in a difficult process, for a consensus in this controversial question.[38]

Yet this is of course only one side of the problem, and the easier side. The other side is very much more difficult ecumenically. And that is the following question: to what extent is the eucharist not merely the actualization of the sacrifice of Jesus Christ, but also a sacrifice on the part of the church? Or it would be better to say: is the sacrifice of the church in thanksgiving the sacramental form of Christ's present sacrifice? And if so, how? This question brings to a head the fundamental problem of whether and in what respect the eucharist has an anabatic dimension (from below upwards) as well as a katabatic one (from above to below) – this anabatic dimension meaning that the church, as the body of Christ, is included in the sacrifice of Christ and, as the bride of Christ, also shares in the realization of his sacrifice in obedient subordination.[39] Scripture testifies that this is fundamentally conceivable, biblically speaking, wherever – as in the psalms, for example – the human response to God's word is understood as being itself, in its turn, God's word. Here giving and receiving are not parallel, let alone opposed to one another; they are intertwined.

If thanksgiving is the fundamental form of the eucharist, then the primal meaning of the eucharist celebration is the *cultus divinus*, the glorification, adoration, praise and exaltation of God in the remembrance of his mighty acts. This aspect – the supreme worship of God in the assembly of his people – is becoming more and more difficult in our society, aligned as it is towards human needs and their satisfaction.

This is surely the real reason for the liturgical crisis and the widespread incapacity for liturgy. Yet in this social situation especially, feast and celebration are healthful, indeed necessary, even from a purely anthropological point of view, as a liberation from the thraldom of what society is able to find comprehensible.⁴⁰ A reduction of the eucharist to its purely anthropological significance would therefore be a false contemporization of the church and its liturgy. The theological arguments already put forward make this sufficiently clear. According to these arguments, to glorify God is the salvation of human beings. Glorification is the making-present of salvation in sacramental form. This second meaning and purpose of the liturgy is therefore not something tacked on to the first. It is an intrinsic part of it. 'The glory of God is the person who is truly alive.'⁴¹

4. The eucharist as *epiklesis*

Thanksgiving as the movement of the human being towards God is of course not a 'meritorious work' on the part of the person himself, and not an independent, autonomous achievement of the person or the church. According to Scripture, it is the work of the Spirit, an *oratio infusa*, so to speak, through which the grace given by God streams back to God.⁴² Thus out of inner necessity the eucharist becomes an *epiklesis*, the prayer for the sending forth of the Spirit, so that he may perfect the acts of salvation which become present in the *anamnesis*. The *epiklesis*⁴³ is therefore *the inmost soul of the eucharist*, as it were. In this sense the eucharist or *prosphora* and *epiklesis* together constitute the form which the Lord's supper takes.⁴⁴

The eucharist as a prayer for God's blessing is ultimately embedded in the biblical understanding of the term *berakah/eulogia* (or *eucharistia*) which is of central importance for the Jewish grace at table, and for the Christian eucharistic celebration. For this word means both God's blessing on human beings and the human being's blessing of God – the praise and adoration of his name.⁴⁵ So Paul talks explicitly about 'the cup of blessing which we bless [over which we speak the blessing]' (I Cor. 10.16).

Because the eucharist is a prayer for blessing and a gift conferring blessing, the ground was already paved in the ancient church for a shift in its significance. In the course of the Middle Ages this new stress increasingly came to prevail, and meant that thanksgiving and adoration no longer *rose up* to God, but that *the descent* of God's blessing was implored. This change of direction comes out with unequivocal clarity when Isidore of Seville translates *eucharistia* as *bona gratia*.[46] It was this interpretation of the eucharist as prayer and gift which led to the description of the eucharist as the mass, a term which later came to be the name most generally used. The original meaning of *missa* is probably derived from the rite of dismissal which was linked with the final benediction: *ite, missa est*. Starting from this conclusion, the whole eucharist was viewed as a blessing.[47] Features of a solemn blessing are part of the Roman canon,[48] in which the Preface (the real prayer of thanksgiving) is immediately followed by the prayer: 'Through him we ask you to accept and bless these gifts we offer you in sacrifice.' The words of institution also are directly preceded by the petition: 'Grant O God these gifts your abundant blessing.' These benedictions are generally speaking little understood today; but without them the eucharist would lose its soul, and would become a soulless, purely external, or at least purely human, act. It is therefore a particular reason for gratitude that in the present ecumenical discussion, the sense of the eucharist as gift has again become central.[49]

According to Scripture, the realization of Jesus Christ's saving work in the world and in individual men and women is the work of the Holy Spirit. The Spirit is *the* eschatological gift *per se*. Thus for Paul, *pneuma* is a key concept for his understanding of the eucharist (cf. I Cor. 10.3f.).[50] Following John 6.52ff. and I Cor. 10.3f., the tension between bodily and spiritual reception puts its stamp on the whole tradition.[51] As a prayer for the coming of the Spirit on the assembled congregation and on the gifts offered, the *epiklesis* explicitly brings out this aspect. Indeed the eucharist as a whole is first and foremost *epiklesis*; the special *epiklesis* (which is located and interpreted differently in the various liturgical traditions) is no more than an explicit expression of the supplicatory character of the whole.[52] The *epiklesis* makes it clear that the eucharist is not at the disposal of the church or the celebrant, and is not something which happens automatically. The eucharist is a humble yet assured and potent prayer for the efficacy of the Holy Spirit. For that reason, the revival of the *epiklesis* in the post-conciliar liturgy of the mass is extremely important, both fundamentally and ecumenically. This is true not only in relation to the Eastern churches (which ascribe to the *epiklesis* a very special importance, which was actually controversial for a long time[53]), but in relation to the Protestant churches too, since they also belong to the Latin liturgical tradition in having no explicit *epiklesis*, yet often criticize the Roman view of the eucharist for its 'objectivism' and 'legalism'.[54]

Stress on the *epiklesis* throws new light on the mass as 'sacrifice'. It enables us to make clear in a new way that, just as Jesus offered his sacrifice on the cross in the Spirit (Heb. 9.14), so the sacrifice of the mass is an offering in the Spirit, an *oblatio rationalis* – a 'reasonable offering' as the liturgical texts say, taking up Rom. 12.1 and I Peter 2.5.[55] The personalization and spiritualization of the Christian interpretation of sacrifice which we have discussed, must therefore ultimately be understood as a 'pneumatologization'. For it is the Spirit who confers openness for God and other human beings. It is the Spirit alone who enables us to pray 'Abba, Father' (Rom. 8.15; Gal. 4.6). So it is the Spirit too who – as the third eucharistic prayer says – makes us acceptable to God, an offering in Spirit and in truth.

5. The eucharist as communion

It is the mission of the Holy Spirit to give universal effect to Christ's work, and so to integrate the world and history 'into Christ'. Consequently the efficacy of the Holy Spirit in the eucharist is directed towards *koinonia* (*communio*) in and with Jesus Christ. This communion is both personal, being participation in Christ and the most intimate personal fellowship with him, and is also, ecclesially, community in Christ.[56] Personal and ecclesial *communio* is the purpose and *the fulfilment of the eucharistic celebration*. It reaches its goal in 'the peace' and in the communion. So the eucharist is, in Augustine's words, a sign of unity and a bond of love.[57]

This aspect too goes back ultimately to Jesus' institution, which took place in the framework of a shared festal meal. The special thing about it was that Jesus departed from custom by letting all those present share the one cup, so giving them all a share in himself, and thereby establishing the new covenant. In the liturgical movement this has often led to the conclusion that the basic form of the eucharist is the meal.[58] In liturgical practice, this thesis about the eucharist as meal has sometimes led to highly wilful experiments in which, in extreme cases – and contrary to I Cor. 11.27ff. – the celebration of the eucharist is hardly to be distinguished from a banquet or a party. But of course the thesis about the 'meal' character overlooks the fact that although the decisive and distinguishing feature of what Jesus did certainly belonged within the framework of a meal, it none the less broke through the usual form in which a meal was held. The repetition of Jesus' special words and gestures then very soon began to replace the normal meal for satisfying hunger. This is already evident in Paul (I Cor. 11.17–34), and the process was already completed by the second century.[59] This is clearly brought out by the fact that the celebration of the eucharist was moved to the early morning.[60] The term 'Lord's Supper' for the eucharist, then, is a complete novelty in Catholic tradition, and in liturgical history too.[61] It would therefore be better to talk about the eucharist as a fellowship, and about its ecclesial dimension, rather than to say that it has the character of a meal.

The connection between the eucharist and the church is explicitly brought out in Scripture. We find it in the accounts of the Last Supper, in the phrase about 'the blood of the covenant' (Mark 14.22; Matt. 26.28), or 'the new covenant in my blood' (Luke 22.20; I Cor. 11.25).[62] This indicates that the eucharist is a sign of the new era of salvation and the new saving order – a sign imbued with fulfilled reality. This new reality of salvation embraces both the relationship of human beings to God, and their relationship to one another. Paul thinks this through to the end. For him, participation in the eucharistic body of the Lord is at the same time fellowship with the body of Christ in the church (I Cor. 10.16f.). When it celebrates the eucharist, the church is therefore the new order of salvation.[63] Hardly anyone has understood this connection as profoundly as Augustine. He could actually say: 'So if you yourselves be the body of Christ and his members, then on the eucharistic table lies your own mystery . . . You shall be what you see, and you shall receive what you are.'[64]

In the context of the second eucharistic dispute in the eleventh century, the connection between the sacramental body of Christ, which up to then had been called Christ's mystical body, and the ecclesial body of Christ was lost. In the disputes of that time, the expression 'Christ's mystical body' had become open to misunderstanding, and was used in a purely symbolic sense; so people talked instead about the true body of Christ. The church was now called the mystical body of Christ. This meant that awareness of the connection between the eucharist and the church was largely lost.[65] Theologians of the stature of Thomas Aquinas were certainly still very much aware of the connection, and stressed it.[66] But in general, eucharistic interpretation and practice came to be individualized and privatized to a disastrous degree.

This one-sided development was only halted by the liturgical movement of our own century, and by the Second Vatican Council, although the ground for the change had been prepared by the romantically influenced theology of the nineteenth century, and especially by J. A. Möhler's interpretation of the church. Now the liturgically gathered people of God was once more seen as the active subject of the eucharistic liturgy, and the *actuosa participatio* of all those present was emphasized as both the norm and the ideal.[67] Admittedly the community mass (as it was called at the beginning of the liturgical movement) was often played off to such a degree against the private mass (which was now disapproved of) that too little attention was frequently given to the indispensable personal element: the personal communion with Christ, which includes personal conversion and personal prayer, personal thanksgiving and adoration.[68] Some present-day forms for administering and receiving the sacrament of the altar would in earlier centuries quite simply have been termed sacrilegious.[69] A proper balance between personal and ecclesial communion has evidently not yet been found.

The ecclesial dimension of the eucharist has consequences for the question about admission to the eucharistic fellowship. A Lord's Supper which is open, not only to the church but to the world as well,[70] would seem from this aspect to be excluded from the outset. The eucharist, as the sacrament of faith and sign of unity, presupposes that those partaking share the same faith and baptism. It purifies, matures and deepens this already given and premised unity.[71] This reciprocal relationship between eucharist and church is constitutive for the question about eucharistic fellowship between churches and church groups with whom the Catholic Church is not in full communion. According to the Catholic view (and even more in Orthodox eyes), the eucharist as the sacrament of unity presupposes the full community of the church. This is expressed especially in fellowship with the diocesan bishop and with the bishop of Rome, as successor of Peter, whose office is a ministry of the church's unity. It is therefore not a purely superficial matter when the names of bishop and pope are included in the canon of the mass. It is an expression of the *communio* within which alone the individual eucharistic celebration is meaningful, in the light of its profoundest essence. It is only in the light of this wider context that we can then understand why the question of eucharistic fellowship should come to a head in the question of the ministry.[72] This question must not be seen in isolation, but must be treated in the total context of the eucharist as *communio*.

To reduce the discussion about the *communio* dimension of the eucharist to the question about the ministry would therefore be extremely one-sided, indeed fatal. The eucharist as *communio* has important ethical aspects as well.[73] Even in the primitive church there were problems about table and eucharistic fellowship between Jewish and Gentile Christians (in Antioch) and between the poor and the rich (in Corinth). There are similar conflicts today in South Africa and Latin America – and not only there! It is certainly contrary to the nature of the eucharist, and contrary to the relevant decisions of the early church, to turn the eucharist into a race or class eucharist, either by making it the exclusive eucharistic celebration of the privileged, or by making it the revolutionary celebration of the under-privileged. But the nature of the eucharist is equally violated if we fail to recognize the ethical presuppositions and consequences of the common celebration: the practically realized *agape* (cf. Matt. 5.23f.), whose minimum requirement is the fulfilment of the demands of social justice. We cannot share the eucharistic bread without sharing our daily bread as well. It is not for nothing that the eucharistic assembly ends with the sending out into the world of those gathered. Gathering and sending forth are two poles which must not be separated or played off against one another. Without the gathering, the going forth becomes inwardly empty and hollow; but the gathering without the going forth becomes sterile and ultimately unconvincing.

6. The eucharist as an eschatological sign

The communion of the eucharist points beyond itself to the world and its eschatological consummation. Consequently it has not merely a social dimension, but a universal and cosmic dimension as well. Here we can do no more than touch on this, indicating the forward direction our glance should take.[74]

For Jesus himself, the eschatological glance forward to the coming kingdom of God was already a constitutive part of the Last Supper (Mark 14.25ff.). Paul talks explicitly about proclaiming the Lord's death 'until he comes' (I Cor. 11.26), and the first congregation in Jerusalem celebrated the daily breaking of bread in joyful anticipation of the *eschaton* (Acts 2.46). Festivity and celebration therefore belong essentially to the eucharistic celebration, and they must not be swept aside from the outset as pomp or triumphalism, or fall victim to a joyless puritanism or a flat de-sacralization. This will affect our attitude to church buildings, church decorations, church music, language, vestments, rites, and so forth. In the whole way it is celebrated, the eucharist should be a foretaste of the coming kingdom of God.

The anticipatory celebration of the heavenly marriage feast draws in the whole creation, in sacramental symbolism. The offering of bread and wine, 'fruits of the earth and of human labour,' looks forward to the eschatological glorification of God through the whole creation, and in the transformation of these gifts anticipates the eschatological transformation of the world. In the first, third and fourth eucharistic prayers, the good gifts of creation which Christ fills with life, and sanctifies, are therefore explicitly drawn into the great closing doxology. In this way the eucharist is what Karl Rahner calls the liturgy of the world, or – in Teilhard de Chardin's words – 'the mass of the world'.

7. The eucharist – the summing-up of the Christian mystery of salvation

Now that we have presented the various different aspects of the eucharist, we have to ask in closing: what, then, *is* the eucharist? The answer can only be: the eucharist makes present the whole Christian mystery of salvation, and sums it up sacramentally. It embraces creation and the eschatological new creation; it expresses the movement of God to human beings, as well as the responding movement of human beings and humanity to God; it is the all-comprehensive legacy of the life, death and resurrection of Jesus Christ; it is the glorification of God and the salvation of men and women, personally and ecclesially; it is gift and charge in one. We cannot therefore understand the eucharist if we start from only one of its manifold aspects. It is not solely, or even primarily, a meal; nor is it only thanksgiving and sacrifice. It is at once God's gift (katabatically) and grateful, sacrificial self-giving (anabatically), because it makes Jesus Christ present in his person and his work – the Christ who is in one person God's gift of himself and the self-giving response to that gift.[75]

But we cannot stop short even at this glorious all-embracing vision, inspired by Origen. Everything depends essentially on a closer understanding of the unity of the two movements within this christological approach. It is only in answering this question that we can discover an answer to the question about the unity of the different aspects of the eucharist. For the God-man Jesus Christ is not the subsequent 'glueing together' of a divine and a human nature. The person of the Logos is rather the ground of subsistence for the human person of Jesus, who is the true and perfected human being – indeed *the* new human being – above all in his radically 'owed', relational existence and in his radical, self-giving obedience. In his ultimate selflessness and in his giving of himself to the Father and to human beings, Jesus Christ is wholly God and wholly man. In analogy to this christological statement about his Being, the katabatic and the anabatic movements in the eucharist do not follow on one another; they are intertwined. In the eucharist, in analogy to the Christ event, the gifts of creation, bread and wine, are possessed, appropriated, in such a way that they lose their own independent substance, become pure signs, and thus sacramentally symbolize Jesus' sacrificial mode of existence.[76] This again comes about when, in the Holy Spirit, the church is drawn into Jesus' sacrificial attitude, and so becomes wholly one with him and in him. The eucharistic Real Presence; the eucharist as sacrifice; the eucharist as sacrament: in scholastic theology these three aspects of the eucharist stand parallel to one another and follow one another, in a rather unrelated way. But these three aspects constitute an indissoluble inner unity. They are aspects of a single whole, the sacramental making-present of the one mystery of salvation, Jesus Christ.

But we can and must go beyond even the christological perspective.

The mystery of Jesus Christ can only be understood as a revelation of the trinitarian mystery; and the same is true of the eucharist. It has an ultimately trinitarian structure.[77] In thanksgiving, it is directed to the Father, the source and origin of all being, and of the whole history of salvation; in thanksgiving, the church also receives in the eucharist the unique gift of God to human beings, his communication of himself in Jesus Christ, so as to be joined with him in innermost communion. And both movements, again, take place in the power of the Holy Spirit, who also prepares us for fellowship with Christ and allows this fellowship to become fruitful in Christian living. Finally, in the eucharist the mutual self-communication and self-giving of the trinitarian persons are sacramentally manifested and become present. If the trinitarian confession is the dogmatic summing up of the whole mystery of salvation, the eucharist is *the sacramental summing up* of that mystery. Both in their different ways are a 'symbol' – both creed and emblem – of the one mystery of God's salvation through Jesus Christ in the Holy Spirit.

If we start from a comprehensive understanding of the eucharist like this, it is possible to develop the basic lines of a eucharistic spirituality. Such a eucharistic spirituality would have to be the most intimate unity of receiving and giving, contemplation and action. It would have to be strong enough to overcome the disastrous antitheses and conflicts in the present life of the church, conflicts which actually threaten the understanding and practice of the eucharist itself. It would have to enable us to understand as a single unity the gathering for worship *and* the sending forth into the world of that gathered congregation.

Notes

Introduction: Systematic Theology Today and the Tasks Before It

1. For a fuller account of the development of dogmatics, cf. W. Kasper, *Die Methoden der Dogmatik. Einheit und Vielfalt*, Munich 1967; also 'Dogmatik als Wissenschaft', *ThQ* 157, 1977, 189–203; also 'Dogmatik' in *NHThG* I 1984, 193–203; also 'Zur Wissenschaftspraxis der Theologie' in W. Kern, H. J. Pottmeyer and M. Seckler (eds.), *Handbuch der Fundamentaltheologie*, vol. 4, Freiburg, Basle and Vienna (in preparation). On the development in the church: W. Kasper, *Zukunft aus der Kraft des Konzils*, Freiburg, Basle and Vienna 1986, 49–54, 64–68.

2. Cf. here W. Kasper, 'Säkularisierung', *Staatslexikon* IV, Freiburg (in preparation). On the closely connected problem of pluralism I have learnt from North American theologians: B. Lonergan, *Theologie im Pluralismus heutiger Kulturen*, QD 67, 1975; D. Tracy, *The Analogical Imagination. Christian Theology and the Culture of Pluralism*, New York 1981.

3. My book *Dogma unter dem Wort Gottes*, Mainz 1965, had a certain tendency in this direction. The distinction (not division) between philosophical and theological truth which is made there (in spite of some clear differentiations) is problematical, in the light of historical findings as well. Hence my critical development 'Das Wahrheitsverständnis der Theologie' in E. Coreth (ed.), *Wahrheit in Einheit und Vielheit*, Düsseldorf 1987. However, I have already clearly stated the fundamental importance of a new metaphysical basis for theology in *Das Absolute in der Geschichte. Philosophie und Theologie der Geschichte in der Spätphilosophie Schellings*, Mainz 1965, and in *Die Methoden der Dogmatik*, Munich 1967. In *Jesus der Christus*, Mainz 1974 (*Jesus the Christ*, trans. V. Green, London 1976), and *The God of Jesus Christ*, trans. M. J. O'Donnell, New York and London 1984, I already took up an unequivocal position in the de-Hellenization debate.

4. Cf. 'Verständnis der Theologie damals und heute' in W. Kasper, *Glaube und Geschichte*, Mainz 1970, 9–32.

5. J. A. Möhler, *Neue Untersuchung der Lehrgegensätze zwischen den Katholiken und Protestanten*, Mainz 1835, 482f.

6. On the discussion about H. Küng's position, cf. my contribution 'Christologie von unten? Kritik und Neuansatz gegenwärtiger Christologie' in L. Scheffczyk (ed.), *Grundfragen der Christologie heute*, QD 72, 1975, 159–165 and 179–183; also 'Christsein ohne Tradition?' in *Diskussion über Hans Küngs 'Christ sein'*, Mainz 1976, 19–34 (ET by P. MacSeumais, *On Being a Christian: the Hans Küng*

debate, Dublin 1982). Also important in this connection is my *Wissenschaftliche Freiheit und lehramtliche Bindung der katholischen Theologie,* Essener Gespräche vol. 16, Münster 1982, 12–44.

7. Resistance to the dogmatistic misunderstanding of dogma led me to say (in *An Introduction to Christian Faith,* trans. V. Green, London and New York 1980, 170) that dogma *can* undoubtedly be one-sided and stupid. (Incidentally I was here following a similar formulation of K. Rahner's.) This was an inappropriate way of expressing what I meant and was open to misunderstanding. What I wished to say was that dogmas may be formulated in the light of a limited historical perspective. That in what they positively say they are none the less true, and therefore binding, is of course made quite plain in the context quoted. What is under discussion is the positive justification and defence of the doctrine of infallibility, which was being keenly discussed at the time. Since (in the tradition of the Tübingen school) I have always stressed the ecclesial bond of theology (see already *Die Lehre von der Tradition in der Römischen Schule,* Freiburg 1962), the unobjective polemic which was directed against this statement, torn out of its context, can hardly be explained as being motivated by an objective interest in the truth. A bishop who had to resign his office because he disputed the doctrine of infallibility was even sought out to act as crown witness against me, who had had to defend this doctrine. This surely speaks for itself. I recently expressed my views on the subject of dogma in the article 'Dogma/ Dogmenentwicklung', *NHThG* I, 1984, 176–193.

8. J. Ratzinger has especially stressed this, and rightly so. Cf. *Theologische Prinzipienlehre. Bausteine zur Fundamentaltheologie,* Munich 1982.

9. Thus J. A. Möhler, *Die Einheit in der Kirche oder das Prinzip des Katholizismus,* 1825, reissued, ed. J. R. Geiselmann, Cologne 1957, 100f., 109, 131, 147ff., 152ff.

10. Cf. here my article 'Dogmatik', *NHThG* I, 1984, 196f., 201f. In this question I have been increasingly influenced by the work of H. U. von Balthasar.

11. The following deserve special mention: W. Pannenberg, *Theology and the Philosophy of Science,* tran. F. McDonagh, London 1976; H. Peukert, *Wissenschaftstheorie – Handlungstheorie – Fundamentale Theologie,* Düsseldorf 1976.

12. On Karl Rahner's profound influence and in enduring gratitude for his theology, see my article 'Theologie in einer Zeit des Umbruchs', *ThQ* 159, 1979, 263–271.

13. Cf. H. Krings, 'Philosophie', *NGThG* III, 361 (although he is talking about philosophy in general).

14. This is the conclusion of my exposition of Schelling in 'Das Absolute in der Geschichte' and 'Freiheit als philosophisches und theologisches Problem in der Philosophie Schellings' in *Glaube und Geschichte,* 33–47. I took this up systematically in *Introduction to Christian Faith,* esp. 28ff., 159ff., *Jesus der Christus,* 62ff., and *The God of Jesus Christ,* esp. 106ff.

15. Following H. Krings and R. Spaemann, I have several times tried to point this out, for example in *Jesus der Christus,* 62ff. and in *The God of Jesus Christ,* 104ff. I have occasionally also given the name 'metahistoric' to such a metaphysics, which takes as starting point not the experience of nature (*physis*) but historically situated freedom. The term attempts above all to bring out the ontological and theological difference. H. Krings' approach has been made fruitful for theology

especially by T. Pröpper, *Erlösungsglaube und Freiheitsgeschichte. Eine Skizze zur Soteriologie*, Munich 1985.

16. For a favourably critical view of liberation theology cf. 'Die Theologie der Befreiung aus europäischer Perspektive' in J. B. Metz (ed.), *Die Theologie der Befreiung. Hoffnung oder Gefahr für die Kirche?*, Düsseldorf 1986, 77–98.

17. On the praxis character of theology cf. 'Zur Wissenschaftspraxis der Theologie', *Handbuch der Fundamentaltheologie* (n. 1 above), vol. 4.

18. Cf. here 'Theologie und Heiligkeit' in W. Kasper (ed.), *Sie suchten die Wahrheit*, Mainz 1985, 7–16.

19. For some hesitant approaches cf. 'Die weltverwandelnde Kraft christlicher Liebe. Grundsatzüberlegungen zum Verhältnis von Christentum und Gesellschaft' in K. Hemmerle (ed.), *Liebe verwandelt die Welt*, Mainz 1980, 25–52.

20. Cf. here 'Gottes Gegenwart in Jesus Christus. Vorüberlegungen zu einer weisheitlichen Christologie', in *Weisheit Gottes – Weisheit der Welt. Festschrift für Kardinal J. Ratzinger*, ed. W. Baier, St Ottilien 1987.

21. Cf. W. Oelmüller (ed.), *Wiederkehr von Religion? Perspektiven, Argumente, Fragen*, Paderborn, Munich, Vienna and Zürich 1984; P. Koslowski (ed.), *Die religiöse Dimension der Gesellschaft. Religion und ihre Theorien*, Tübingen 1985.

22. Cf. 'Christentum und Mythos' in P. Koslowski (ed.), *Die religiöse Dimension der Gesellschaft*, 264–271.

I. Revelation and Mystery: The Christian Understanding of God

1. The most important recent literature on the subject is cited in W. Kasper, *The God of Jesus Christ*, ET New York 1984.

2. H. Diels and W. Kranz (eds.), *Die Fragmente der Vorsokratiker*, vol. 1, 5th ed., Berlin 1934, 79, lines 26f.

3. Fragment 31; 67: H. Diels and W. Kranz, op. cit., 158 and 165.

4. Thomas Aquinas, *STh* I q 16 a. 1 c.

5. Fragment 23; H. Diels and W. Kranz, op. cit., 135.

6. Plato, *Apology* 23b.

7. *De caelesti hierarchia* II, 3, Sources Chrétiennes 58, Paris 1958, 77–80.

8. '... quia inter creatorem et creaturam non potest similitudo notari, quin inter eos maior sit dissimilitudo notanda' in H. Denzinger and A. Schönmetzer (eds.), *Enchiridion Symbolorum* ... (henceforward DS), 33rd ed., Freiburg 1965, para. 806.

9. Pastoral Constitution on the Church in the Modern World (*Gaudium et Spes*), article 10.

10. Ibid., article 45.

11. Ibid., article 22.

12. Manlius Severinus Boethius, *Liber de persona et duabus naturis*, cap. III, PL 64, 1343.

II. Autonomy and Theonomy: The Place of Christianity in the Modern World

1. On the history of the autonomy problem cf. R. Pohlmann, 'Autonomie' in *Historisches Wörterbuch der Philosophie*, ed. J. Ritter, I, 1971, 701–720;

G. Rohrmoser, 'Autonomie' in *Handbuch philosophischer Grundbegriffe*, ed. H. Krings et al. I, 1973, 155–170; K. Hilpert, 'Autonomie' in *Wörterbuch christlicher Ethik*, ed. B. Stoeckle, Freiburg 1975, 28–34; M. Welker, *Der Vorgang der Autonomie. Philosophische Beiträge zur Einsicht in theologische Rezeption und Kritik*, Neukirchen–Vluyn 1975; C. J. Pinto de Oliveira et al., *Dimensions éthiques de la liberté*, Études d'éthique chrétienne. Stud. christl. Ethik 4, Fribourg and Paris 1978.

2. Cf. A. Auer, *Autonome Moral und christlicher Glaube*, Düsseldorf 1971; also 'Nach dem Erscheinen der Enzyklika "Humanae vitae". Zehn Thesen über die Findung sittlicher Weisungen', *ThQ* 149, 1969, 75–85; also 'Autonome Moral und christlicher Glaube', *KatBl* 102, 1977, 60–72; also 'Das Vorverständnis des Sittlichen und seine Bedeutung für eine theologische Ethik' in *In libertatem vocati estis (Miscellanea B. Häring)*, ed. H. Boelaars and R. Tremblay, Studia Moralia 15, Rome 1977, 219–244.

3. Cf. already his *Autonome Moral*, 12. He makes the point more fully in 'Interiorisierung der Transzendenz. Zum Problem Identität und Reziprozität von Heilsethos' in *Humanum. Moraltheologie im Dienst des Menschen*, ed. J. Gründel, F. Rauh and V. Eid, Düsseldorf 1972, 47–65, where Auer specifically secures his position against the futuristic, evolutionistic and anthropological reduction of transcendence. Finally Auer brings out the failure of radical autonomism in 'Die Bedeutung der christlichen Botschaft für das Verständnis und die Durchsetzung der Grundwerte' in *Werte, Rechte, Normen*, ed. A. Paus, Kevelaer and Graz 1978, 50–53. Many of the all too undifferentiated objections made by B. Stoeckle in *Grenzen der autonomen Moral*, Munich 1974, have therefore already been accepted by Auer and miss their mark.

4. Cf. Pastoral Constitution *Gaudium et spes*, 36, 59.

5. Cf. Declaration on Religious Liberty *Dignitatis humanae*, 1.

6. Cf. *Gaudium et spes*, 3, 12–17, 27 and frequently; *Dignitatis humanae*, 1f. and frequently.

7. Cf. *Gaudium et spes*, 21, 36.

8. The reflections that follow are therefore not intended to intervene directly in the present discussion of the moral theologians. They merely aim to make a contribution to that discussion indirectly by pointing to parallel questions arising in dogmatic theology and by trying to come closer to a solution of a fundamental problem shared by all theological disciplines. Direct statements about the discussion in moral theology based on dogmatic theology may be found in Küng, who takes a positive and affirmative view of the programme of an autonomous morality in the Christian context; cf. H. Küng, *On Being a Christian*, trans. E. Quinn, New York 1976, London 1977, 530–553; also *Existiert Gott? Antwort auf die Gottesfrage der Neuzeit*, Munich 1978, 635–641 (*Does God Exist? An answer for today*, trans. E. Quinn, London 1980, 578–583); E. Schillebeeckx, 'Glaube und Moral' in *Ethik im Kontext des Glaubens*, ed. E. Mieth and F. Compagnoni, Freiburg and Vienna 1978, 17–45. For a critical view cf. L. Scheffczyk in *MThZ* 25, 1974, 336–358; J. Ratzinger and H. U. von Balthasar in *Kirchliches Lehramt – Glaube – Moral*, ed. J. Ratzinger, Einsiedeln 1975. For comment cf. D. Mieth, 'Autonome Moral im christlichen Kontext. Zu einem Grundlagenstreit der theologischen Ethik', *Orientierung* 40, 1976, 31–34; B. Schüller, 'Zur Diskussion über das Proprium einer christlichen Ethik', *Th Ph* 51, 1976, 321–343.

9. Cf. R. Pohlmann, 'Autonomie', 701.

10. Cf. M. Pohlenz, *Die Stoa*, vol. 1, 3rd ed., Göttingen 1964, 135.

11. Cf. H. Diels, *Fragmente der Vorsokratiker*, Hamburg 1957, n. 22; similarly Heraclitus, cf. Diels, op. cit., n. 9; also Plato, *Nomoi* 899b.

12. Cf. Plato, *Timaios* 92b.

13. Cf. *'kosmos'* in *TDNT* III, 872.

14. Cf. *'theos'* in *TDNT* III, 67–68.

15. Cf. W. F. Otto, *Die Götter Griechenlands*, Frankfurt 1961; K. Kerényi, 'Die griechischen Götter' in A. Schäfer (ed.), *Der Gottesgedanke im Abendland*, Urban-Bücher 79, Stuttgart 1964, 13–20.

16. Cf. Aristotle, *Metaphysics*, 1075 a. This comes out most clearly in the basic formula of Stoic ethics: 'to live in harmony with nature'; cf. *'physis'* in *TDNT* IX, 263f.

17. C. Westermann, *Genesis. A Commentary*, trans. J. J. Scullion, vol. 1, Minneapolis and London 1984, 25.

18. Cf. the summing-up of the discussion about this question in W. Kern, *Atheismus – Marxismus – Christentum*, Innsbruck, Vienna and Munich 1976, 23f.

19. K. Rahner, *Foundations of Christian Faith: an Introduction to the Idea of Christianity*, trans. W. V. Dych, London 1978, 78f.

20. Ibid., 79.

21. Cf. Westermann, *Genesis*, 151ff.; also his 'Das Alte Testament und die Menschenrechte' in *Zum Thema Menschenrechte. Theologische Versuche und Entwürfe*, ed. J. Baur, Stuttgart 1977, 5–18.

22. Cf. R. Hasenstab, *Modelle paulinischer Ethik. Beiträge zu einem Autonomie-Modell aus paulinischem Geist*, Tübinger Theologische Studien 11, Mainz 1977, 188ff.

23. Cf. M. D. Chenu, *La théologie au douzième siècle*, Études de philosophie médiévale 45, Paris 1957, 21–51.

24. Cf. Thomas Aquinas, Prol. to *STh* 1 q. 2 and to I/II. On the following passage cf. M. D. Chenu, *Introduction à l'étude de Saint Thomas d'Aquin*, Montreal and Paris 1950, German ed. revised by the author, *Das Werk des hl. Thomas von Aquin*, Graz, Vienna and Cologne 1960; M. Seckler, *Das Heil in der Geschichte. Geschichtstheologisches Denken bei Thomas von Aquin*, Munich 1964.

25. Cf. M. Seckler, *Das Heil*, 66–79.

26. Cf. Aquinas, *Contra gentiles* II, 46, with the comments by Seckler, op. cit., 92f.

27. Cf. Aquinas, Prol. to *STh* I/II.

28. Cf. J. B. Metz, *Christliche Anthropozentrik. Über die Denkform des Thomas von Aquin*, Munich 1962, 47.

29. Cf. A. Auer, 'Die Autonomie des Sittlichen nach Thomas von Aquin' in *Christlich Glauben und Handeln*, ed. K. Demmer and B. Schüller, Düsseldorf 1977, 31–54; W. Korff, *Norm und Sittlichkeit. Untersuchungen zur Logik der normativen Vernunft*, Tübinger theologische Studien 1, Mainz 1975, 42–61; also his *Theologische Ethik. Eine Einführung*, Theologisches Seminar, Freiburg, Basle and Vienna 1975, 79–86; S. Pinckaers, 'Autonomie et hétéronomie en morale selon S. Thomas d'Aquin' in *Der Vorgang der Autonomie* (see n. 1 above), 104–123; K. W. Merks, *Theologische Grundlegung der sittlichen Autonomie. Struktur-*

momente eines 'autonomen' Normbegründungsverständnisses im lex-Traktat der Summa theologiae des Thomas von Aquin, Moraltheologische Studien, Systematische Abt. 5, Düsseldorf 1978.

30. Cf. W. Kluxen, *Philosophische Ethik bei Thomas von Aquin*, Walberberger Studien 2, Mainz 1964, 234; O. H. Pesch in *Die deutsche Thomasausgabe*, vol. 13, Heidelberg, Vienna and Cologne 1977, 566.

31. Cf. Aquinas, *STh* I/II q. 106 a. 1; q. 108 a. 1–4. Comment by U. Kühn, *Via caritatis. Theologie des Gesetzes bei Thomas von Aquin*, Göttingen 1965; O. H. Pesch, *Die Theologie der Rechtfertigung bei Martin Luther und Thomas von Aquin*, Mainz 1967.

32. This may be said both of the doctrine of natural law in the sixteenth century and of the definition of the relationship between God and human beings in the dispute about grace in the same period. On the first of these cf. J. T. Arntz, 'Die Entwicklung des naturrechtlichen Denkens innerhalb des Thomismus' in *Das Naturrecht im Disput*, ed. F. Böckle, Düsseldorf 1966, 87–120; A. Hollerbach, 'Das christliche Naturrecht im Zusammenhang des allgemeinen Naturrechtsdenken' in *Naturrecht in der Kritik*, ed. F. Böckle and E. W. Böckenförde, Mainz 1973, 16–21. On the second problem cf. H. Holz, 'Omnipotenz und Autonomie. Zur Frage des Wirkungsverhältnisses zwischen einem absoluten und einem endlichen Subjekt', *NZSTh* 16, 1974, 257–284. Admittedly Holz also attempts to suggest that Thomas too tried to 'demythicize' to some degree.; cf. also his *Thomas von Aquin und die Philosophie*, Munich, Paderborn and Vienna 1975.

33. Cf. F. Hoffmann, *Die theologische Methode des Oxforder Dominikanerlehrers Robert Holcott*, Beiträge zur Geschichte der Philosophie und Theologie des Mittelalters, Neue Folge 5, Münster 1972; K. Bannach, *Die Lehre von der doppelten Macht Gottes bei Wilhelm von Ockham. Problemgeschichtliche Voraussetzungen und Bedeutung*, Wiesbaden 1975.

34. Cf. *Die Kirche und die Menschenrechte. Ein Arbeitspapier der Päpstlichen Kommission Justitia et Pax (1974)*, Entwicklung und Frieden. Dokumente – Berichte – Meinungen 5, Mainz 1976, 8 (No. 18).

35. The view maintained in G. Jellinek's famous if one-sided investigation 'Die Erklärung der Menschen- und Bürgerrechte' (1895), now in R. Schnur (ed.), *Zur Geschichte der Erklärung der Menschenrechte*, 2nd ed., Darmstadt 1974, 1–77. For a different view see e.g. G. Ritter, 'Ursprung und Wesen der Menschenrechte' in Schnur, ibid., 202–237.

36. Cf. B. M. Biermann, *Las Casas und seine Sendung*, Walberberger Studien 5, Mainz 1968.

37. Cf. R. Pohlmann, 'Autonomie' (see n. 1 above), 702, on the development of the juristic concept of autonomy by Franciscus Burgcardus in the context of the Peace of Augsburg (1555). For the wider context cf. E. Hirsch, *Geschichte der neueren evangelischen Theologie im Zusammenhang mit den allgemeinen Bewegungen des europäischen Denkens*, vol. 1, Gütersloh 1960, 1–110.

38. Cf. H. Grotius, *The Law of War and Peace*, trans. F. W. Kelsey et al., Classics of International Law, Washington and Oxford 1913–27, Prolegomena 11.

39. This aspect was stressed above all by W. Dilthey, *Weltanschauung und Analyse des Menschen seit Renaissance und Reformation*, Gesammelte Schriften 2, Leipzig 1914, 254ff. and frequently elsewhere.

40. This is the opinion maintained by H. Blumenberg, *Säkularisierung und Selbstbehauptung*, Frankfurt 1974. For a critical view of his thesis cf. W. Pannenberg, 'Die christliche Legitimität der Neuzeit' in his *Gottesgedanke und menschliche Freiheit*, Göttingen 1972, 114–128. The wider background of Blumenberg's viewpoint in its bearing on the problem becomes clear in *Subjektivität und Selbsterhaltung. Beiträge zur Diagnose der Moderne*, ed. H. Ebeling, Frankfurt 1976. Pannenberg's criticism is justified in some respects, but Blumenberg is correct in so far as the attempt to derive modern secularization from Christianity as if this were the single cause, remains' abstract. It can only interpret as a mutual misunderstanding the fact that, largely speaking, all the major churches for a long time judged modern movements for liberty negatively and polemically; while modern strivings for freedom had specifically to prevail in the face of mainstream Christianity. The aspect that Christian impulses had to make themselves felt through protest against the mainstream churches is insisted upon especially by H. Küng, *Does God Exist?*, 9ff., 83ff. and frequently.

41. E. Troeltsch's view; cf. *Aufsätze zur Geistesgeschichte und Religionsgeschichte, Gesammelte Schriften* 4, 1925, reissued Aalen 1966, 334.

42. There was hence an interesting shift in the concept of emancipation, from graciously granted liberty to autonomous self-liberation. Cf. M. Greiffenhagen, 'Emanzipation' in *Historisches Wörterbuch der Philosophie* (n. 1 above), II, 448f.; G. Rohrmoser, *Emanzipation und Freiheit*, Munich 1970; R. Spaemann, 'Autonomie, Mündigkeit, Emanzipation', in *Kontexte* 7, Stuttgart and Berlin 1971, 94–102.

43. R. Descartes, *Meditation* II (*Philosophical Works*, trans. E. S. Haldane and G. R. T. Ross, vol. I, Cambridge 1911, 150; cf. 159).

44. Cf. R. Descartes, *Discourse on Method*, Part IV (*Philosophical Works* I, 101–103); also *Meditation* II (*Philosophical Works*, vol. I, 150).

45. Cf. R. Descartes, *Meditation* V (*Philosophical Works*, 179ff.). On this new form of the ontological proof cf. D. Henrich, *Der ontologische Gottesbeweis. Sein Problem und seine Geschichte in der Neuzeit*, 2nd ed., Tübingen 1967, 10–21.

46. Cf. E. Troeltsch, *Aufsätze zur Geistes- und Religionsgeschichte, Gesammelte Schriften*, vol. 4, 1925, reissued Aalen 1966, 324–327. For a different view cf. W. Dilthey, *Die Autonomie des Denkens . . ., Werke*, vol. 2, Göttingen 1969, 260–267 (with his well-known Stoic thesis).

47. Cf. G. Ebeling, 'Die Evidenz des Ethischen und die Theologie' in his *Wort und Glaube*, vol. 2, Tübingen 1969, 1–41. For a critical view cf. W. Pannenberg, 'Die Krise des Ethischen und die Theologie' in his *Ethik und Ekklesiologie*, Göttingen 1977, 41–55. For Ebeling's reply cf. *Wort und Glaube*, 42–55; for Pannenberg's rejoinder, *Ethik*, 55–69.

48. Cf. I. Kant, *Grundlegung zur Metaphysik der Sitten, Werke*, ed. W. Weischedel, 2nd ed., Darmstadt 1966, vol. 4, 74; cf. 8of. (*The Moral Law; or Kant's Groundwork of the Metaphysic of Morals*, trans. H. J. Paton, London 1948, 100, 103f.); *Kritik der praktischen Vernunft*, ibid., 144 (*Critique of Practical Reason*, trans. L. W. Beck, Chicago 1949, 33f.)

49. Cf. *Grundlegung*, 66, 71f. (*Groundwork*, 92, 99). Cf. J. Schwartländer, *Der Mensch ist Person. Kants Lehre vom Menschen*, Stuttgart 1968.

50. Cf. *Grundlegung*, 91ff. (*Groundwork*, 110ff.); *Kritik der reinen Vernunft*, ed. Weischedel, op. cit., vol. 2, 673ff. (*Critique of Pure Reason*, trans. J. M. D. Meiklejohn, London 1860, often reprinted).

51. *Grundlegung,* 51 (*Groundwork,* 88); cf. *Kritik der praktischen Vernunft,* 140 (*Critique of Practical Reason,* 30).
52. Cf. *Grundlegung,* 65 (*Groundwork* 96).
53. Cf. *Kritik der praktischen Vernunft,* 139 (ET 29).
54. J. Schwartländer, 'Staatsbürgerliche und sittlich-institutionelle Menschenrechte. Aspekte zur Begründung und Bestimmung der Menschenrechte' in *Menschenrechte. Aspekte ihrer Begründung und Verwirklichung,* ed. J. Schwartländer, Tübinger Universitätsschriften 1, Tübingen 1978, 87.
55. *Kritik der praktischen Vernunft,* 261 (ET 134).
56. *Die Religion innerhalb der Grenzen der bloßen Vernunft, Werke,* vol. 4, 838 (*Religion within the Limits of Reason Alone,* trans. T. M. Greene and H. H. Hudson, 1934).
57. Cf. ibid. 842.
58. Cf. *Kritik der reinen Vernunft,* 677ff. (ET 451f.), *Kritik der praktischen Vernunft,* 254ff. (ET 128ff.).
59. Following Kant, therefore, in neo-Protestantism (as represented by A. Ritschl, W. Hermann and others) ethics became the prime way of access to an understanding of religion and Christianity. Cf. here the controversy between Ebeling and Pannenberg cited in n. 47 above. For similar Catholic approaches (esp. S. Mutschelle) and the way in which they were critically surmounted in Catholic theology, cf. C. Keller, *Das Theologische in der Moraltheologie. Eine Untersuchung historischer Modelle aus der Zeit des Deutschen Idealismus,* Göttingen 1976, esp. 65–86.
60. Modern thinking moves dialectically between these two basic possibilities, as is shown in W. Schulz, *Der Gott der neuzeitlichen Metaphysik,* 3rd ed., Pfullingen 1957.
61. This basic form of religious criticism has been so often stressed in recent years that a more detailed discussion of it may be dispensed with here; but cf. W. Kern, *Atheismus* (see n. 18 above), 39–78 and H. Küng, *Does God Exist?,* 189–339; for the ethical problem, cf. F. Böckle, *Fundamentalmoral,* Munich 1977, 49–69.
62. Cf. F. Nietzsche, *Die fröhliche Wissenschaft, Werke,* ed. K. Schlechta, Munich 1954–56, vol. 2, 127; *Also sprach Zarathustra,* ibid., 523 (ETs *The Joyful Wisdom* and *Thus spake Zarathustra* in *Complete Works,* vols 10 and 11, ed. O. Levy, Edinburgh and London, 1909–13).
63. *Aus dem Nachlaß der Achzigerjahre, Werke,* vol. 3, 557f.
64. *Also sprach Zarathustra,* 281, 523.
65. *Ecce homo, Werke,* vol. 2, 1098 (*ET Ecce homo, Complete Works,* vol. 17; *Aus dem Nachlaß,* 834.
66. *Also sprach Zarathustra,* 408, 415, 463, 473f., 588.
67. Ibid., 449; cf. 431.
68. Ibid., 283ff.
69. For the effect on Catholic theology cf. H. Maier, *Revolution und Kirche. Zur Frühgeschichte der christlichen Demokratie,* 3rd ed., Munich 1973, 145–173; H. J. Pottmeyer, *Unfehlbarkeit und Souveränität. Die päpstliche Unfehlbarkeit im System der ultramontanen Ekklesiologie des 19. Jahrhunderts,* Tübinger theologische Studien 5, Mainz 1975. Where Protestant theology is concerned cf. R. Strunk, *Politische Ekklesiologie im Zeitalter der Revolution,* Gesellschaft und Theologie, Systematische Beiträge 5, Munich and Mainz 1971.

70. Cf. R. Guardini, *The Church and the Catholic*, trans. A. Lane, London 1935, 11, 17.

71. R. Guardini, *The End of the Modern World*, trans. J. Theman and H. Burke, London 1957, 104.

72. K. Adam, *Das Wesen des Katholizismus*, 12th ed., Düsseldorf 1949, 18f. (*The Spirit of Catholicism*, trans. J. McCann, London 1929, revised 1934, reissued 1969). Adam speaks more sharply still in his essay 'Der moderne Mensch und der katholische Glaube' in *Glaube und Glaubenswissenschaft im Katholizismus*, Rottenburg 1923, 143–165.

73. Cf. J. Lortz, *Geschichte der Kirche in ideengeschichtlicher Betrachtung*, 18th/19th ed., Münster 1953, 216–223, 333–338; H. E. Hengstenberg, *Autonomismus und Transzendentalphilosophie*, Heidelberg 1950; A. Hartmann, 'Autonomismus' in *LThK*, 2nd ed. I, 1131f. Interestingly enough, even in its new edition, the *LThK* only has an entry under 'Autonomismus'; the heading 'Autonomie' is treated only in the context of canon law.

74. Cf. P. Eicher, *Die anthropologische Wende. Karl Rahners philosophischer Weg vom Wesen des Menschen zur personalen Existenz*, Dokimion vol. 1, Fribourg 1970.

75. Cf. notes 19 and 20 above.

76. J. B. Metz, *Theology of the World*, trans. W. Glen-Doepel, London and New York 1969, 19f.

77. Ibid., 49.

78. J. B. Metz, *Faith in History and Society*, trans. D. Smith, London 1980, 68. Cf. *Diskussion zur 'politischen Theologie'*, ed. H. Peukert, Mainz and Munich 1969.

79. Metz, *Faith in History*, 62.

80. Cf. F. Gogarten, *Verhängnis und Hoffnung der Neuzeit. Die Säkularisierung als theologisches Problem*, Stuttgart 1953. A survey of other positions may be found in Metz, *Theology of the World*, 14 n. 1 and 20 n. 10. Important for an understanding of the term secularization is H. Lübbe, *Säkularisierung. Geschichte eines ideenpolitischen Begriffs*, 2nd ed., Freiburg and Munich 1975.

81. T. Rendtorff, *Theorie des Christentums. Historisch-theologische Studien zu seiner neuzeitlichen Verfassung*, Gütersloh 1972.

82. Cf. J. Moltmann, 'Wer vertritt die Zukunft des Menschen? Fragen zur theologischen Basis der Menschenrechte', *EvKomm* 8, 1975, 399–402; also his 'Welches Recht hat das Ebenbild Gottes?' *EvKomm* 9, 1976, 280–282; also 'Theologische Erklärung zu den Menschenrechte' in *Gottes Recht und Menschenrechte – Studie und Empfehlungen des Reformierten Weltbundes*, ed. J. M. Lochmann and J. Moltmann, Neukirchen-Vluyn 1976, 44–60.

83. Cf. M. Honecker, 'Recht oder ethische Forderung – Aporien der Menschenrechtsdiskussion', *EvKomm* 8, 1975, 737–740; also 'Grundwerte und christliches Ethos' in his *Sozialethik zwischen Tradition und Vernunft*, Tübingen 1977, 145–174.

84. Cf. G. Gutiérrez, *A Theology of Liberation*, trans. C. Inda and J. Eagleson, Maryknoll, N.Y. 1973, London 1974, 45ff., 153ff. Gutiérrez certainly rejects a complete identification between the two. On the hermeneutical problem and on the relationship between human well-being and Christian salvation, cf. Internationale Theologenkommission: K. Lehmann et al., *Theologie der*

Befreiung, Einsiedeln 1977.

85. M. Horkheimer and T. W. Adorno, *Dialektik der Aufklärung. Philosophische Fragmente*, Frankfurt 1969.

86. Cf. P. L. Berger, *A Rumour of Angels. Modern Society and the Rediscovery of the Supernatural*, Harmondsworth 1971; also his 'Soziologische Betrachtungen über die Zukunft der Religion. Zum gegenwärtigen Stand der Säkularisierungsdebatte' in O. Schatz (ed.), *Hat die Religion Zukunft?*, Graz, Vienna and Cologne 1971, 49–68; also *The Social Reality of Religion*, London 1969 (*The Sacred Canopy*, New York 1969).

87. Cf. *Concilium* 9, January 1973, No. 1 (vol. 81): *The Persistence of Religion*, with contributions by G. Baum, A. Greeley, M. Marty, J. Brothers, W. and N. McCready, J. Remy/E. Servais, B. van Iersel, D. Power, J. Shea, E. Kennedy, D. Tracy, R. Ruether and R. Laurentin.

88. Cf. E. Schillebeeckx, *Gott – Die Zukunft des Menschen*, Mainz 1966, 142ff. (*God the Future of Man*, trans. N. D. Smith, London and Sydney 1969); R. Spaemann, 'Gesichtspunkte der Philosophie' in *Wer ist das eigentlich – Gott?*, ed. H. J. Schulz, Munich 1969, 63. This danger becomes especially acute in the so-called theology after the death of God. On the various outlines of G. Vahanian, T. J. J. Altizer, D. Sölle and J. Cardonell, cf. J. Bishop, *Die Gott-ist-tot-Theologie*, Düsseldorf 1968; S. M. Daecke, *Der Mythos vom Tod Gottes*, Hamburg 1969; L. Scheffczyk, *Gottloser Gottesglaube? Die Grenzen des Nichttheismus und ihre Überwindung*, Regensburg 1974; W. Kern, *Atheismus* (see n. 18 above), 134–151; J. Figl, *Atheismus als theologisches Problem. Modelle der Auseinandersetzung in der Theologie der Gegenwart*, Tübinger Theol. Studien 9, Mainz 1977.

89. J. B. Metz, *Faith in History*, 76 (ET altered).

90. Cf. as summing up P. Tillich, *Systematic Theology*, trans. J. L. Adams, vol. 1, Chicago 1951, 59–66 (London 1953, 67–73).

91. Cf. K. Barth, CD III/2, 220ff., 322f.

92. Cf. Barth, CD IV/3, 112ff. For a further development cf. C. Link, *Die Welt als Gleichnis. Studien zum Problem der natürlichen Theologie*, Beiträge zur ev. Theologie 73, Munich 1973.

93. Cf. E. Jüngel, 'Freiheitsrechte und Gerechtigkeit' in his *Unterwegs zur Sache. Theologische Bemerkungen*, Munich 1972, 246–256. On the wider context cf. also his *God as the Mystery of the World*, trans. D. L. Guder, Grand Rapids, Mich., and Edinburgh 1983.

94. Cf. W. Huber and H. E. Tödt, *Menschenrechte. Perspektiven einer menschlichen Welt*, Suttgart and Berlin 1977, 64ff., 160ff.

95. This was D. Bonhoeffer's view; cf. *Letters and Papers from Prison*, ed. E. Bethge, trans. R. H. Fuller, [4th] enlarged ed., London and New York 1971, 281f., 283, 325–329 (letters to Bethge, 30 April, 5 May and 8 June 1944). From the Catholic point of view and also more differentiated, H. U. von Balthasar, *Karl Barth. Darstellung und Deutung seiner Theologie*, 2nd ed., Cologne 1962.

96. For the history and meaning of this axiom, cf. J. Beumer, 'Gratia supponit naturam. Zur Geschichte eines theologischen Prinzips', *Gregorianum* 20, 1939, 381–406; 535–552; E. Przywara, 'Der Grundsatz "Gratia non destruit sed supponit et perficit naturam". Eine ideengeschichtliche Interpretation', *Scholastik* 17, 1942, 178–186; J. Alfaro, 'Gratia supponit naturam' in *LThK* IV, 2nd ed., 1960, 1169–1171; J. Ratzinger, 'Gratia praesupponit naturam. Erwägungen über

Sinn and Grenze eines scholastischen Axioms' in *Einsicht und Glaube*, ed. J. Ratzinger and H. Fries, Freiburg, Basle and Vienna 1962, 135–149; B. Stockle, *'Gratia supponit naturam.' Geschichte und Annalyse eines theologischen Axioms*, Rom 1962.

97. Cf. H. Krings' important contribution, 'Freiheit. Ein Versuch, Gott zu denken', *PhJ* 77, 1970, 225–237.

98. Pastoral Constitution *Gaudium et spes*, 22.

99. Irenaeus, *Against the Heresies*, V, 26, 2.

100. Ibid. III, 20, 2.

101. Cf. E.-W. Böckenförde, *Einleitung zu: Zweites Vatikanisches Konzil. Erklärung über die Religionsfreiheit*, Münster 1968, 9.

102. Cf. Declaration on Religious Liberty *Dignitatis humanae*, 1, 9.

103. For the church's position on human rights today, cf. the document issued by the papal commission *Justitia et Pax*, 1974. Cf. here n. 34.

104. Cf. R. Spaemann, 'Natur' in *Handbuch philosophischer Grundbegriffe* (see n. 1 above), II, 956–969; also his 'Die Aktualität des Naturrechts' in *Naturrecht in der Kritik*, ed. F. Böckle and E.-W. Böckenförde, Mainz 1973, 262–276.

105. Cf. A. Hollerbach, 'Das christliche Naturrecht im Zusammenhang des allgemeinen Naturrechtsdenkens' in *Naturrecht in der Kritik*, 9–38.

106. E. Bloch, *Naturrecht und menschliche Würde*, Frankfurt 1961.

107. On the christological determination of human nature cf. W. Kasper, *Jesus der Christus*, Mainz 1974, 290–295 *(Jesus the Christ*, trans. V. Green, London 1976), with (on p.61) a general discussion of the dialectic of determination, following J. E. Kuhn.

III. The Modern Sense of Freedom and History and the Theological Definition of Human Rights

1. *Die Kirche und die Menschenrechte. Ein Arbeitspapier der Päpstlichen 'Kommission Justitia et Pax'*, (Entwicklungen und Frieden. Dokumente, Berichte, Meinungen, 5), Munich and Mainz 1976, 8, No. 18.

2. For the reasoning in detail, cf. 'Autonomy and Theonomy', pp. 32–53 above.

3. R. Guardini, *The End of the Modern World*, trans. J. Theman and H. Burke, London 1957, 104.

4. J. B. Metz, *Theology of the World*, trans. W. Glen-Doepel, London and New York 1969, 49.

5. J. B. Metz, *Faith in History and Society*, trans. D. Smith, London 1980, 62.

6. Allen O. Miller (ed.), *A Christian Declaration on Human Rights*, Grand Rapids 1977, 144 (includes texts and preparatory papers).

7. Metz, *Faith in History*, 76.

8. Cf. the historical survey in W. Kluxen, 'Analogie' in *Historisches Wörterbuch der Philosophie*, ed. J. Ritter, I, 1971, 214–227. On the importance of the analogy model for the theological determination of human rights, cf. especially W. Huber and H. E. Tödt, *Menschenrechte. Perspektiven einer menschlichen Welt*, Suttgart and Berlin 1977, 16off.

9. K. Rahner, *Foundations of Christian Faith: an Introduction to the Idea of Christianity*, trans. W. V. Dych, London 1978, 79.

10. Cf. R. Hasenstab, *Modelle paulinischer Ethik. Beiträge zu einem Autonomie-Modell aus paulinischem Geist*, Tübinger Theologische Studien 11, Mainz 1977, 188ff.

11. Cf. E. W. Böckenförde, 'Das neue politische Engagement der Kirche. Zur "politischen Theologie" Johannes Pauls II.', *StZ* 105, 1980, 219–234; O. von Nell–Breuning, 'Politische Theologie Papst Johannes Pauls II.', *StZ* 105, 1980, 675–686.

12. Cf. M. D. Chenu, *La théologie au douzième siècle*, Études de philosophie médiévale 45, Paris 1957, 21–51.

13. Cf. Thomas Aquinas, Prol. to *STh* I q. 2 and to I/II. On the following passage cf. M. D. Chenu, *Introduction à l'étude de Saint Thomas d'Aquin*, Montreal and Paris 1950; German ed. revised by the author, *Das Werk des hl. Thomas von Aquin*, Graz, Vienna and Cologne 1960; M. Seckler, *Das Heil in der Geschichte. Geschichtstheologisches Denken bei Thomas von Aquin*, Munich 1964.

14. Cf. Seckler, op. cit., 66–79.

15. Cf. Aquinas, *Contra gentiles* II, 46, and the comments in Seckler, op. cit., 92f.

16. Cf. Aquinas, Prol. to *STh* I/II.

17. Cf. J. B. Metz, *Christliche Anthropozentrik. Über die Denkform des Thomas von Aquin*, Munich 1962, 47.

18. Cf. K. W. Merks, *Theologische Grundlegung der sittlichen Autonomie. Strukturmomente eines 'autonomen' Normbegründungsverständnisses im lex-Traktat der Summa theologiae des Thomas von Aquin*, Moraltheologische Studien, Systematische Abt. 5, Düsseldorf 1978.

19. Cf. W. Kluxen, *Philosophische Ethik bei Thomas von Aquin*, Walberberger Studien 2, Mainz 1964, 234; O. H. Pesch in *Thomas von Aquin, Das Gesetz*, kommentiert von O. H. Pesch, I–II, 90–105, in *Die deutsche Thomas Ausgabe* 13, Heidelberg, Graz, Vienna and Cologne 1977, 566.

20. Cf. Aquinas, *STh* I/II q. 106 a. 1; q. 108 a. 1–4. Cf. also the comments by U. Kuhn in his. *Via caritatis. Theologie des Gesetzes bei Thomas von Aquin*, Göttingen 1965; O. H. Pesch, *Die Theologie der Rechtfertigung bei Martin Luther und Thomas von Aquin*, Mainz 1967.

21. See ch. II n. 96 pp. 204f. above.

22. Cf. H. Krings, 'Freiheit. Ein Versuch Gott zu denken', *PhJ* 77, 1970, 225–237.

23. Cf. John Paul II, Encyclical *Redemptor hominis*, 17.

24. Cf. Vatican II, Pastoral Constitution *Gaudium et spes*, 76.

25. W. Dilthey, 'Die drei Grundformen der Systeme in der ersten Hälfte des 19. Jahrhunderts', *Gesammelte Schriften* IV, 5th ed., Stuttgart and Göttingen 1974, 529.

26. Cf. W. Kasper, 'Vernunft and Geschichte (Diskussionsvotum)' in J. Schwartländer (ed.), *Menschenrechte. Aspekte ihrer Begründung und Verwirklichung*, Tübinger Universitätsschriften 1, Tübingen 1978, 232f.

27. Cf. 'Autonomy and Theonomy' above, pp. 34–38.

28. Cf. here W. Kasper, *An Introduction to Christian Faith*, trans. V. Green, London and New York 1980, 159ff.

29. Cf. W. Kasper, *Jesus der Christus*, Mainz 1974, 290ff. (*Jesus the Christ*, trans. V. Green, London 1976).

30. Cf. G. Greshake, *Geschenkte Freiheit. Einführung in die Gnadenlehre*, Freiburg, Basle and Vienna 1977.

31. On this discussion, which was started above all by A. Auer, cf. B. Schüller, 'Zur Diskussion über das Proprium einer christlichen Ethik', *ThPh* 51, 1976, 321–343; F. Böckle, *Fundamentalmoral*, Munich 1977, passim.

32. Cf. K. Rahner, 'Existential, übernatürliches', in *LThK*, 2nd ed., III, 1301.

33. Cf. H. Schlier, *'eleutheros'* in *TDNT* II, 496–502.

34. Cf. M. Kehl, *Kirche als Institution. Zur theologischen Begründung des institutionellen Charakters der Kirche in der neueren deutschsprachigen katholischen Ekklesiologie*, Frankfurter Theologischen Studien 22, Frankfurt 1976.

35. Cf. J. Neumann, *Menschenrechte auch in der Kirche?*, Zürich, Einsiedeln and Cologne 1976.

IV. Christology and Anthropology

1. The biblical, dogmatic and historical foundations can be presented briefly here, in the form of key words or intimations, because the most important points have already been made in 'Quaestiones selectae de Christologia I', *Gregorianum* 4, 1980, 609–632 (in Latin); German text in *HerKorr* 35, 1981, 137–145. What is said there is presupposed in the present essay, where it is developed under the aspect of the present theme.

2. Pastoral Constitution *Gaudium et spes*, 22.

3. Cf. for example O. Cullmann, *The Christology of the New Testament*, trans. C. M. Guthrie and C. A. M. Hall, 2nd ed., London and Philadelphia 1963, 326: 'Therefore, in the light of the New Testament witness, all mere speculation about his natures is an absurdity. Functional Christology is the only one that exists.' Many other testimonies may be found in Y. Congar, 'Christ in the Economy of Salvation and in our Dogmatic Tracts', *Concilium* no. 2, vol. 1, January 1966, 4–15.

4. Among earlier work, cf. A. Gilg, *Weg und Bedeutung der altkirchlichen Christologie*, Munich 1961; most recently A. Grillmeier, *Jesus Christus im Glauben der Kirche*, vol. 1, Freiburg, Basle and Vienna 1979.

5. R. Schnackenburg's view in *Das Johannesevangelium*, Pt. I, HThK 4/1, Freiburg, Basle and Vienna 1965, 211. E. Käsemann, *Commentary on Romans*, trans. G. W. Bromiley, Grand Rapids 1980, 2nd impression London 1982, 5, 10, maintains quite unequivocally that the Sonship in the metaphysical sense is presupposed by the whole of the New Testament as a matter of course. M. Hengel, *The Son of God*, trans. J. S. Bowden, London 1976, sees the real pre-existence as security against the road to docetism.

6. Y. Congar, op. cit., 11.

7. Cf. for example R. Bultmann, 'The Christological Confession of the World Council of Churches' in his *Essays Philosophical and Theological*, trans. J. C. G. Grieg, London and Philadelphia 1955, 273–90. On p.275 we find the characteristic Bultmann alternative: 'If Christ is termed "God", is this a description of his nature, his metaphysical essence or his significance? Is this a soteriological statement or a cosmological one, or both?' Or p.280: 'Does he help me because he is the Son of God, or is he the Son of God because he helps me?'

8. Cf. H. Braun, 'Der Sinn der neutestamentlichen Christologie' in his *Gesammelte Studien zum Neuen Testament und seiner Umwelt*, Tübingen 1962, 272.

9. Thus H. Küng, *On Being a Christian*, trans. E. Quinn, New York 1976, London 1977, 442: 'But does any reasonable person today want to become God? . . . Our problem today is not so much the deification of human beings as their humanization.' In line with this, on pp. 554ff. being a Christian is interpreted as the radical form of being human. Of course all these statements are open to various interpretations and are therefore hard to judge. Similarly, in E. Schillebeeckx, *Christ: the Christian Experience in the Modern World*, trans. J. S. Bowden, London and New York 1980, the systematic fourth part is entitled 'God's Glory and Truth, Man's Wellbeing and Happiness' (646ff.). In the exegetical part the theologically important aspects are certainly mentioned, but there is a decline in the systematic evaluation, only particular points from the historical material presented being brought out. It must, however, be said that Schillebeeckx's expositions are so complex that it is difficult to 'place' them with complete clarity. Cf. here K. Lehmann, 'Heiliger Geist, Befreiung zum Menschsein – Teilhabe am göttlichen Leben' in *Gegenwart des Geistes*, QD 85, Freiburg, Basle and Vienna 1979, 193f.

10. K. Adam, *Jesus Christus*, 8th ed., Düsseldorf 1949, 17 (cf. *The Son of God*, trans. P. Hereford, London 1934, 7).

11. Cf. J. Moltmann, *The Crucified God. The Cross of Christ as the Foundation and Criticism of Christian Theology*, trans. R. A. Wilson and J. S. Bowden, London 1974, 7–31; W. Kasper, *Jesus der Christus*, Mainz 1974, 13f. (*Jesus the Christ*, trans. V. Green, London 1976).

12. Cf. H. U. von Balthasar, *Love Alone*, ET London 1968, New York 1969, where the cosmological and the anthropological reductions are set over against one another and both are surpassed in a third way, that of self-interpreting and self-manifesting love.

13. Justin Martyr, *Apology* 46; *Second Apology* 8, 13.

14. Cf. A. Grillmeier, op. cit., 222ff., 403ff.

15. This is classically the case in Aquinas' *Summa theologiae*, where within the Thomist world formula of *exitus* and *reditus* Christ is described in the *Tertia Pars* as the practical way.

16. Cf. I. Kant, *Critique of Pure Reason*, B XVI.

17. Ibid. B 93.

18. Cf. E. Cassirer, *Substance and Function*, trans. W. C. and M. C. Swabey, Chicago and London 1923; reprint 1953.

19. I. Kant, *Der Streit der Fakultäten*, A 50.

20. Unfortunately from this point of view *HDG* vol. 3, Fasz. 2 c: *Soteriologie. Von der Reformation bis zur Gegenwart*, 1972, is completely inadequate. Still helpful, on the other hand, in spite of the well-known Hegelian construction, is F. C. Baur, *Lehrbuch der christlichen Dogmengeschichte*, Leipzig 1867, reprint Darmstadt 1974; also A. Ritschl, *The Christian Doctrine of Justification and Reconciliation*, trans. H. R. Mackintosh and A. B. Macaulay, Edinburgh and New York 1900, sections 44ff., 48ff., 56ff., 62ff.

21. H. J. Iwand, 'Wider den Mißbrauch des pro me als methodisches Prinzip in der Theologie', *ThLZ* 79, 1954, 433–458.

22. Cf. H. J. Birkner, 'Natürliche Theologie und Offenbarungstheologie. Ein theologiegeschichtlicher Überblick', *NZSTh* 3, 1961, 279–295.

23. Cf. K. Rahner and K. Lehmann, 'Kerygma und Dogma' in *Mysterium Salutis*

1, Einsiedeln, Zürich and Cologne 1970, 657–660; G. Söll, 'Dogma und Dogmenentwicklung', in *HDG* I/5, 40–44.

24. Cf. H. Albert, *Traktat über kritische Vernunft*, 2nd ed., Tübingen 1969, 111, 119, 121.

25. Cf. L. Feuerbach, *The Essence of Christianity*, trans. George Eliot, London 1854, New York 1855, 49: 'The Incarnation is nothing else than the practical, material manifestation of the human nature of God. God did not become man for his own sake. The need, the want of man . . . was the cause of the Incarnation. . . . But the incarnate God is only the apparent manifestation of deified man; for the descent of God to man is necessarily preceded by the exaltation of man to God.'

26. Cf. Hegel, *Glauben und Wissen* in *Werke*, ed. H. Glockner, Stuttgart 1927, I, 281f. and frequently elsewhere. Similar analyses may be found in J. Paul, Jacobi, Novalis, Fichte and Schelling; though Schelling scented this nihilism in Hegel's own philosophy (*Werke* X, 151ff.). In this case, as Heidegger interpreted the matter, Nietzsche would have correctly thought the modern era through to its logical conclusion.

27. Cf. the interpretation in H. Jonas, *Gnosis und spätantiker Geist*, vol. 1, Göttingen 1964, 94ff. (on the subject of dread and thrownness), 221ff., 238ff. (on the revolutionary character of gnosticism); H. M. Schenke, *Der Gott 'Mensch' in der Gnosis*, Göttingen 1962.

28. On the history of the reception and the different forms it took, see 'Autonomy and Theonomy', pp. 45–53 above. For a recent discussion of the relationship of Christianity to the Enlightenment, cf. M. Seckler, 'Aufklärung und Offenbarung' in *Christlicher Glaube in moderner Gesellschaft*, vol. 21, Freiburg, Basle and Vienna 1980, 5–78.

29. Cf. K. Rahner, *Geist in Welt. Zur Metaphysik der endlichen Erkenntnis bei Thomas von Aquin*, 2nd ed. Munich 1957.

30. K. Rahner, 'Zur Theologie der Menschwerdung' in *Schriften zur Theologie*, vol. 4, Einsiedeln, Zürich and Cologne 1960, 137–155, esp. 150f. (cf. 'On the Theology of the Incarnation', *Theological Investigations* IV, London 1966, 105–120, esp. 117). Also his *Foundations of Christian Faith*, trans. W. V. Dych, London 1978, 224–7. More recently, H. Fries, 'Theologie als Anthropologie' in K. Rahner and H. Fries, *Theologie in Freiheit und Verantwortung*, Munich 1981, 30–69.

31. On the criticism of the secularization thesis cf. especially H. Blumenberg, *Säkularisierung als Selbstbehauptung*, Frankfurt 1974, where the modern era is understood as a humane self-assertion against theonomy, interpreted in a Nominalist sense. Cf. here W. Pannenberg's criticism in 'Die christliche Legitimität der Neuzeit' in his *Gottesgedanke und menschliche Freiheit*, Göttingen 1972, 114–128. Pannenberg's criticism is justifiable in certain cases. But Blumenberg must be considered right inasmuch as any monocausal derivation of modern times from Christianity is bound to remain abstract. It cannot plausibly present as a mere mutual misunderstanding the fact that the modern freedom movement was specifically directed against the church – and was bound to be so directed, largely speaking; or that all the major churches assumed a negative and polemical attitude towards the struggle for freedom. It is of course true that the modern history of freedom was again mediated through Christianity, in its very antithesis. That is what makes it so tragic that Christianity's liberating impulses were so often forced to prevail in the face of Christianity in its established form.

32. Cf. K. Rahner, 'Transzendentaltheologie' in *Sacramentum Mundi*, Freiburg 1967–, IV, 986–992.

33. Cf. K. Rahner and W. Thüsing, *Christologie – systematisch und exegetisch*, QD 55, 1972, 22f.

34. B. Pascal, *Oeuvres de Pascal*. Pensées II, ed. L. Brunschvieg, Paris 1904, reprint Vaduz 1965, no. 397: 'La grandeur de l'homme est grande en ce qu'il se connâit misérable. Un arbre ne se connâit pas misérable. C'est donc être misérable que de [se] connâitre misérable; mais c'est être grand que de connâitre qu'on est misérable.'

35. Cf. W. Schulz, *Philosophie in einer veränderten Welt*, Pfullingen 1972, 602–609 and frequently elsewhere.

36. W. Dilthey, *Die drei Grundformen der Systeme in der ersten Hälfte des 19. Jahrhunderts* in *Gesammelte Schriften*, Leipzig 1911–, IV, 529.

37. Cf. K. Barth, *Christ and Adam. Man and Humanity in Romans 5*, trans. T. A. Smail, Edinburgh and London 1956, 43.

38. H. U. von Balthasar, *Karl Barth. Darstellung und Deutung seiner Theologie*, 2nd ed., Cologne 1962, 263ff. More recently, on Barth's anthropology: K. Stock, *Anthropologie der Verheißung. Karl Barths Lehre vom Menschen als dogmatisches Problem*, Munich 1980, which shows the failure of a christologically conceived anthropology in Barth's sense.

39. See ch. II n. 96 (pp 204f. above). (Ratzinger's article reappears in his *Dogma und Verkündigung*, Munich and Freiburg 1973, 161–181.) More recently: M. Figura, *Der Anruf der Gnade. Über die Beziehung des Menschen zu Gott nach Henri de Lubac*, Horizonte NF 13, Einsiedeln 1979.

40. The controversy between Barth and Bultmann is still of fundamental importance for the interpretation of the Adam-Christ typology. Cf. K. Barth, *Christ and Adam*; R. Bultmann, 'Adam und Christus nach Römer 5', ZNW 50, 1959, 145–165 (reprinted in *Der alte und der neue Mensch in der Theologie des Paulus*, Darmstadt 1964, 41–66). More recent literature (apart from the general commentaries) include: E. Brandenburger, *Adam und Christus. Exegetisch-religionsgeschichtliche Untersuchung zu Röm 5.12–21 (I Kor 15)*, WMANT 7, Neukirchen 1962; E. Jüngel, 'Das Gesetz zwischen Adam und Christus' in his *Unterwegs zur Sache*, Munich 1972, 145–172.

41. Cf. G. Bornkamm, 'Paulinische Anakoluthe im Römerbrief' in his *Das Ende des Gesetzes. Gesammelte Aufsätze*, vol. 1, Munich 1963, 80–90.

42. Cf. E. Jüngel, op. cit., 167f.

43. For a different view cf. U. Wilckens, *Der Brief an die Römer*, EKK VI/1, Zürich and Neukirchen 1978, 335ff. He interprets Paul in line with Hegel's dialectical *Aufhebung*, and not in the analogical sense.

44. Pastoral Constitution *Gaudium et spes*, 36, 41, 56.

45. Declaration on Religious Liberty *Dignitatis humanae*, 1, 10f.

46. Pastoral Constitution *Gaudium et spes*, 76.

47. J. E. Kuhn developed this determination dialectic in *Katholische Dogmatik*, vol. 1, 2nd ed., Tübingen 1859, 228ff. Cf. here W. Kasper, *Jesus der Christus*, 61, 292f.

48. This 'dialectical' formula probably meets Aquinas' concept best. On the one hand, for him God is the material and the formal object of faith and theology (*STh* I q. 1 a. 7; II/II q. 1 a. 1). On the other hand, faith is the anticipation of the beatific

vision (II/II q. 2 a. 3; q. 4 a. 1). Consequently, according to Aquinas, the statement of faith that God is the salvation of human beings and wills that salvation, implicitly contains all other truths of faith (II/II q. 2 a. 5).

49. Cf. J. Ratzinger, *Dogma und Verkündigung*, 148f.

50. Cf. J. Alfaro, 'Die Heilsfunktionen Christi als Offenbarer, Herr und Priester' in *Mysterium Salutis* (see n.23) 3/1, 677–781.

51. Cf. F. Mussner, 'Ursprünge und Entfaltung der neutestamentlichen Sohnes-christologie. Versuch einer Rekonstruktion' in *Grundfragen der Christologie heute*, QD 72, 1975, 97–104.

52. Cf. here J. Alfaro, 'Christo glorioso, rivelatore del Padre' in *Cristologia e antropologia*, Assisi 1972, 156–204.

53. Cf. J. Ratzinger, 'Licht' in *HThG* II, 44–54.

54. Cf. Thomas Aquinas, *STh* I/II q. 85 a. 3.

55. Pastoral Constitution *Gaudium et spes*, 22.

56. John Paul II, sermon preached in Victory Square, Warsaw, on June 2, 1979, printed in *Predigten und Ansprachen von Papst Johannes Paul II. bei seiner Pilgerfahrt durch Polen*, ed. Sekretariat der Deutschen Bischofskonferenz, Bonn 1979, 14.

57. Cf. DS 3004f.

58. Cf. Pastoral Constitution *Gaudium et spes*, 3f., 10f., 22, 40, 42f., 44, 62.

59. Cf. P. Ricoeur's interpretation of parable and metaphor in *Stellung und Funktion der Metapher in der biblischen Sprache*, EvTh Sonderheft 1974, 45–70.

60. J. Simon, 'Leben' in *HThG* II, 844.

61. Thomas Aquinas, *STh* III q. 48 a. 2 and 3.

62. Cf. K. Rahner, 'Opfer' in *LThK* VII, 1174f.

63. Hegel, *Vorlesungen über die Philosophie der Religion*, ed. G. Lasson, I/1, 227ff.

64. Characteristic of this are K. Marx's remarks in *Zur Judenfrage*, *Werke*, I, Darmstadt 1962, 459 (translated in *Karl Marx: Selected Writings*, ed. D. McLellan, Oxford 1977, 39–62) where, starting from the idea of emancipation, any mediation is excluded from the outset.

65. Cf. O. Marquard, 'Wie irrational kann Geschichtsphilosophie sein?' in his *Schwierigkeiten mit der Geschichtsphilosophie*, Frankfurt 1973, 66–82.

66. Barnabas 8, 5; Justin, *1st Apol.* 41; *Dial.* 73.

67. Cf. Pius XI, Encyclical *Quas primas* (1925) No. 71 (quoted in DS 3676).

68. Augustine, *De civ. Dei*, 19. 26.

69. Ibid., 14. 28; 19. 24.

70. Thomas Aquinas, *STh* III q. 8 a. 3. Cf. M. Seckler's interpretation, 'Das Haupt aller Menschen. Zur Auslegung eines Thomastextes' in *Virtus politica. Festschrift für A. Hufnagel*, Stuttgart-Bad Cannstatt 1974, 107–125.

71. Thus John Paul II in *Papst Johannes Paul II in Deutschland*, ed. Sekretariat der Deutschen Bischofskonferenz, Bonn 1980, 204; cf. W. Kasper, 'Die weltver-wandelnde Kraft christlicher Liebe. Grundsatzüberlegungen zum Verhältnis Christentum und Gesellschaft' in *Liebe verwandelt die Welt*, Mainz 1980, 25–52.

72. The pre-condition for an adequate discussion of political theology is awareness of the complicated history of this programmatic term. This reaches from its use in the ancient world (Panaitios, Varro), down to writers belonging to modern times (Macchiavelli and Hobbes on the one hand, and the traditionalism

of de Maistre etc. on the other), as well as the present-day problems encountered in C. Schmitt, and the largely new definition given to political theology by J. B. Metz and J. Moltmann especially. Attention must also be given to the precise context in which the term is at present used: for it is itself ambiguous and often open to misunderstanding. Consequently what is at issue here is not a limited theological sector (a political ethic for example). This is a fundamental theological concern: a definition of theology as a whole which no longer starts from the relationship between faith and reason, or dogma and history, but from a new relationship between theory and praxis. Faith then appears as a configuration or *Gestalt* of a socially critical freedom, and the church as the place of that freedom. This raises many individual problems; but apart from these, it seems to me that the fundamental question must be put to this comprehensive claim itself, because – by defining faith as the '*Gestalt* of . . .' it is pressing theology into an already given scheme, and failing to see it adequately in its own essential nature, which transcends the sphere of political praxis, and is relevant for that praxis because of that very fact. Consequently it misses the mark of the triple definition of the relation between christology and anthropology developed above. This criticism by no means diminishes the service rendered by political theology, which has stimulated and deepened theological reflection and drawn attention to urgent questions of political ethics.

73. On this definition of the relationship on the lines of analogy, and on its meaning for a theological elucidation of human rights, cf. W. Huber and H. E. Tödt, *Menschenrechte. Perspektiven einer menschlichen Welt*, Stuttart and Berlin 1977, 64ff., 160ff. On the total theological context of this question see 'Autonomy and Theonomy', pp. 32–53 above.

V. 'One of the Trinity . . .': Re-establishing a Spiritual Christology in the Perspective of Trinitarian Theology

1. Vatican II, *Lumen gentium*, 8. Cf. Y. Congar, 'Dogme christologique et Ecclésiologie. Vérité et limites d'un parallèle' in *Das Konzil von Chalkedon. Geschichte und Gegenwart* III, ed. A. Grillmeier and H. Bacht, Würzburg 1954, 239–286; F. X. Arnold, 'Das gottmenschliche Prinzip der Seelsorge und die Gestaltung der christlichen Frömmigkeit', ibid., 287–340.

2. Cf. A. Grillmeier, 'Moderne Hermeneutik und altkirchliche Christologie. Zur diskussion um die chalkedonische Christologie heute' in his *Mit ihm und in ihm. Christologische Forschungen und Perspektiven*, Freiburg 1975, 489.

3. J. Hick (ed.), *The Myth of God Incarnate*, London and Philadelphia 1977.

4. B. Sesboüé, 'Le procès contemporain de Chalcédoine. Bilan et perspectives', *RSR* 65, 1977, 45–79.

5. M. Luther, Sermon 520 of 14 May, 1525 (WA 16, 228f.). Cf. Melanchthon, *Loci communes* (1521) Intro.: 'hoc est Christum cognoscere beneficia eius cognoscere, non, quod isti docent, eius naturas, modos incarnationis contueri' (*Werke*, II/1, ed. R. Stupperich, Gütersloh 1952, 7). ['To know Christ is to know his benefits, not – as they teach – to consider his natures and the mode of his incarnation.']

6. F. Schleiermacher, *The Christian Faith*, trans. H. R. Mackintosh and J. S. Stewart, Edinburgh 1928, 391–8.

7. A. von Harnack, *History of Dogma* vol. IV, trans. E. B. Speirs and J. Millar, London 1898, 223.

8. Individual examples in B. Sesboüé, op. cit. Cf. also C. von Schönborn, 'Aporie der Zweinaturenlehre. Überlegungen zur Christologie von W. Pannenberg', *FZPhTh* 24, 1977, 428–445, and Pannenberg's reply, 'Zur "Aporie der Zweinaturenlehre". Brief an C. von Schönborn', *FZPhTh* 25, 1978, 100–103.

9. A. Grillmeier, op. cit., 89f. This was precisely the fundamental question in the debate on infallibility triggered off by H. Küng.

10. Cf. Y. Congar, 'Regards et réflexions sur la christologie de Luther' in *Chalkedon* III, 457–486; also his *Martin Luther. Sa foi, sa réforme*, Paris 1983, 105–134; M. Lienhard, *Luther témoin de Jésus-Christ*, Paris 1973; T. Beer, *Der fröhliche Wechsel und Streit. Grundzüge der Theologie Martin Luthers*, Einsiedeln 1980.

11. On the Nicaeno-Constantinopolitan creed, cf. J. N. D. Kelly, *Early Christian Creeds*, London 1950. K. Lehmann, 'Dogmenhermeneutik am Beispiel der klassischen Christologie' in *Jesus – Ort der Erfahrung Gottes*, with contributions by B. Casper et al., Freiburg 1976, 180–209; also the survey of literature and research on the subject by W. D. Hauschild, *Grundprobleme altkirchlicher Dogmengeschichte*, Beihefte zu *EvTh* 28, 1984, 4–32, esp. 25–32.

12. On these two models cf. A. Grillmeier, 'Die theologische und sprachliche Vorbereitung der christologischen Formel von Chalcedon' in *Chalkedon* I, Würzburg 1951, 67ff.; also his *Jesus der Christus im Glauben der Kirche* I, Freiburg 1979.

13. For a new judgment on Nestorius cf. A. Grillmeier, 'Das Scandalum occumenicum des Nestorios in kirchlich-dogmatishcher und theologiegeschichtlicher Sicht' in *Mit ihm und in ihm*, 245–282; also his *Jesus der Christus im Glauben der Kirche*, I, 642ff., 707ff.

14. On Tertullian cf. R. Cantalamessa, *La christologia di Tertulliano*, Paradosis 18, Freiburg 1962; A. Grillmeier, *Jesus der Christus*, 241–257.

15. On Augustine, cf. W. Geerlings, *Christus Exemplum. Studien zur Christologie und Christusverkündigung Augustinus*, (= TThSt 13), Mainz 1978; A. Grillmeier, *Jesus der Christus*, 594–604.

16. The modern situation in research with regard to neo-Chalcedonianism would be an important subject of its own in this context, but it is impossible to enter into it here. An excellent summing up and evaluation of the discussion may be found in A. Grillmeier, 'Der Neu-Chalkedonismus' in his *Mit ihm und in ihm*, 371–385. According to Grillmeier, the neo-Chalcedonian interpretation of Chalcedon, as this was accepted at the Second Ecumenical Council of Constantinople (533) and as it came to prevail in later tradition (in the West, especially through Aquinas' influence) was in clear continuity with Chalcedon, especially if this council is interpreted in the light of the modern research considered here. In so far it is distinct from the mediating, temporary and historically conditioned two-track terminology of neo-Chalcedonian theology in its narrower sense.

17. On this formula cf. A. Lachenschmid, 'Theopaschismus', *LThK* X, 83; J. Meyendorff, *Le Christ dans la théologie byzantine*, Paris 1969, 91–120; A. M. Ritter, 'Dogma und Lehre der Alten Kirche' in C. Andresen (ed.), *Handbuch der Dogmen- und Theologiegeschichte* I, Göttingen 1982, 274ff.

18. Thus for example P. Schoonenberg, *Der Gott der Menschen*, Einsiedeln

1969, 52ff. K. Rahner is much more cautious; cf. 'Jesus Christus – Sinn des Lebens' in his *Schriften zur Theologie* 15, Zürich, Einsiedeln and Cologne 1983, 206–213, esp. 210ff. Rahner's characterization of neo-Chalcedonianism is historically inaccurate. From a dogmatic and systematic standpoint, however, this is precisely the point where the difference from H. U. von Balthasar's christology is to be found, and consequently the heart of the difference in the doctrine of the Trinity. If the views put forward here about the dogmatic history are correct, one must assent to Balthasar's dogmatic point of departure. At the same time, Balthasar's speculative elaboration of these existing dogmatic facts (which is deeply influenced by the mysticism of Adrienne von Speyr) would require separate discussion. This is particularly true when the kenosis belonging to the economy of salvation is introduced into the immanent Trinity itself – an idea especially influenced by the sophiology of S. Bulgakow and ultimately by Hegel. On questions arising here cf. H. U. von Balthasar, *Theodramatik* IV, Einsiedeln 1983, 11, and the comments by W. Breuning and W. Löser in *Trinität. Aktuelle Perspektiven der Theologie*, ed. W. Breuning, QD 101, 1984, 18, 26ff.

19. Recent literature on the christological dogma of Chalcedon: M. Richard, 'L'introduction du mot "hypostase" dans la théologie de l'incarnation', *Mélanges de Science religieuse* 2, 1945, 5–32; 243–270; A. Grillmeier and H. Bacht, *Das Konzil von Chalkedon. Geschichte und Gegenwart*, 3 vols., Würzburg 1951–54 (the contributions by A. Grillmeier, U. Ortiz de Urbina, C. Moeller, and K. Rahner are important for our present subject); R. V. Sellers, *The Council of Chalcedon. A Historical and Doctrinal Survey*, London 1953; H. M. Diepen, 'Les Trois Chapitres au concile de Chalcédon', *Mél. de Science rel.* 11, 1954, 89–92; also his *Douze dialogues de christologie ancienne*, Rome 1960; H. Dörrie, 'Ὑπόστασις (Hypostasis). Wort- und Bedeutungsgeschichte', Nachrichten der Akademie der Wiss., Philolog.-hist. Klasse, Göttingen 1955, 35–92; E. L. Fortin, 'The Definitio Fidei of Chalkedon and its Philosophical Sources' in *Stud. Patr.* 5.3 (= TU 80), Berlin 1962, 489–498; P.T. Camelot, *Ephesus und Chalkedon* (= *Geschichte der ökumenischen Konzilien* 2), Mainz 1963; T. Šagi-Bunić, '"Duo perfecta" et "duae naturae" in definitione dogmatica Chalcedonensi', *Laurentianum* 5, 1964, 3–70; 203–244; 321–362; also his *"Deus perfectus et homo perfectus" a Concilio Ephesino (a. 431) ad Chalcedonense (a. 451)*, Rome 1965; J. Liébaert, 'Christologie' in *HDG* III/1a, Freiburg 1965; R. Cantalamessa, 'Tertullian et la formule christologique de Chalcédoine' in *Stud. Patr.*, 9.3 (= TU 94), Berlin 1966, 139–150; J. I. Gonzalez-Faus, 'La discussión holandese sobre Calcedonia' in *Selecciones di Teologia* 1972, 168–182; also his 'Relectura de Calcedonia', ibid. 183ff.; A. Grillmeier, *Mit ihm und in ihm. Christologische Forschungen und Perspektiven*, Freiburg 1975; J. Sanna, 'Indicazioni per una interpretazione del dogma di Calcedonia' in *Miscellanea Lateranense* 50/51, Rome 1975, 226–253; A. de Halleux, 'La définition christologique à Chalcédoine', *RTL* 7, 1976, 3–23; 155–170; R. Marlé et al. in *RSR* 65, 1977; J. Hick (ed.), *The Myth of God Incarnate*, London and Philadephia 1977; A. Grillmeier, *Jesus der Christus im Glauben der Kirche* I, Freiburg 1979; P. Stockmeier, 'Das Konzil von Chalkedon' in *Glaube an Jesus Christus*, ed. J. Blank and G. Hasenhüttl, Düsseldorf 1980, 102–116; P. Schoonenberg, 'Denken über Chalkedon', *ThQ* 160, 1980, 295–305; L. Abramowski, *Drei christologische Untersuchungen*, Berlin 1981; L. R. Wickham, 'Chalkedon' in *TRE* VII, 1981, 668–675; B. Sesboüe, *Jésus-Christ dans la tradi-*

tion de l'Eglise, Pour une actualisation de la christologie de Chalcédoine, Paris 1982; A. M. Ritter, 'Dogma und Lehre in der alten Kirche' in C. Andresen (ed.), *Handbuch der Dogmen- und Theologiegeschichte* I, Göttingen 1982, esp. 261–270.

20. Thus rightly E. Schlink, *Ökumenische Dogmatik. Grundzüge*, Göttingen 1983, 533.

21. The trinitarian perspective of the creed has been especially stressed anew by H. de Lubac, *La foi chrétienne. Essai sur la structure du Symbole des Apôtres*, Paris 1969. Lubac defends this trinitarian stress against the narrow christocentric interpretation of O. Cullmann in *The Earliest Christian Confessions*, trans. J. K. S. Reid, London 1949.

22. Thus A. Grillmeier, 'Moderne Hermeneutik und altkirchliche Christologie' in *Mit ihm und in ihm*, 538–540.

23. Cf. n. 19.

24. Cf. esp. W. Beierwaltes, *Proklos. Grundzüge seiner Metaphysik*, Philosophische Abhandlungen 24, Frankfurt 1965.

25. Cf. H. U. von Balthasar, *Kosmische Liturgie. Das Weltbild Maximos' des Bekenners*, Einsiedeln 1961; L. Thunberg, *Microcosm and Mediator. The Theological Anthropology of Maximus the Confessor*, Lund 1965; J. Meyendorff, *Le Christ dans la théologie byzantine*, Paris 1969, 177–206; A. Riou, *Le monde et l'église selon Maxime le Confesseur*, Théologie historique 22, Paris 1973.

26. J. Ratzinger, *Schauen auf den Durchbohrten. Versuche zu einer sprituellen Christologie*, Einsiedeln 1984, 33–37.

27. H. G. Beck, 'Die frühbyzantinische Kirche' in H. Jedin (ed.), *Handbuch der Kirchengeschichte*, II/2, Freiburg 1975, 41. On the background as a whole cf. W. Elert, *Der Ausgang der altkirchlichen Christologie*, Berlin 1957, esp. 230–257.

28. Cf. K. Rahner, 'Probleme der Christologie von heute' in *Schriften zur Theologie* I, Zürich, Einsiedeln and Cologne 1954, 169f. (cf. 'Current Problems in Christology', *Theological Investigations* I, London 1961, 149).

29. F. Schleiermacher, *The Christian Faith*, 385–389.

30. This was the concern, and also the great merit, of K. Rahner, to whom I have been greatly indebted here from the beginning. Cf. *Das Absolute in der Geschichte. Philosophie und Theologie der Geschichte in der Spätphilosophie Schellings*, Mainz 1965. Any criticism which is directed only towards the result of modern subjectivity and censures this as Idealism fails to grasp this ontological concern, and the fact that it takes up the Realist position.

31. Cf. M. Müller, *Existenzphilosophie im geistigen Leben der Gegenwart*, 3rd ed., Heidelberg 1964, 160ff.

32. Cf. M. Heidegger, *Being and Time*, trans. J. Macquarrie and E. Robinson, London 1962. pp. 32ff.

33. This new approach is generally accepted, even though individual emphases differ. We find it in most fundamental and detailed form in W. Pannenberg, *Jesus – God and Man*, trans. L. L. Wilkins and D. A. Priebe, London 1968, 324ff.; as well as in K. Rahner, 'Probleme der Christologie von heute', *Schriften* I, 181f. ('Current Problems in Christology', *Theological Investigations* I, 158f.); also in K. Rahner and W. Thüsing, *Christologie – systematisch und exegetisch. Arbeitsgrundlage für eine interdisziplinäre Vorlesung*, QD 55, 1972, 28ff.; W. Kasper, *Jesus der Christus*, Mainz 1974, 195f. (*Jesus the Christ*, trans.

V. Green, London 1976); also *The God of Jesus Christ*, New York and London 1984, 170f.; H. U. von Balthasar, *Theodramatik* II/2, Einsiedeln 1978, 136ff.; D. Wiederkehr, 'Entwurf einer systematischen Christologie' in *Mysterium Salutis*, Einsiedeln, Zürich and Cologne, 1965– , III/1, 566ff.; also in *Mysterium Salutis* Ergänzungs-Band, 220ff.; J. Ratzinger, *Schauen auf den Durchbohrten*, 15ff.

34. J. Jeremias, *The Prayers of Jesus*, trans. J. S. Bowden, C. Burchard and J. Reumann, London and Naperville, Ill., 1967. The interpretation of the cry of desolation 'My God, my God, why hast thou forsaken me?' (Mark 15.34) is important for Jesus' preservation of his 'Abba' relationship, even when he was dying. Since this saying is a quotation from the opening of Psalm 22, it must not be interpreted as an utterance of despair, but must be understood as an expression of trust. 'In the darkness of "God-forsakenness", he turns to God in prayer' (R. Pesch, *Das Markusevangelium*, Pt. II, Freiburg 1977, 495). H. Gese's interpretation is very helpful; cf. 'Psalm 22 und das Neue Testament. Der älteste Bericht vom Tode Jesus und die Entstehung des Herrenmahles' in his *Vom Sinai zum Zion. Alttestamentliche Beiträge für biblische Theologie*, Munich 1974, 180–201.

35. It is unfortunately impossible to develop the pneumatological aspect here. Cf. W. Kasper, *Jesus der Christus*, 298f., 302f. and *The God of Jesus Christ*, 202ff.; U. von Balthasar, *Theodramatik* II/2, 167ff.

36. Cf. especially John 5.20; 8.26–28, 38, 40; 15.15; 17.8, 11f., 22.

37. Cf. Thomas Aquinas, *STh* I, q. 43, a. 1.

38. These lines are dedicated to W. Breuning, who early on, following M. Schmaus and K. Rahner, especially stressed this close connection between Christology and the doctrine of the Trinity. Cf. W. Breuning, 'Trinitätslehre' in *Bilanz der Theologie im 20. Jahrhundert*, ed. H. Vorgrimler and R. van der Gucht, vol. 3, Freiburg 1970, 21–36; also his article 'Gott/Trinität' in *NHThG* 2, 133–149.

39. Cf. here W. Kasper, 'Neuansätze gegenwärtiger Christologie' in J. Sauer (ed.), *Wer ist Jesus Christus?*, Freiburg 1977, 123ff.; also Kasper, 'Neuansätze gegenwärtiger Christologie' in W. Kasper (ed.), *Christologische Schwerpunkte*, Düsseldorf 1980, 17ff.

40. Cf. K. Rahner, 'Probleme der Christologie', 183.

41. The neo-scholastic question about Jesus' human consciousness, which reached a deadlock, could probably be much more easily solved in a christology which starts from Jesus' 'Abba' relationship than it was in tradition.

42. A. von Harnack, *History of Dogma* 4, 222f.

43. Cf. here A. Grillmeier, 'Quod non assumptum – non sanatum', LThK VIII, 954–956.

44. Cf. H. U. von Balthasar, *Theodramatik* III, Einsiedeln 1980, 224ff.

45. Important suggestions for a trinitarian spirituality of this kind may be found in K. Hemmerle, *Thesen zu einer trinitarischen Ontologie*, Einsiedeln 1976. For a survey and an important stimulus for further discussion cf. L. Oeing-Hanhoff, 'Trinitarische Ontologie und Metaphysik der Person' in W. Breuning (ed.), *Trinität*, (see n. 18), 143–182.

46. Cf. W. Kasper, 'Autonomy and Theonomy', pp. 32–53 above.

47. Cf. W. Kasper, 'Christology and Anthropology', pp. 73–93 above.

VI. The Church as a Universal Sacrament of Salvation

1. Cf. as summing up, K. Rahner, *Foundations of Christian Faith*, trans. W. V. Dych, London 1978, 116–126.
2. Ibid. 126–133.
3. Cf. K. Rahner, 'Das Grundwesen der Kirche' in *Handbuch der Pastoraltheologie* I, Freiburg, Basle and Vienna 1964, esp. 132f.; also his *Kirche und Sakramente*, QD 20, 1960, 11–18 (*The Church and the Sacraments*, trans. W. J. O'Hara, Freiburg, Edinburgh and London 1963); also 'The New Image of the Church' in *Theological Investigations* X, 1973, 3–29.
4. Cf. K. Rahner, 'Considerations of the Active Role of the Person in the Sacramental Event' in *Theological Investigations* XIV, 1976, 169f.
5. *Lumen gentium* 48; *Gaudium et spes* 45.
6. Talk about the church as a sign has also been ecumenical language ever since the General Assembly of the World Council of Churches in Uppsala (1968). Cf. *The Uppsala Report 1968*, ed. N. Goodall, Geneva 1968, 17: 'The church is bold in speaking of itself as the sign of the coming unity of mankind.' However this usage is a matter of considerable dispute ecumenically, as may be seen in E. Käseman's essay 'Zur ekklesiologischen Verwendung der Stichworte "Sakrament" und "Zeichen"' in his *Kirchliche Konflikte* I, Göttingen 1982, 46–61.
7. The most important literature is as follows: O. Semmelroth, 'Die Kirche als sichtbare Gestalt der unsichtbaren Gnade', *Scholastik* 28, 1953, 23–39; also his *Die Kirche als Ursakrament*, Frankfurt 1953; also 'Die Kirche als Sakrament des Heils' in *Mysterium Salutis* IV/1, Einsiedeln, Zürich and Cologne 1972, 309–356; P. Smulders, 'A Preliminary Remark on Patristic Sacramental Doctrine', *Bijdragen* 15, 1954, 25–30; also his 'Die sakramental-kirchliche Struktur des christlichen Gnade', ibid., 18, 1957, 333–341; also 'Die Kirche als Sakrament des Heils' in G. Baraúna (ed.), *De Ecclesia* I, Freiburg 1966, 289–312; E. Schillebeeckx, *Christ the Sacrament of Encounter with God*, trans. P. Barrett and N. D. Smith, London and New York 1963; J. Witte, 'Die Kirche als sacramentum unitatis für die ganze Welt' in G. Baraúna, op. cit., 420–452; J. Alfaro, 'Cristo sacramento de Diós Padre. La iglesia, sacramento di Cristo glorificado', *Gregorianum* 58, 1967, 5–28; L. Boff, *Die Kirche als Sakrament im Horizont der Welterfahrung. Versuch einer Legitimation und einer strukturfunktionalistischen Grundlegung der Kirche im Anschluß an das II. Vatikanische Konzil*, Paderborn 1972; Y. Congar, *Un Peuple messianique. L'Église, sacrement du salut. Salut et libération*, Paris 1975; J. Ratzinger, 'Kirche als Heilssakrament' in J. Reicherstorfer (ed.), *Zeit des Geistes*, Vienna 1977, 59–70; W. Beinert, 'Die Sakramentalität der Kirche im theologischen Gespräch' in *Theologische Berichte* IX, Einsiedeln and Zürich 1980, 13–63; J. Auer, 'Die Kirche – Das allgemeine Heils-sakrament', *Kleine katholische Dogmatik* VIII, Regensburg 1983, 84–96.
8. On the following passage see esp. L. Boff, op. cit., 228–295; J. Ratzinger, op. cit., 59ff.
9. For the history cf. L. Boff, op. cit., 49–123; 295–330; Y. Congar, op. cit., 27–55; M. Bernards, 'Zur Lehre von der Kirche als Sakrament. Beobachtungen aus der Theologie des 19. und 20. Jahrhunderts', *MThZ* 20, 1969, 29–54; J. Auer, *op. cit.*, 85–92.

10. H. de Lubac, *Catholicism. A study of dogma in relation to the corporate destiny of mankind*, trans. L. C. Sheppard, London 1950, 291; cf. also his *Méditation sur l'Église*, 2nd ed., Paris 1953 (*Betrachtung über die Kirche*, Graz, Vienna and Cologne 1954, 137).

11. Cf. G. Alberigo and F. Magistretti, *Constitutionis Lumen gentium Synopsis historica*, Bologna 1975, 381.

12. Ibid., 3.

13. Ibid., 436f.

14. Cf. K. Rahner, *Symbole der Kirche. Die Ekklesiologie der Väter*, Salzburg 1964, esp. 91ff. The concept of sacrament expresses the fact that the church goes beyond itself in the direction of Christ and the world. This is especially stressed by H. U. von Balthasar, *Theodramatik* II/2, Einsiedeln 1978, 394ff.

15. G. Alberigo and F. Magistretti, op. cit., 436f.

16. J. Finkenzeller, 'Die Lehre von den Sakramenten im allgemeinen' in *HDG* IV/1a, 123ff.

17. Ibid., 24ff.

18. Thus especially E. Jüngel, 'Das Sakrament – Was ist das?' in E. Jüngel and K. Rahner, *Was ist ein Sakrament? Vorstöße zur Verständigung*, Freiburg, Basle and Vienna 1971, 50ff.

19. Augustine, *Ep.* 187, 34: 'Non est enim aliud Dei mysterium nisi Christus' (PL 33, 846). On this subject cf. W. Geertings, *Christus exemplum. Studien zur Christologie und Christus Verkündigung Augustins*, Tübinger Theol. Studien 13, Mainz 1978, esp. 220ff. For Leo the Great the cross of Christ is the *sacramentum et exemplum* (*Sermo* 72. 1; PL 54, 390). But his view is also 'quod Redemptoris conspicuum fuit in sacramenta transivit' (*Sermo* 74. 2; PL 54, 398).

20. Cf. above all G. Bornkamm, 'μυστήριον' in *TDNT* IV, 802–28; Y. Congar, op. cit., 27ff.; J. Finkenzeller, op. cit., 8ff.

21. Cf. K. Rahner, 'The Concept of Mystery in Catholic Theology', *Theological Investigations* IV, 1966, 36–73.

22. K. Rahner, 'Das Grundwesen der Kirche' in *Handbuch der Pastoraltheologie* I, 129.

23. K. Rahner, op. cit., 137ff.

24. Ibid., 122, 133f.

25. H. R. Schlette takes a different view; cf. his *Die Religionen als Thema der Theologie*, QD 22, 1963, 85f.

26. It is of course impossible to develop here the problem of anonymous Christians in Rahner. The volume designed as a Festschrift for his 75th birthday was devoted to this subject; cf. *Christentum innerhalb und außerhalb der Kirche*, ed. E. Klinger, QD 73, 1976.

27. K. Rahner, 'Anonymous Christians', in *Theological Investigations* VI, 1969, 396: 'The doctrine of "anonymous Christianity" . . . is not a hermeneutical principle critically to reduce the whole corpus of traditional theology and dogmatics . . .; from a dogmatic point of view this doctrine is perhaps even a peripheral phenomenon, whose necessity, lawfulness and correctness derive from many other individual data of ecclesiastical teaching.'

28. Augustine, *In Joan.* tr. 80.3 (CC 36, 529).

29. Thomas Aquinas, *STh* III q. 61 a. 4 c. a.: 'Sunt autem sacramenta quaedam

signa protestantia fidem, qua homo iustificatur.' Further references and literature in Y. Congar, op. cit., 51 n. 9.

30. O. Casel has again brought this aspect into prominence with his mystery theology. Cf. A. Schilson, *Theologie als Sakramententheologie. Die Mysterientheologie Odo Casels*, Tübinger Theol. Studien 18, Mainz 1982.

31. Cf. R. Holz, *Sakramente – im Wechselspiel zwischen Ost und West*, Ökumenische Theologie 2, Zürich, Cologne and Gütersloh 1979.

32. Cf. Y. Congar, 'Die Lehre von der Kirche. Von Augustinus bis zum abendländischen Schisma' in *HDG* III/3c, 106; 110f.

33. Cf. J. Finkenzeller, op. cit., 119ff.

34. This finds expression in, among other things, the new reception of the scholastic distinction between *sacramenta maiora* and *sacramenta minora*. Cf. here Y. Congar, 'The Idea of "Major" or "Principal" Sacraments', *Concilium* 4, January 1968, 12–17.

35. Cf. K. Rahner, *Kirche und Sakramente* (see n. 3), 37–67 (*Church and Sacraments*, 41–74).

36. On the discussion about this point cf. Y. Congar, *Un peuple messianique* (n. 7 above), 67–69.

37. Cf. F. Schupp, *Glaube – Kultur – Symbol. Versuch einer kritischen Theorie sakramentaler Praxis*, Düsseldorf 1974, 123–131.

38. Cf. K. Rahner, 'Considerations of the Active Role of the Person in the Sacramental Event' (see n. 4 above), 161ff.

39. Ibid., 177f.

40. Ibid., 180.

41. Cf. K. Rahner, 'Concerning the Relationship between Nature and Grace', *Investigations* I, 1961, 302ff.; also 'Nature and Grace' in *Investigations* IV, 1966, 165–188; also 'Existential, übernatürliches' in *LThK* III, 1301, and frequently.

42. Cf. K. Rahner, 'Erbsünde' in *Sacramentum Mundi* I, 1113f.

43. H. U. von Balthasar especially has worked out this theodramatic aspect in *Theodramatik* II/2, 380ff.; III, 203–209. For its liturgical significance, cf. C. Vagaggini, *Theologie der Liturgie*, Einsiedeln, Zürich and Cologne 1959, 233–263. From the point of view of political theology, J. B. Metz points anew to the importance of apocalyptic; cf. his *Faith in History and Society: towards a practical fundamental theology*, trans. D. Smith, London 1980, 169–79. This probably also covers E. Käsemann's fundamental concern (cf. n. 6 above).

44. Augustine, *civ. Dei* 19–26 (CSEL 40/2, 421).

45. Irenaeus of Lyons, *Adv. haer.* IV 34, 1. Cf. ibid., III 17, 1, according to which it is the task of the Holy Spirit to renew human beings, bringing them out of the old into the newness of Christ.

46. Cf. 'Christology and Anthropology', pp. 73–93 above. On Rahner's theology in general, cf. W. Kasper, 'Karl Rahner – Theologe in einer Zeit des Umbruchs', *ThQ* 159, 1979, 263–271.

VII. The Church as the Place of Truth

1. Cf. R. Guardini, *Berichte über mein Leben. Autobiographische Aufzeichnungen, aus dem Nachlaß*, ed. F. Henrich, Düsseldorf 1984, 70–73.

2. Quoted in H. B. Gerl, *Romano Guardini. 1885–1968. Leben und Werk*, Mainz 1985, 60.

3. Cf. P. L. Berger, *The Heretical Imperative: Contemporary Possibilities of Religious Affirmation*, New York 1979, London 1980.

4. Cf. R. Guardini, *The Church and the Catholic and The Spirit of the Liturgy*, trans. A. Lane, London 1935, 199–211 (cit. from 205).

5. Cf. H. Küng, *Infallible? An Enquiry*, trans. E. Mosbacher, London 1972.

6. Cf. G. Gutiérrez, *A Theology of Liberation*, trans. C. Inda and J. Eagleson, London and New York 1974, 11–15.

7. J. Pieper, 'Der Verderb des Wortes und die Macht. Platons Kampf gegen die Sophistik', *Hochland* 57, 1964/65, 12–25.

8. Cf. J. Pieper, *Die Wahrheit der Dinge. Eine Untersuchung zur Anthropologie des Hochmittelalters*, Munich 1957.

9. Cf. M. Heidegger, *Platons Lehre von der Wahrheit*, Bern 1954; also his *Vom Wesen der Wahrheit*, 3rd ed., Frankfurt 1954.

10. G. von Rad, *Wisdom in Israel*, trans. J. D. Martin, Nashville 1972, London 1975.

11. Irenaeus of Lyons, *Adv. haer.* III, 24, 1.

12. Ibid., IV, 33, 8.

13. R. Guardini, *The Church and the Catholic*, 11.

14. Cf. Dogmatic Constitution on the Church, *Lumen gentium*, 12; 35 and frequently.

15. Cf. J. H. Newman, 'On Consulting the Faithful in Matters of Doctrine', an essay in *The Rambler*, vol. I, July 1859, published separately, London 1961.

16. Cf. P. M. Zulehner, *Religion nach Wahl. Grundlegung einer Auswahl-christenpastoral*, Vienna 1974; also his 'Auswahlchristen' in *Volkskirche – Gemeindekirche – Parakirche*, Theologische Berichte 10, ed. J. Pfammatter and F. Furger, Zürich etc., 1981, 109–137.

17. M. Weber, *Wissenschaft als Beruf*, 6th ed., Berlin 1975, 28.

18. Cf. J. A. Möhler, *Die Einheit in der Kirche oder das Prinzip des Katholizismus*, ed. J. R. Geiselmann, Cologne 1957, 152–157.

19. Here lies the justifiable concern, and also the fundamental problem, of the suggestion made by H. Fries and K. Rahner in their book *Einigung der Kirchen – reale Möglichkeit*, QD 100, 1983.

20. See also H. Meyer and L. Vischer (eds.), *Growth in Agreement. Reports and Agreed Statements of Ecumenical Conversations on a World Level*, WCC, Geneva and New York 1984.

VIII. The Church as Communion: Reflections on the Guiding Ecclesiological Idea of the Second Vatican Council

1. R. Guardini, *The Church and the Catholic*, trans. A. Lane, London 1935, 11.

2. For the rediscovery of the church as *communio*, the following work is important (for biblical and historical studies relating to the subject cf. nn. 9 and 16 below): Yves Congar, *Divided Christendom. A Catholic study of the problem of reunion*, trans. M. A. Bousfield, London 1939; H. de Lubac, *Catholicism. A study of dogma in relation to the corporate destiny of mankind*, trans. L. C. Sheppard, London 1950; M.-J. Le Guillou, *Mission et unité. Les exigences de la communion*,

Unam sanctam 33, Paris 1960; J. Hamer, *The Church is a Communion*, trans. R. Matthews, London 1964.

3. Thus the secretary of the theological commission, G. Philips; cf. his *L'Église et son mystère au IIe concile du Vatican*, Paris 1966, vol. 1, 7, 59; vol. 2, 24f., 54, 159 and frequently; also Philips in *LThK* Vat. II, vol. 1, 139; also A. Grillmeier, ibid., 161. The extraordinary synod of bishops of 1985 has meanwhile taken up the conciliar approaches to a *communio* ecclesiology and has resolutely taken them further. Cf. *Zukunft aus der Kraft des Konzils. Die außerordentliche Bischofssynode '85. Die Dokumente mit einem Kommentar von W. Kasper*, Freiburg, Basle and Vienna 1986, 89–97.

4. H. U. von Balthasar, 'Communio – Ein Programm', *IKZ Communio* 1, 1972, 8.

5. Important studies on Vatican II's concept of *communio* are the following: O. Saier, *'Communio' in der Lehre des Zweiten Vatikanischen Konzils. Eine rechtsbegriffliche Untersuchung*, Münchner Theologische Studien, 3. Abt. vol. 32, Munich 1973; H. Rossi, *Die Kirche als personale Gemeinschaft. Der kommunitäre Charakter der Kirche nach den Dokumenten und Akten des Zweiten Vatikanischen Konzils*, Grenzfragen zwischen Theologie und Philosophie, vol. 25, Cologne 1976.

6. Cf. *Constitutionis Dogmaticae Lumen gentium Synopsis historica*, ed. G. Alberigo and F. Magistretti, Bologna 1975, 436f. For the interpretation of the church as *mysterium*/ sacrament, cf. 'The Church as a Universal Sacrament of Salvation', pp. 111–128 above.

7. Cf. Cyprian, *De oratione dominica* 23, PL 4, 553. Cf. here G. Philips, *L'Eglise et son mystère*, 91–93; H. de Lubac, *Les églises particulières dans l'Eglise universelle*, Paris 1971 (German trans. *Quellen kirchlicher Einheit*, Einsiedeln 1974, 172–187); *La Santissima Trinidad fuente de salvacion en la Constitucion sobre le Iglesia*, Salamanca 1968; N. Silanez, *'La Iglesia de la Trinidad.' La Santissima Trinidad en el Vaticani II. Estudio genetico-teologico*, Salamanca 1981.

8. Cf. here H. Müller, 'Communio als kirchenrechtliches Prinzip im Codex Juris Canonici von 1983' in *Im Gespräch mit dem Dreieinen Gott. Elemente einer trinitarischen Theologie. (Festschrift für W. Breuning)*, ed. M. Böhnke and H. Heinz, Düsseldorf 1985, 495f.

9. Cf. H. Seesemann, *Der Begriff KOINΩNIA im Neuen Testament*, Gießen 1933; F. Hauck, 'κοινός' in *TDNT* III, 789–797; C. Bori, *KOINΩNIA. L'idea della comunione nell'ecclesiologia recente e nel Nuova Testamento*, Brescia 1972.

10. J. R. Geiselmann, *Die theologische Anthropologie Johann Adam Möhlers. Ihr geschichtlicher Wandel*, Freiburg 1955, 56–105; W. Elert, *Eucharist and Church Fellowship in the first four centuries*, trans. N. E. Nagel, St Louis 1966; H. de Lubac, 'Credo . . . Sanctorum Communionem', *IKZ Communio* 1, 1972, 18–32.

11. Augustine, *In Joan.* tr. 26. 13 (CC 36, 266).

12. Cf. O. Saier, *Communio*, 48ff.

13. Cf. H. de Lubac, *Corpus mysticum. L'Eucharistie et l'Eglise au Moyen Age*, 2nd ed., Paris 1949; A. Gerken, *Theologie der Eucharistie*, Munich 1973,'111ff.

14. Cf. 'Aspects of the Eucharist in their Unity and Variety' pp. 189–191 below.

15. Cf. O. Saier, *Communio*, 36ff.

16. Cf. L. Hertling, *Communio und Primat*, Miscellanea Historia Pontificiae VII, 9, Rome 1943; W. Elert, *Eucharist and Church Fellowship*.

17. On this development cf. Y. Congar, 'De la communion des Eglises à une

ecclésiologie de l'Eglise universelle' in *L'Episcopat et l'Eglise universelle*, ed. Y. Congar and B. D. Dupuy, Unam sanctam 39, Paris 1962, 229–260.

18. K. Rahner and J. Ratzinger, *Episkopat und Primat*, QD 11, 1961; W. Bertrams, *De relatione inter episcopatum et papstum*, Rome 1963; J. Colson, *L'épiscopat catholique: collégialité et primauté dans les trois premiers siècles*, Unam sanctam 43, Paris 1963; Y. Congar, *La collégialité épiscopale*, Unam sanctam 52, Paris 1965; also his *Ministères et communion ecclésiale*, Paris 1971; U. Betti, *La dottrina sull'episcopato del capitolo III della costituzione dommatica Lumen gentium*, Rome 1968.

19. G. Ghirlanda, *'Hierarchica communio.' Significato della formula nella Lumen gentium*, Rome 1980.

20. Cf. here the commentary by J. Ratzinger in *LThK* Vat. II, vol. 1, 348–359.

21. Cf. above all A. Acerbi, *Due ecclesiologie. Ecclesiologia giuridica ed ecclesiologia di communione nella 'Lumen gentium'*, Bologna 1975.

22. Cf. 'The Continuing Challenge of the Second Vatican Council. The Hermeneutics of the Conciliar Statements', pp. 166–175 below.

23. Cf. here M.-J. Le Guillou, *Mission et unité*, (German trans., *Sendung und Einheit der Kirche*, Mainz 1964, 560–614); J. Hamer, *L'Eglise est une communion*, Unam sanctam 40, Paris 1962, 207ff. (ET *The Church*, 190ff.)

24. H. de Lubac, *Les églises particulières* (German trans. *Quellen kirchlicher Einheit*, 31ff.).

25. Cf. H. U. von Balthasar, *Der antirömische Affekt*, Freiburg, Basle and Vienna 1974.

26. J. J. von Allmen, quoted in H. de Lubac, *Les églises*, 55 (*Quellen*, 54); cf. *Ad gentes* 9: 'Whatever goodness is found in the minds and hearts of men, or in the particular customs and cultures of peoples, far from being lost, is purified, raised to a higher level and reaches its perfection . . .'

27. H. de Lubac, *Les églises*, 50f., (*Quellen*, 49f.).

28. W. Kasper, *The God of Jesus Christ*, New York and London 1984, 293–296, 305f., 315f.

29. B. Forte, *La chiesa – icona della Trinità. Breve ecclesiologia*, Brescia 1984.

30. Cf. H. Müller, 'Communio als kirchenrechtliches Prinzip', (n. 8 above).

31. H. J. Pottmeyer, 'Kontinuität und Innovation in der Ekklesiologie des II. Vatikanums' in *Kirche im Wandel. Eine kritische Zwischenbilanz nach dem Zweiten Vatikanum*, ed. S. Alberigo, Y. Congar and H. J. Pottmeyer, Düsseldorf 1982, 89–110; M. Legrand, 'Die Entwicklung der Kirchen als verantwortliche Subjekte. Eine Anfrage an das II. Vatikanum', ibid., 141–174.

32. J. A. Möhler, *Die Einheit in der Kirche oder das Prinzip des Katholizismus*, ed. J. R. Geiselmann, Darmstadt 1957.

33. Ibid., 237.

34. Cf. H. Peukert, *Wissenschaftstheorie – Handlungstheorie – Fundamentale Theologie. Analysen zu Ansatz und Status theologischer Theoriebildung*, Düsseldorf 1976.

X. Aspects of the Eucharist in their Unity and Variety: On the Recent Discussion about the Fundamental Form and Meaning of the Eucharist

1. This is not the place to describe the whole discussion, which is endless, or to

enter into it in any detail. Cf. the survey of the exegetical research in H. Lessig, *Die Abendmahlsprobleme im Lichte der neutestamentlichen Forschung seit 1900*, diss. Bonn 1953; E. Schweizer, 'Das Herrenmahl im Neuen Testament. Ein Forschungsbericht' in his *Neotestamentica*, Zürich and Stuttgart 1963, 344–370; H. Patsch, *Abendmahl und historischer Jesus*, Stuttgart 1972; F. Hahn, 'Zum Stand der Erforschung des urchristlichen Herrenmahls', *EvTh* 35, 1975, 553–563; H. Feld, *Das Verständis des Abendmahls*, Beiträge der Forschung, vol. 50, Darmstadt 1976, 4–76.

2. R. Bultmann's view; cf. *History of the Synoptic Tradition*, trans. J. Marsh, Oxford 1963, 265–266; also his *Theology of the New Testament* vol. I, trans. K. Grobel, London 1952, 40f., 57f., 144ff., 313f.

3. The Jewish background was stressed above all by J. Jeremias in *The Eucharistic Words of Jesus*, trans. N. Perrin, London 1966. In doing so, however, Jeremias based his own interpretation in a one-sided way on the disputed thesis that the Last Supper was the passover supper. This view is also found in H. L. Strack and P. Billerbeck, *Kommentar zum Neuen Testament aus Talmud und Midrasch*, vol. IV, 74–76. On this question cf. R. Feneberg, *Christliche Passafeier und Abendmahl. Eine biblisch-hermeneutische Untersuchung der neutestamentlichen Einsetzungsberichte*, Studien zum Alten und Neuen Testament 27, Munich 1971. Important for the Old Testament background in general is F. Hahn, 'Die alttestamentlichen Motive in der urchristlichen Abendmahlsüberlieferung', *EvTh* 27, 1967, 337–374.

4. Cf. Strack-Billerbeck, op. cit., IV, 620f., 627ff.; J. Jeremias, *Eucharistic Words*, 108f.

5. Cf. above all H. Schürmann, 'Die Gestaltung der urchristlichen Eucharistiefeier' in his *Ursprung und Gestalt. Erörterungen und Besinnungen zum Neuen Testament*, Düsseldorf 1970, 79ff.; also 'Das Weiterleben der Sache Jesus im nachösterlichen Herrenmahl. Die Kontinuität der Zeichen in der Diskontinuität der Zeiten' in his *Jesu ureigener Tod. Exegetische Besinnungen und Ausblicke*, Freiburg, Basle and Vienna 1975, 76ff. Also G. Delling, 'Abendmahl II. Urchristl. Mahl-Verständnis' in *TRE* I, 1977, 49.

6. Cf. J. Betz in *Mysterium Salutis* IV/2, Einsiedeln, Zürich and Cologne 1973, 193ff.

7. H. Conzelmann has pointed to the resulting heremeneutical circle, and to the limits of the attempt to reconstruct Jesus' original words at the Last Supper; cf. his *An Outline of the Theology of the New Testament*, trans. J. S. Bowden, London 1969, 59. This circle must admittedly be understood more profoundly against the background of Jesus' own transmission in and through the tradition of the church; while against the background of the solidarity between Christ and the church it must be evaluated positively.

8. A different view has been taken recently by R. Pesch, who sees the narrative account in Mark as situated in the life of Jesus, in distinction from the cultic aetiology of Paul, which had its *Sitz im Leben* in the life of the primitive church. Cf. *Das Markusevangelium. II. Teil*, HThK 2, 1977, 354ff.; cf. also Pesch, *Wie Jesus das Abendmahl hielt. Der Grund der Eucharistie*, Freiburg, Basle and Vienna 1977, esp. 54. At the same time the view held by many other scholars must be remembered: that Mark and Matthew (Matthew being dependent on Mark) present a more liturgically stylized text than Paul and Luke inasmuch as they

already put together the sayings over the bread and the wine, and no longer – like Paul and Luke – separate them by the meal that lies between. Cf. among others G. Bornkamm, 'Herrenmahl und Kirche bei Paulus' in his *Studien zu Antike und Christentum, Gesammelte Aufsätze*, vol. 2, Munich 1959, 150ff.; H. Conzelmann, *Outline*, 57; G. Delling, 'Abendmahl', 48, 51, 54.

9. This continuity is stressed in different ways by J. Betz, H. Schürmann, H. Patsch, G. Delling and others. They also provide the detailed reasoning for the following passage.

10. Cf. here K. Kertelge (ed.), *Der Tod Jesu. Deutungen im Neuen Testament*, QD 74, 1976.

11. Thus J. Ratzinger, *Eucharistie – Mitte der Kirche*, Munich 1978, 10, 18.

12. J. Betz's view, op. cit., 263f.

13. This comes out very clearly in *De captivitate Babylonica ecclesiae* (1520), WA 6, 512–526.

14. It is impossible to enter here into the complicated individual exegetical questions about sacrificial ideas in Jesus. Cf. n. 10 above and nn. 32f. below. Also F. Hahn, 'Das Verständnis des Opfers im Neuen Testament' in K. Lehmann and E. Schlink (ed.), *Das Opfer Jesu Christi und seine Gegenwart in der Kirche. Klärungen zum Opfercharakter des Herrenmahles*, Dialog der Kirchen 3, Freiburg and Göttingen 1983, 51–91.

15. For the functional view cf. H. Küng, *On Being a Christian*, trans. E. Quinn, New York 1976, London 1977, 322–325; for the existential approach cf. W. Marxsen, *Das Abendmahl als christologisches Problem*, Gütersloh 1963.

16. Cf. the survey in P. Neuenzeit, *Das Herrenmahl. Studien zur paulinischen Eucharistieauffassung*, Studien zum Alten und Neuen Testament 1, Munich 1960, 136–147.

17. The derivation from the Hellenistic memorial meal for the dead was maintained especially by H. Lietzmann, *Mass and Lord's Supper. A Study in the History of the Liturgy*, trans. Dorothea Reeve, Leiden 1954–79 (published in 11 pts.). The derivation from the mystery religions was important for O. Casel's mystery theology, which is summed up in his book *The Mystery of Christian Worship*, ET ed. by B. Neunheuser, London 1962. The Old Testament and Jewish background is stressed by J. Jeremias, *Eucharistic Words*, 237–255; by M. Thurian, *The Eucharistic Memorial*, trans. J. G. Davies, 2 pts., London 1960, 1961; and by L. Bouyer, *Eucharistie. Théologie et spiritualité de la prière eucharistique*, Paris 1966, 87f., 107f. (*Eucharist. Theology and Spirituality of the Eucharistic Prayer*, trans. C. U. Quinn, London 1968).

18. Strack-Billerbeck IV/1, 68.

19. Cf. J. Betz, *Die Eucharistie in der Zeit der griechischen Väter*, I/1, Freiburg 1955, 197ff.; G. Kretschmar, 'Abendmahl III/1. Alte Kirche' in *TRE* I, 1977, 62ff., 78ff. This raises the problem of Hellenization in the sense of a hermeutically necessary translation; cf here Kretschmar, ibid., 84–86.

20. Thomas Aquinas, *STh* III q. 60 a. 3.

21. Cf. A. Gerken, *Theologie der Eucharistie*, Munich 1973, 61ff., 97ff.

22. Cf. E. Iserloh, 'Abendmahl III/2. Mittelalter' in *TRE* I, 1977, 100f., 128ff.

23. Cf. DS 1740.

24. Cf. particularly P. Brunner, 'Zur Lehre vom Gottesdienst der im Namen Jesu versammelten Gemeinde' in *Leiturgia. Handbuch des evangelischen Gottes-*

dienstes, I, Kassel 1954, 209ff., 229ff.; J. J. von Allmen, *Ökumene im Herrenmahl*, Kassel 1968, 25ff., 98ff. (*The Lord's Supper*, trans. W. Fletcher Fleet, London 1969) and M. Thurian, *Eucharistic Memorial*. Cf. the survey in W. Averbeck, *Der Opfercharakter des Abendmahls in der neueren evangelischen Theologie*, Konfessionskundliche und kontroverstheologische Studien 19, Paderborn 1967; U. Kühn, 'Abendmahl IV. Das Abendmahlsgespräch in der ökumenischen Theologie der Gegenwart' in *TRE*, 1977, 157ff., 164ff., 192ff.; K. Lehmann and E. Schlink (ed.), *Das Opfer Jesus Christi*.

25. Constitution on the Sacred Liturgy *Sacrosanctum concilium*, 6, 47.

26. Cf. H. Schlier, 'Die Verkündigung im Gottesdienst der Kirche' in his *Die Zeit der Kirche. Exegetische Aufsätze und Vorträge*, 2nd ed., Freiburg 1958, 246ff.; K. Rahner, 'The Word and the Eucharist' in *Theological Investigations* IV, London 1966, 253–86.

27. It is impossible to enter here into discussion about the various modes of the presence of Jesus Christ in the eucharist. Cf. J. Betz in *Mysterium Salutis* IV/2, 267ff.; and recently F. Eisenbach, *Die Gegenwart Jesu Christi im Gottesdienst. Systematische Studien zur Liturgiekonstitution des II. Vatikanischen Konzils*, Mainz 1982. It is even less possible in the present context to go into the recent discussion about a deepened understanding of the Real Presence (transubstantiation, transignification, transfinalization). But cf. n. 76.

28. H. Beyer, 'eulogéo' in *TDNT* II, 759ff.; H. Conzelmann, 'eucharistéo' in *TDNT* IX, 411ff.; L. Lies, *Wort und Eucharistie bei Origines. Zur Spiritualisierungstendenz des Eucharistie-verständnisses*, Innsbrucker Theologische Studien 1, Innsbruck, Vienna and Munich 1978, 11–36.

29. Ignatius of Antioch, *Ad Smyrn.* 8, 1; *Ad Philad.* 4; Justin, *Dial. c. Trypho* 41, 117. Cf. J. A. Jungmann, 'Von der "Eucharistia" zur "Messe"', *ZKTh* 89, 1967, 29f.; H. Conzelmann, *TDNT* IX, 415.

30. J. A. Jungmann, *Missarum Solemnia. Eine genetische Erklärung der römischen Messe*, 5th ed., Vienna 1962, vol. 1, 20f., 38; vol. 2, 138ff.

31. Thus J. A. Jungmann, ibid., vol. 1, 27f.; J. Ratzinger, 'Gestalt und Gehalt der eucharistischen Feier' in his *Das Fest des Glaubens*, Einsiedeln 1981, 31–46; L. Bouyer tries in an impressive way to interpret the whole eucharist from the aspect of the *berakah*; cf. *Eucharist* (n. 17). For a summing up and development cf. L. Lies, 'Eulogia. Überlegungen zur formalen Sinngestalt der Eucharistie', *ZKTh* 100, 1978, 69–97.

32. H. Gese, 'Die Herkunft des Herrenmahls' in his *Zur biblischen Theologie*, Munich 1977, 107–127; taken up by J. Ratzinger, op. cit., 47–54.

33. J. Betz, *Die Eucharistie in der Zeit der griechischen Väter*, (n. 19), II/1, 40.

34. J. A. Jungmann, *Missarum Solemnia*, I, 31ff.; also his 'Von der "Eucharistia" zur "Messe"', *ZThK* 89, 29f.; H. Conzelmann, 'eucharistéo', op. cit., 415.

35. J. A. Jungmann, 'Von der "Eucharistia" zur "Messe"', 33. Cf. H. Moll, *Die Lehre von der Eucharistie als Opfer. Eine dogmengeschtliche Untersuchung vom Neuen Testament bis Irenäus von Lyon*, Theophaneia 26, Cologne and Bonn 1975.

36. Of decisive importance here was the fact that Isidore of Seville cut off the Preface (the thanksgiving in the narrower sense) from the rest of the canon, thus breaking up the canon's organic unity. Cf. J. R. Geiselmann, *Die Abendmahlslehre*

an der Wende der christlichen Spätantike zum Frühmittelalter. Isidor von Sevilla and das Sakrament der Eucharistie, Munich 1933.

37. *Apologia Confessionis Augustanae* XXIV (cf. *Apology of the Augsburg Confession [Article XXIV]: 'The Mass'* in *The Book of Concord*, trans. and ed. by T. G. Tappert, Philadelphia 1959, 16th printing 1987). On the other hand the Council of Trent maintains that the eucharist is a true sacrifice (DS 1751), not merely of praise and thanksgiving but in the expiatory sense (DS 1753).

38. Cf. J. Ratzinger, 'Is the Eucharist a Sacrifice?', *Concilium* no. 3, vol. 4, April 1967, 35–40; cf. also n. 24.

39. Thus Augustine, *Civ. Dei* 10.20; 10.6. On the question in general cf. H. U. von Balthasar, 'Die Messe, ein Opfer der Kirche?' in his *Spiritus Creator. Skizzen zur Theologie* III, Einsiedeln 1967, 166–217.

40. Cf. T. Schneider, *Zeichen der Nähe Gottes. Grundriß der Sakramententheologie*, Mainz 1979, 144ff.

41. Irenaeus of Lyons, *Adv. haer.*, IV, 19. The inward unity of theocentricism and anthropocentricism is stressed and justified especially by E. Lengeling, 'Liturgie' in *HThG* II, 81ff., 88ff.

42. H. Conzelmann, *TDNT* IX, 413.

43. On the interpretation of the epiklesis cf. O. Casel, 'Zur Epiklese' in *Jahrbuch für Liturgiewissenschaft* 3, 1923, 100–102; also his 'Neue Beiträge zur Epiklesenfrage', ibid. 4, 1924, 169–178; J. A. Jungmann, *Missarum Solemnia*, vol. 2, 238ff.; J. Betz, *Die Eucharistie in der Zeit der greichischen Väter*, vol. I/ 1, 320–346; J. P. de Jong, 'Epiklese' in *LThK* III, 935–937.

44. Thus J. Betz, op. cit., 319.

45. H. Beyer, *TDNT* II, 754ff.; L. Lies, *Wort und Eucharistie*, 61f.

46. J. A. Jungmann, 'Von der "Eucharistia" zur "Messe"', 37. We already find this meaning in Origen, although certainly in the still wider concept of the whole. Cf. L. Lies, ibid., 261ff., 294ff.

47. J. A. Jungmann, ibid., 38; also his 'Zur Bedeutungsgeschichte des Wortes "Missa"' in his *Gewordene Liturgie*, Innsbruck und Leipzig 1941, 34–52; other interpretations in J. J. von Allmen, *Ökumene im Herrenmahl*, 120f.

48. J. A. Jungmann, 'Von der "Eucharistia" zur "Messe"', 39.

49. This applies above all to 'the Lima document': *Baptism, Eucharist and Ministry*, Faith and Order Paper No. 111, World Council of Churches, Geneva 1982, 10ff. Cf. U. Kühn, op. cit. (n. 24), 197.

50. Cf. above all E. Käsemann, 'The Pauline Doctrine of the Lord's Supper' in *Essays on New Testament Themes*, trans. W. J. Montague, London 1964, 108–135; cf. P. Neuenzeit, op. cit. (n. 16) 48f., 185f.

51. H. R. Schlette, *Kommunikation und Sakrament*, QD 8, 1960.

52. J. Betz., op. cit., 328ff.

53. Cf. among others J. Meyendorff, 'Notes on the Orthodox Understanding of the Eucharist', *Concilium* no. 3, vol. 4, April 1967, 27–30.

54. Cf. J. J. von Allmen, op. cit., 32ff.

55. O. Casel, 'Die Logiké thysia der antiken Mystik in christlich-liturgischer Umdeutung', *Jahrbuch für Liturgiewissenschaft* 4, 1924, 37–47.

56. F. Hauck, 'koinonós' in *TDNT* III, 797–809; P. C. Bori, KOINΩNIA. *L'idea della comunione nell'ecclesiologie recente e il Nuovo Testamento*, Brescia 1972.

57. Augustine, *In Ioan.* tr. 26. 13 (CC 36, 266). This statement had a wide and longstanding influence in the doctrinal documents: DS 802; 1635; Vatican II, Constitution on the Liturgy *Sacrosanctum concilium* 47.

58. R. Guardini, *Besinnung vor der Feier der Heiligen Messe*, pt. 2, 2nd ed., Mainz 1939, 73ff. Of course Guardini was not intending to define the essence of the eucharist (ibid. 75), let alone to dispute the sacrificial character as source and premise (ibid. 77). Similarly J. Pascher, *Eucharistia. Gestalt und Vollzug*, Münster 1947; also his 'Um die Grundgestalt der Eucharistie', *MThZ* 1, 1950, 64–75. On the dispute at that time cf. T. Maas-Ewerd, *Die Krise der Liturgischen Bewegung in Deutschland und Österreich. Zu den Auseinandersetzungen um die 'liturgische Frage' in den Jahren 1939 bis 1944*, Studien zur Pastoralliturgie 3, Regensburg 1981, esp. 343–348. On the present discussion cf. n. 31.

59. Cf. the important contribution, already mentioned more than once, by H. Schürmann, 'Die Gestalt der urchristlichen Eucharistiefeier' (cf. n. 5).

60. Thus already in Pliny's famous letter to Trajan, 10, 9; also in Justin, *Apology* I, 67.

61. J. A. Jungmann, '"Abendmahl" als Name der Eucharistie', *ZKTh* 93, 1971, 91–94.

62. Cf. P. Neuenzeit, *Das Herrenmahl*, 191ff.; F. Lang, 'Abendmahl und Bundesgedanke im Neuen Testament', *EvTh* 35, 1975, 524–538: V. Wagner, 'Der Bedeutungswandel von berit hadascha bei der Ausgestaltung der Abendmahlsworte', *EvTh* 35, 1975, 538–552.

63. Cf. P. Neuenzeit, op. cit., 201–219; E. Schweizer, '*soma*' in *TDNT* VII, 1067f.; E. Käsemann, 'The Theological Problem Presented by the Motif of the Body of Christ' in *Perspectives on Paul*, trans. Margaret Kohl, London and Philadelphia 1971, 102–121.

64. Augustine, *Sermo* 272 (PL 38. 1217).

65. Cf. above all H. de Lubac, *Corpus mysticum. L'eucharistie et l'Eglise au moyen âge*, 2nd ed., Paris 1949; following him, A. Gerken, op. cit. (n. 21 above), 122ff.

66. Thomas Aquinas, *STh* III q. 73 a. 6: 'in hoc sacramento tria considerare possumus: scilicet id quod est sacramentum tantum, scilicet panis et vinum; et id quod est res et sacramentum, scilicet corpus Christi verum; et id quod est res tantum, scilicet effectus huius sacramenti.' q. 80 a. 4: 'Duplex autem est res huius sacramenti . . . una quidem quae est significata et contenta, scilicet ipse Christus; alia autem est significata et non contenta, scilicet corpus Christi mysticum, quod est societas sanctorum.' Cf. q. 60. a. 3 sed contra; q. 73 a. 2 sed contra.

67. Vatican II, Constitution on the Liturgy *Sacrosanctum concilium*, 11, 14, 48. This renewed understanding of the connection between the eucharist and the church had important results for a eucharistic ecclesiology which no longer takes the universal church as starting point, but instead the local church in its celebration of the eucharist, and sees the unity of the universal church as a *communio* of local churches.

68. Cf. K. Lehmann, 'Persönliches Gebet in der Eucharistiefeier', *IKZ Communio* 5, 1977, 401–406. It is impossible here to enter into the important subject of the veneration of the eucharistic elements outside the eucharistic celebration.

69. On the question of a new secret discipline cf. H. Spaemann, *Und Gott schied*

das Licht von der Finsternis. Christliche Konsequenzen, Freiburg, Basle and Vienna 1982, 93–140.

70. J. Moltmann's view; cf. *The Church in the Power of the Spirit. A Contribution to Messianic Ecclesiology*, trans. Margaret Kohl, London and New York 1977, 244ff., 258ff.

71. Vatican II, Constitution on the Church *Lumen gentium* 3: 'Likewise, in the sacrament of the eucharistic bread, the unity of believers, who form one body in Christ (cf. I Cor. 10:17), is both expressed and brought about.' 11: 'Strengthened by the body of Christ in the eucharistic communion, [the faithful] manifest in a concrete way that unity of the People of God which this holy sacrament aptly signifies and admirably realizes.'

72. According to Catholic doctrine, the eucharist presupposes validly consecrated ministers. Cf. DS 802; 1752; Vatican II, Constitution on the Church *Lumen gentium* 26, 28; Decree on Ecumenism *Unitatis redintegratio* 22. On this question cf. P. Bläser et al., *Amt und Eucharistie*, Konfessionskundliche Schriften 10, Paderborn 1973; for a different view cf. H. Küng, *Why priests?*, trans. J. Cumming, London and Glasgow 1972; E. Schillebeeckx, *Das kirchliche Amt*, Düsseldorf 1981.

73. Cf. here the survey given by G. Wingren in 'Abendmahl V. Das Abendmahl als Tischgemeinschaft nach ethischen Gesichtspunkten' in *TRE* I, 1977, 212–229.

74. Cf. G. Wainwright, *Eucharist and Eschatology*, New York 1981.

75. Thus L. Lies, 'Eulogia' (n. 31 above), 94–97, following up the approaches of J. A. Jungmann and J. Ratzinger.

76. Thus J. Betz in *Mysterium Salutis*, IV/2, 264f. For the corresponding interpretation of the doctrine of transubstantiation, cf. J. Ratzinger, 'Das Problem der Transsubstantiation und die Frage nach dem Sinn der Eucharistie', *ThQ* 147, 1967, esp. 152f.

77. Cf. Vatican II, Constitution on the Liturgy *Sacrosanctum concilium* 6.

Index of Names